Research on Teacher Thinking: Understanding Professional Development

Research on Teacher Thinking:
Understanding Professional Development

Edited by

Christopher Day
James Calderhead
and
Pam Denicolo

The Falmer Press
(A member of the Taylor & Francis Group)
London · Washington, D.C.

UK   The Falmer Press, 4 John St, London WC1N 2ET
USA   The Falmer Press, Taylor & Francis Inc., 1900 Frost Road,
      Suite 101, Bristol, PA 19007

First published 1993

**A catalogue record of this publication is available from the
British Library**

ISBN 0 75070 177 3 cased
ISBN 0 75070 178 1 paper

**Library of Congress Cataloging-in-Publication Data are
available on request**

Jacket design by Caroline Archer

Typeset in 9.5/11 pt Bembo by
Graphicraft Typesetters Ltd., Hong Kong

*Printed in Great Britain by Burgess Science Press, Basingstoke on paper
which has a specified pH value on final paper manufacture of not less than
7.5 and is therefore 'acid free'.*

Contents

Contents

Introduction

Christopher Day, James Calderhead and Pam Denicolo

In the introduction to the previous book (Day, Pope and Denicolo, 1990) in the series derived from the biennial conferences of ISATT, we noted three areas of growth in the conceptualisation and practice of research on teachers' thinking and action:

1 the increasing complexity of the subject matter of teacher thinking research;
2 the impact of this upon methodology and the associated debates regarding strategies of research employed; and
3 that the calls for 'ethical' research which produced benefits for all its participants were becoming increasingly loud.

Issues were raised in the first part of that book: about the traditional ways in which research is disseminated; about the role of contemplation on or reflection in practice; about the moral imperative in teachers' thinking and concomitant demands on the researcher. That section closed with a plea that we should consider the potential alienation which can result when the sender and the receiver, researchers and the researched in either order, interpret the message differently. The chapters in Part 1 of this book move the debate on by presenting a series of inter-related challenges. Whilst each paper in the previous compilation recognised implicitly the dynamic between theory and action, between research and practice, that interface is the explicit focus of the chapters by Calderhead, Pope, Huberman and Letiche in this volume as they ask us to risk the discomfort inherent in conceptual reorganisation of espoused theory and theory-in-practice. All four chapters acknowledge the interactive and multifaceted relationship between research and practice but urge us to think beyond the traditional conceptions of the linkages. Lest we become too complacent in the security of established practice, whether as researchers or teachers — no matter how radical that practice seemed when we first espoused its underpinning theory — each chapter confronts us with provocative perspectives.

In 1987 Handal and Lauvas warned us that teachers are in danger of either becoming too rigid or becoming 'passengers on any educational bandwagon that happens to pass their school' (p. 22). These chapters, in reflecting our theory and practice as researchers back to us and in proposing alternative scenarios, provide us with the opportunity to become more knowledgeable and to exercise more broadly-based critical judgment, not as passengers but in a way congruent with our own critical evaluation of those alternatives.

James Calderhead addresses the issue of the role played by research in the professional education of teachers, exploring what its potential might be if a metaperspective were taken. His arguments derive from a concern with pre-service education, and his chapter begins with a justification for that concern in terms of the plethora of changes or 'imposed theories' which currently impinge on teaching and, thereby, on teacher education. Nevertheless, as he evaluates the range of views on the relationship between research and education, it becomes apparent that his arguments have relevance for all stages of professional development. In seeking to provide an answer to the charge that research has not contributed to the defence of current good practice nor to its further development in times of uncertainty, he presents a range of views about the relationship between research and practice and discusses how different epistemologies of each result in a variety of interactions between them. He posits the value of a metaperspective which acknowledges the complexity of the two activities. In exemplifying this viewpoint, he demonstrates how restricted views from either domain can limit the development of truly reciprocal relationships which could result from more appropriate recognition of the diversity of each. It is clear that clashes of paradigm in which one does not recognise the fundamental concerns and values of the other are unproductive; whereas great potential derives when the research paradigm is complementary to the view of teacher education.

His proposals that we should, as researchers, take the lead in the latter are echoed in the chapter by Maureen Pope which begins by addressing how a 'constructive alternativistic' approach may act as a means of breaking free from the prison of confining paradigms and ideologies. As a prelude to, and as a basis for, reviewing current research on teacher thinking and for anticipating alternative directions for future research, Pope draws an analogy with the Lakatosian (1970) philosophy about the progress of science. She suggests that teacher thinking research has adopted a different paradigm to that embraced by traditional research in education, proposing that it could be considered as pre-paradigmatic since there exists a diversity of approaches and methods in currency which share a common focus and ideology. In describing the various purposes which such research serves, and how these have shifted over time for individual researchers and the research community, she advocates that it is an appropriate time for us to critically review the congruency of methods.

She focuses upon one constellation of techniques, which aims to make the tacit knowledge of teachers articulate so that it can be appraised, and raises a caveat about the importance of authenticating research by grounding it collaboratively with the teachers in their own practice by action research (a theme later reiterated by Huberman). This requires reconsideration of the complementary roles of the teacher and the researcher with greater communication and reciprocity advised. She also suggests that, to truly represent the reality of teaching, we need to extend the range of teachers with whom we work. In this respect she particularly regrets the scarcity of comparative studies, though, as we shall see from Letiche's chapter, these should not be undertaken without cognisance of the limitations of language for conveying constructs.

One particular form of evolution is proposed by Michael Huberman who begins his chapter by addressing one of the connecting threads between research and practice, the dissemination and utilisation of knowledge. He, too, notes the transformations of meaning during the process of transfer between domains in which language registers and primary objectives differ. He interprets the dominant practice to be one in which the typical research community connects with practitioners at two points, dependent on the aim of the research, i.e. when the body of knowledge is increased and then accessed by the practice group (the classic pattern) and when that group articulates a need to which their research counterparts respond (more reminiscent of simple forms of action research).

The main thrust of his chapter is to define, explain and evaluate an alternative operational mode which he terms 'sustained interactivity'. Users of research in this form are not 'subjects' of the research but play a key role in a conversation which takes place over the whole course of the project. During this conversation relevant areas of focus and meanings attributed to words and acts are negotiated so that what is germane and valid within the complexity of the relevant context is acknowledged, as are the micro-politics of information use. Using an example from the vocational training field, Huberman demonstrates that not only were ephemeral effects and distortions reduced by subjective interactivity, but also conceptual mastery was increased and real practices changed, even in initially relatively hostile settings. Reciprocal influences pervaded the study, and researchers gained from the changed process.

He illustrates this latter effect by a fictitious example of what could happen if the model were followed in other areas of research and practice. In essence the proposition is that if all parties engaged in research can tolerate the initial discomfort of entertaining alternative conceptions, and live with the time and effort demands of using such techniques, then the product will be the professional growth and development of all concerned alongside more refined and authenticated theories.

The preceding three chapters have a strong constructivist base. The final chapter in this section, by Hugo Letiche, advocates that we also consider a deconstructivist approach. The chapter provides an example in which the world views of individuals, though seemingly similar, never meet, and so alerts us to the difficulties of interpreting between superficially equivalent, and purportively interacting, domains. His chapter confronts us with the paradox that, in choosing to remain within the safety of conventional approaches to research, we are lured into ignoring, or not even being aware of, discontinuities or mismatches between the understandings of the various actors in the process. Beginning at the inception of the research process, as opposed to the later stage of dissemination of findings, he notes that one artefact of the traditional process is that it is generally organised around themes selected by researchers while other possible query areas are suppressed. This leads to a consideration of the ambiguity about what teacher and researcher reflexivity is/is not and what their respective roles are/are not. Taking an example from a research project in higher education involving two differing national and professional cultures he uses what he terms his 'authorial' voice, one which distrusts all perspectives including his own, to examine the tensions between expectations and events in a situation. In this scenario, adherence to pretended certainty, contributed to by the use of the same verbal label being used to describe very different processes and events, leads to frequent disjunctions of understanding.

In Part 2, 'Exploring Teachers' Knowledge and Beliefs', the chapters are concerned with the relationship between teachers' thinking and practice and the particular contexts in which teachers work, exploring in particular the situated nature of teachers' knowledge and the cultural influences upon teachers' knowledge and beliefs.

Rosa Laffitte's study examines how teachers in Spanish schools feel about their roles and responsibilities. This is of particular interest because these schools have recently undergone dramatic changes in moving toward a much more democratic culture, with several implications for the expectations commonly held for teachers' roles. The data that Laffitte has collected from teachers in one region of Spain, Catalonia, are compared with similar data from teachers in Britain and France. Interestingly, Spanish teachers were found to experience a higher sense of responsibility to the community both within and beyond the school; they also reported being more influenced by them. Headteachers, who in Spain are democratically elected from the teaching staff for a three-year period, appeared to be much less influential. Spanish teachers were also found to hold more positive views of teaching, and were more likely than their English or French counterparts to view teaching as a collaborative activity rather than a task in which they worked alone. Laffitte's study raises several questions about the values embedded within the educational culture of a school and its potential to influence the ways in which teachers think about their work and the roles and responsibilities that they are, in consequence, prepared to accept.

Mary Lynn Hamilton's chapter, in contrast, describes an ethnographic study of one school where the school culture has been deliberately manipulated to influence teachers' and children's beliefs and practices. School district administrators took on the task of developing a culture of self-efficacy within one multi-racial, inner-city school. Teachers who were appointed to the school had to express a commitment to ideas of positive change, teamwork and the ability of the students to improve themselves through effort and self-esteem. A great deal of emphasis was placed within the school on 'The Efficacy Seminar' which all teachers were expected to attend and which reinforced the intellectual work ethic that pervaded espoused beliefs within the school. Hamilton, however, points out that the need to state explicitly that teachers and students need to work hard to be successful carries the implicit message that at least some teachers and students are not working hard and are not successful. Within the school, some staff went along with the culture only in a superficial sense — they could 'talk the talk but not walk the walk'. Nevertheless, Hamilton suggests that the culture did have quite profound effects upon both children and parents and did influence children's sense of their own worth and potential, which reinforced some teachers' beliefs in the work ethic.

The chapter by Bob Yinger and Martha Hendricks-Lee questions conventional conceptions of teachers' working knowledge and suggests that rather than knowledge residing in the individual teacher, much of the knowledge concerning teaching resides in systems. Yinger and Hendricks-Lee term this: 'ecological intelligence' and describe how it is located in cultural, material, social, historical and personal systems. In practice these different systems interact to create new meanings and actions, and the teacher may be viewed as engaged in a variety of conversations with different systems. The authors propose that viewing the classroom as an ecosystem involving a number of different interacting systems in which both teachers and children are involved provides a new way of looking at the task of the teacher and an alternative perspective on what might be done to prepare teachers to take on this task. Rather than developing expert knowledge, teachers must be prepared in the art of conversation. Yinger and Hendricks-Lee raise a number of questions to challenge some current ideas about teachers' expertise and teachers' professional development, though the full implications of an ecological intelligence approach for teachers and teacher educators have still to be thought through.

The issue addressed by Bridget Somekh's chapter is how teachers' knowledge is generated and shared amongst practitioners whose own experiences and working contexts differ. Somekh identifies a problem in reporting case studies of action research where teachers who have explored and written about their own practice are communicating their experience with the intention of helping others to share this knowledge. Frequently the reader's and writer's appreciation of the case studies appears to differ widely. After an examination of action research case studies, and a detailed analysis of one in particular, Somekh argues that learning from case studies is an active process in which the reader must reconstruct and question the author's meaning and construct a new meaning in response. In the process of reconstruction, teachers bring their own knowledge and understandings of their own contexts to bear on the case study. Somekh argues that much of teachers' knowledge is person and context dependent and therefore the reader needs to analyse and re-contextualise a case study in order for it to become meaningful and relevant to the reader's own practice. Extracting meaning from a case study is seen as a continuous process of questioning and testing out one's interpretation. Recognising the way in which case studies might contribute to the professional development of teachers clearly has implications for the way in which teachers' case studies are written, an issue that Somekh explores in some depth.

Part 3, 'Developing Knowledge and Practice', contains examples of small-scale qualitative studies undertaken with serving teachers. The chapters focus upon professional development and provide examples of the kinds of 'connective' or interactive research to which we referred earlier in this introduction. In 'Teachers' Stories: An Analysis of the Themes', Marguerite Hansen Nelson discusses 'what it means to be a teacher', from the teachers' perspective. The work adds to the young but growing tradition of research which seeks to learn from teachers themselves, to listen to their 'voices' through, for example, narrative inquiry.

One hundred and forty-six independently taped stories of memorable or meaningful moments in the lives of fifty-five classroom teachers with a range of experience were analysed. Eight themes, which were 'evoked' from within the stories rather than imposed, were identified. The themes highlight teaching qualities as perceived by teachers themselves — their willingness to go 'above and beyond' the call of duty; the importance they attach to effective communication; the satisfaction gained from influencing their pupils; the challenges and responsibilities of teaching; relationships; the importance of student perspective; the satisfaction from particular student successes; and the importance of learning through reflecting on the action. Much of the chapter is devoted to providing exemplars of these themes, giving value to the teachers' words. The significance of this research is that, whilst it confirms findings of other researches into, for example, teacher attributes, it provides also an agenda for those involved in leading pre-service and in-service education. Essentially, these teachers' perceptions of 'worthwhileness' as revealed in their stories, provide a crucial indicator of values which underpin considerations of individual teacher effectiveness and thus school improvement.

Michael Kompf's chapter, 'Construing Teachers' Personal Development: Reflections on Landmark Events Through Career Mapping', contributes to research which focuses upon the examination of long-term reflection and anticipation. As in Nelson's work, teachers were asked to recall past 'landmark' events through narratives which focused upon significant personal and professional events and the relationships between these, where appropriate. In addition they were asked to anticipate future events. The narratives were fed back to the teachers and their responses sought. In this and other ways, Kompf addresses issues for researchers who seek to establish ethical contracts with their subjects such that both parties gain from the enterprise, a theme raised in Part 1 of this book. The chapter presents a closely argued theoretical framework which underpins the constructionist techniques of career-mapping used. The work is grounded in personal construct psychology, and much of the discussion centres upon the need for 'epistemological permeability' and 'constructive developmentalism' (cf. Pope in this book) in work concerned with revealing the sophisticated 'inner lives' of developing adults. The paper makes a significant theoretical and methodological contribution to career mapping.

In, 'The Identification, Development and Sharing of Professional Craft Knowledge', Margaret Batten reports a small-scale study undertaken with twelve secondary school teachers in Australia. All were acknowledged, by their pupils, to be 'good' teachers. The teachers were observed teaching *in situ* and interviewed in order to construct 'pedagogical profiles' and establish 'criteria for successful teaching'. Whereas Nelson and Kompf focus upon teachers' constructs of significant events in their own development, Batten uses stimulated recall techniques to assist teachers in reflecting upon specific classroom action. Within elements of successful teaching which were identified, differences in emphasis were found to exist between teachers of 'practical subjects' and those of maths/science and humanities, the latter being more concerned with teaching processes and the former with outcomes. When students in these classes were asked to assess the teaching, whilst there were constructs common to all teachers, again, differences in pattern emerged for each area. The research raises the possibility, not surprisingly, that teachers in different subject disciplines teach in different ways; and that students themselves look for and value different things in different subjects. Whilst these findings offer few surprises, they provide additional evidence of the need in the detailed consideration of criteria for the assessment of teaching to take into account teachers' craft knowledge, student perspectives, and differences in content and pedagogy.

'Transferring Knowledge to Classroom Teaching: Putting Knowledge into Action' provides a similar focus to others in this section, but represents a different research tradition. Whereas the other authors construct knowledge through analysis and interpretation of information provided by teacher practitioners, Hannelore Börger and Harm Tillema begin from a recognition of a 'lack of usability' in teaching of knowledge acquired during teacher training. The paper offers a detailed critique of traditional theories of knowledge acquisition (the what), strategic theories (the how) and their transfer and suggests ways in which 'theory' can better be transferred into 'practice'. Börger and Tillema identify two generic and contrasting approaches to knowledge transfer, from the literature. They label these, 'embedding' and 'immersion'; and they combine what they consider to be the strengths of each approach in a detailed research proposal. The paper is unusual in that it reveals what for many researchers is a first step in the construction of a rational research model i.e. problem identification, hypothesis construction, literature review and research design. It remains to be seen whether the 'rational' approach will be adequate in the investigation of what is, essentially, a highly complex non-rational process.

The two final contributions to this book focus upon teacher biography. In 'Teachers and their Career Story: A Biographical Perspective on Professional Development', Geert Kelchtermans reports research in Belgium with twelve primary school teachers from six schools which aimed to test and refine a framework for conceptualising the factors which influence the movement of teachers through identifiable phases or stages of development. Through the analysis of interview data he examines key notions of 'self' and 'subjective educational theory' which result from individual biography, arguing that they are idiosyncratic and that they result from the interaction of three key factors; critical incidents, critical persons and critical phases. Teachers' careers can only be understood, therefore, in relation to the several aspects of the professional self which his research reveals. The research points to the importance of recognising the complexity of teacher development. This is reinforced in the final contribution to the book, which illustrates the ways in which professional development is influenced by biography. In 'The Importance of Learning Biography in Supporting Teacher Development', Christopher Day reports the results of research carried out over a two-year period with teachers from eleven primary schools in England. An investigation of the effects of devolved in-service budgets upon schools revealed the importance of three interacting cultures upon teacher development — leadership (nature of intervention); organisation (context and variables); and individual teacher cultures (professional learning assumptions), and provides evidence that in the 'market-led' model of in-service education predominant now in English schools opportunities for long-term teacher growth are being lost. Through interviews with teachers, Day identifies the importance to the development of teacher thinking and practice of 'critical learning stages'.

At the beginning of this introduction we stated that three years ago, in the previous volume of papers selected from an ISATT (International Study Association on Teacher Thinking) conference, a number of areas of growth in teachers' thinking research were identified. The chapters in this volume provide evidence of the continuing intensity of thought, activity and debate about how best to conceptualise research of this kind — how best to generate knowledge for understanding and action; and a concern for the ethical basis for undertaking research into the inner lives of teachers. They are not presented as 'best practice', for definitions of this will be inevitably value laden, but rather as contributions from scholars in eight countries which together indicate and anticipate key areas for the development of our understanding of teachers' thinking and action in the 1990s.

Reference

HANDAL, G. and LAUVAS, P. (1987) *Promoting Reflective Teaching: Supervision in action*, Milton Keynes: SRHE and Open University Educational Enterprises Ltd.

Part 1　Research Issues

Chapter 1

The Contribution of Research on Teachers' Thinking to the Professional Development of Teachers

James Calderhead

Research on teachers' thinking has been pursued for many reasons, though pro-minent amongst these has been a concern with the improvement of the professional education of teachers. Given the current concern in many countries with the quality of teacher education, particularly in the pre-service phase, one might reasonably turn to this body of research for some insight into the problems and some suggestions for possible solutions. Commentators on teacher education, however, have frequently not viewed research as particularly helpful in resolving teacher education's difficulties.

This chapter will first of all address the question of why the present crisis in confidence in teacher education has occurred, and what the current issues are that confront teacher education. It will then consider the different ways in which researchers have suggested research might inform policy and practice in teacher education, and will explore, through a variety of examples, what the potential of research on teacher's thinking might be. The chapter will conclude with a typology of the roles research might fulfil in teacher education, and some emerging issues in the professional education of teachers that demand urgent enquiry if research is to establish itself as intrinsic to future developments in this field. It argues for a more eclectic and interactive relationship between research and practice in developing further our understanding of the processes involved in teachers' professional education.

Teacher Education — A Recent Context

Teacher education as we know it today has a surprisingly brief history. In Britain, the first B.Ed. courses appeared in 1965. Polytechnics and universities only became substantially involved in teacher training around the same time, coinciding with an expansion of the higher education system. And for maths and science teachers in secondary schools, where there have traditionally been shortages, teacher training only became compulsory as late as 1982.

The utility and value for money of teacher education have been questioned on numerous occasions in recent decades. But it has only been during the past five years that, in several countries, pressures upon teacher training have particularly intensified, and it is now being called to account perhaps more than ever before. Questions about its nature, its effectiveness, its cost, and whether it is actually needed at all are seriously being asked. In Britain, this trend can be partly explained in terms of a powerful political ideology of Thatcherite enterprise and account-ability and its blanket application to public and professional services — the health service, education, the legal profession, and even the water supply — though clearly other factors are involved in similar trends in other countries (e.g. Australia).

Official policy views concerning the content and organisation of teacher training have, not surprisingly, changed radically in these times. There has grown an increased emphasis on the importance of subject matter knowledge rather than pedagogy, classroom experience rather than college experience, the practical rather than the theoretical, and the notion of apprenticeship has re-emerged, with the development of various school-based alternative training schemes.

In several countries it seems that teacher education is not only being called more fully to account for itself, but policies are being drafted which impose particular views of professional development on the way teachers are trained, with the effect of reducing the 'academic' demands of training and promoting the immediately 'practical'. The relatively easy imposition of these views, and their receptive, even enthusiastic, support in the media, may well highlight the fact that teacher education is not widely understood, and teacher educators themselves, although they may have an intuitive understanding of good practice, are hampered in the defence of their work by the absence of any coherent theoretical account, or even precise language, for describing what they do. It appears, in fact, to be extremely difficult to articulate the basis of good practice in teacher education, and extremely difficult to defend good practice in the face of a simple, dominant ideology.

Teacher Education and Research on Teachers' Thinking

In this situation, one could reasonably ask what contribution research on teacher thinking might play. How might research help to illuminate, guide or justify teacher education practices? According to some commentators, its contribution has, in the past, been limited and disappointing. Shulman (1986) for example, in his contribution to the *Third Handbook of Research on Teaching*, suggests that research on teachers' thinking has been narrowly focused, too influenced by pre-vious process-product research, and unproductive for teaching and teacher edu-cation. More recently, McNamara (1990) criticises research on teacher thinking for failing to generate 'a corpus of findings which student educators can incorporate into their teaching so as to foster student teachers' capacity to reflect critically upon their practice and thereby improve their teaching' (p. 153).

In order to evaluate these general criticisms, we need to consider what the possible relationships might be between research and practice in teacher education. There is, in fact, quite a range of views about the relationship of research in general, and about research on teacher thinking in particular, to teacher education. Fenstermacher (1986), for example, has argued that educational research findings inform practice through practical arguments, where empirical research serves the function of clarifying, testing and informing the premises on which everyday judgments are based. Clark (1988) has argued that research on teachers' thinking serves to sensitise teacher educators to the ways in which they might think about professional education, encouraging them to ask questions of their own practice and thereby to guide their efforts to help beginning teachers. To this, Floden and Klinzing (1990) have replied, claiming that research might not at the moment offer more than sensitisation to issues, but, as our understanding of teachers' thinking improves, it has the potential to offer principles for action in teacher education in the future. In fact, within the literature on the relationship between research and practice in education, there are clearly many models to characterise how these inform one another or interact. McIntyre (1980), Elliott (1980) and Furlong, Pocklington, Hirst and Miles (1988) are others who have contributed to this debate. As one might expect, these models present a wide range of different conceptions both of research and of practice.

Epistemologies of Research and Practice

At this point, it may be useful to consider what some of the common views of research and practice are. Typically research has been categorised as falling into one of three traditions, each characterised by its own epistemology or assumptions about the nature of knowledge and how it is acquired: the *positivist*, the *phenomenological* and the *critical*. Gibson (1986) provides a useful summary of these traditions in terms of their focus of enquiry, interests and organisation of knowledge. What is seen as characterising positivism is the striving for principles or generalisations, a set of 'law-like' accounts that enable action to be predicted and controlled. Phenomenology, in contrast, is aiming for an understanding of particular individuals' perspectives through case studies or ethnographies that focus in particular on the language and interaction of participants. And critical science is seen as having a greater interest in emancipation, the sensitising of people, through a critical analysis, to the power relations in their own context and the causes and consequences of their own actions.

Zeichner (1983) has similarly produced a classification of the ways in which classroom practice and its development have been viewed in what he terms the four paradigms of teacher education. The *behaviourist paradigm* views teaching in terms of a series of competencies or technical skills that have to be practised and learned by the student teacher. The *personalistic paradigm* views teaching as a process of personal growth from the student teacher's own beliefs and commitments. The *traditional craft paradigm* views teaching as a body of craft knowledge and skill that can only be acquired through apprenticeship. And the *inquiry oriented paradigm* views teaching in a wider social context of which the teacher must become aware in order to make judgments about the appropriateness of their own values and actions. These paradigms might also be regarded as reflecting different epistemologies of practice, different ways of thinking about the nature of knowledge that teachers possess and how it is acquired.

Because there are numerous ways of thinking both about research and about practice, it then becomes possible for McNamara, for instance, to conceive of research on teacher thinking in positivist terms as a body of theoretical knowledge and principles about how teachers plan and make decisions, and at the same time to consider classroom practice in terms of a craft in which teachers' knowledge is tacit and contextualised, and therefore to come to the conclusion that research on teacher thinking has no contribution whatever to make to teacher education. Similarly, it is possible for Floden and Klinzing, who appear to view research on teacher thinking as falling into a positivist tradition and view teacher education as a collection of technical skills, to come to the conclusion that research on teacher thinking has enormous potential to lay the basis for teacher education programs.

Going Beyond Existing Paradigms

It is argued here that much of the debate about whether and how research on teaching might be of use in teacher education rests on narrow, stereotyped assumptions both about the nature of research and the nature of practice. Depending upon the assumptions one cares to make one could argue either for or against the contribution that research on teachers' thinking might provide.

There are two reasons why the above classifications of research and practice could be useful. First of all, they help us understand where the protagonists are coming from and the assumptions they make in their arguments, and to recognise some of the essentially straw man arguments that are being presented. Secondly, it raises the possibility of looking beyond fixed standpoints. McCutcheon (1981), for example, suggests that the division of research approaches into the positivist, the phenomenological and the critical doesn't reflect so much a set of three discrete categories as much as the parameters within which researchers work, and that these stereotypes might be represented schematically as the apexes of a triangle. Whilst one might well find some examples of research which typify each stereotype, the vast majority of research actually combines elements of two or even all three. The diverse range of research on teachers' thinking, therefore, does not fall within any one tradition but could be represented in terms of points within the triangle.

Similarly, if we take Zeichner's classification of views of classroom practice, it is extremely difficult to find examples of teacher training programs that typify any one paradigm. A teacher training program may be far more likely to reflect a combination of these. Classroom practice itself involves aspects of the knowledge emphasised in each of the paradigms. To complicate matters, it may be that different student teachers learn in different ways at different times, and therefore the process of learning to teach is far more complex than is acknowledged by any one paradigm. Some student teachers, for example, may need to adopt some basic survival strategies and be taught how to reflect before they can begin to be oriented to development through self-enquiry, whereas others may be well oriented to learn through enquiry from the start (Korthagen, 1988). Technical skills, craft, personalistic and inquiry oriented approaches to professional development may therefore be appropriate at different times in a teacher's career and at different times for different teachers.

The Inter-relationship of Research and Practice

If we accept that both research and practice are highly complex activities that are not at present accountable for in terms of single specific paradigms, we can begin to appreciate that:

(a) the relationship between research and practice is also inevitably complex;
(b) that an individual area of research might relate to different aspects of practice in different ways;
(c) that teacher educators might usefully take a more eclectic view both of research and practice in order to improve their understanding of teacher education.

The significance of each of these points can be explored further. For example, the topic of teacher planning has in the past attracted research activity and has also been an area that has presented numerous difficulties in teacher education. We have a body of research evidence on experienced teachers' planning that tells us that planning is not a rational, linear process as depicted in the commonly pre-scribed rational planning models, but a much more creative, interactive, problem-finding and problem-solving process, where teachers may start with an idea, a child's difficulty, a textbook or a curriculum guide and draw upon an enormous range of knowledge about children, teaching strategies, how particular activities might be organised, how long children take to do certain things, teaching mater-ials, children's learning, accepted ways of doing things within the school and so on to construct eventually a conception of a classroom activity or series of activities (see McCutcheon, 1980; Clark and Peterson, 1986; Sardo-Brown, 1990). And in teacher education we have a body of painful experience that tells us that planning is something that is difficult to teach to students. Typically, we ask student teachers to plan a scheme of work before going out into schools, and to use objectives models when planning individual lessons. We can offer good reasons for such prescriptions — we want students to think of lessons in the context of a curricular framework and long-term goals, and we want them to think about what children are going to learn from individual lessons. But it is also well recognised amongst teacher educators that this approach has many drawbacks. Student teachers, when they take their schemes of work into schools, often find that they have misjudged children's abilities or failed to take account of the context in which they will be working, the materials available, or the expectations of the school, and in con-sequence have to abandon their plans. And when asked about objectives models, they generally confess that they do not actually plan that way, and see the rational planning frameworks more as a constraint than a facilitator.

If we take a simple view of research and practice and the relationship between them, there is an apparent easy solution to this problem. Research tells us how experienced teachers plan, student teachers do not know how to plan, therefore we can tell them about the research and the problem will be solved. Such an approach has generally not been found to be effective either.

However, once it is acknowledged that classroom practice is in fact much more complex, and that much of the research on teacher planning offers a fairly restricted and partial account of the issues concerning planning, then it becomes possible to use that research more constructively and to recognise, for instance, that the knowledge teachers use in planning is highly specific, relating to particu-lar children, school contexts or curriculum materials; to recognise that planning also involves issues of values and beliefs; to recognise that much of the knowledge that teachers use can only have been abstracted from lengthy experience (e.g. learning appropriate expectations for a practical science lesson); that the ways in which beginning teachers learn to plan may differ; and that there are other areas of research (such as student teachers' learning) that might be equally informative for teacher educators. Once that greater complexity of research and practice is appreciated, we can start to think about the design and evaluation of potentially useful professional development activities that more adequately reflect the difficult and multi-faceted task of learning to teach: activities, for instance, that enable student teachers and experienced teachers to work collaboratively in planning, where each attempts to make the expert's knowledge explicit and explore how and when it is used; or activities that enable the exploration of how alternative values influence teachers' planning.

It is all too common, however, for research to be interpreted in teacher education in line with one particular, and often very restricted, view of classroom practice. This is evident, for instance, in the current vogue for reflective teaching. The term has become a widely used slogan in teacher education, and some have even described it as a movement, reacting against more centralised policy views of teachers as technicians (Copeland, 1991). The term has been used to refer to widely differing practices, however, and there are examples of reflective teacher education programmes that embody each of Zeichner's four paradigms, ranging from reflection as a component of skill and a means to effective teaching, to reflection as a heightening of one's awareness of social justice in educational practice.

Different conceptions of reflective practice seem to have channelled teacher educators to draw upon specific areas of research to inform their ideas of reflection and also to provide methods, such as narratives and journal writing, stimulated recall, action research and ethnographies, that might be transposed from a research to a practice setting. For example, the Maryland reflective teacher education program, described by McCaleb, Borko and Arends (1992), views reflection primarily in terms of evaluation skills and draws on research on teaching, and especially teacher thinking, in the program as a means of increasing student teachers' repertoire of concepts that can be used in analysis and evaluation. Ross, Johnson and Smith's (1992) account of the Florida reflective teacher education program, on the other hand, sees reflection in terms of personal and professional growth and adopts a series of processes to promote student teachers' examination of their own educational values and beliefs. Many reflective teacher education programs appear in fact to draw upon fairly narrow conceptions both of research and practice. It is also infrequent for the relationship between research and practice to be viewed as interactive. Perhaps understandably, teacher educators writing about reflective teaching have generally employed research selectively to illustrate or support their standpoints or provide a methodology for teacher education. For instance, work on narratives and journal writing has been used to justify reflective practices in some programs and also to provide a methodology, but the use of such approaches in teacher education itself raises many questions that are important to explore in order to extend our understanding of professional development. For instance, how does journal writing contribute to students' professional development — is it inspiring confidence through valuing the person? Is it making educational values and assumptions explicit and therefore more amenable to critical scrutiny? Is it essentially cathartic in alleviating anxiety about classroom experiences? Does it promote greater autonomy and self-direction in professional development by thrusting greater responsibility upon the students themselves? Does it facilitate problem-solving by helping teachers make their problems explicit? Both for teacher education and for research, it is important to pursue these questions so that the processes of professional development are more fully understood and so that the ways in which it can be structured and facilitated can also be appreciated, leading perhaps in turn to other practices in teacher education and other questions for research.

Conclusion

The conclusion this paper is leading to is first of all that it is not surprising that teacher educators have in the past not turned in vast numbers to research to develop fuller conceptualisations of their work, because this is itself an extremely problematic task. Secondly, in order to explore, conceptualise and defend teacher education practices, there is a need to develop much closer links between research, widely defined, and practices in teacher education. Thirdly, the relationship between research and practice in teacher education has tended in the past to be characterised by fairly insular conceptions of both research and practice and a tendency to view research purely as a means of supporting and informing practice rather than in terms of a reciprocal questioning and exploration. At present, we lack a well established epistemology of practice, and it is suggested that an eclectic, exploratory approach to its development will avoid the inevitable imprisonment in restricted ways of thinking about teaching and learning to teach. The development of further understanding of professional development may be dependent on recognising the complexity and diversity of both research and practice and acknowledging that the relationship between the two is interactive and multifaceted. To do otherwise would be to support very partial accounts of what teacher education is about, and to be ill equipped to counter, or see beyond some of the constraints and ideologies that are being foisted upon teacher education at the present time.

References

CLARK, C.M. (1988) 'Asking the right questions about teacher preparation: contributions of research on teacher thinking', *Educational Researcher*, **17**(2), pp. 5–12.

CLARK, C.M. and PETERSON, P.L. (1986) 'Teachers' thought processes', in WITTROCK, M.C. (Ed.) *Handbook of Research on Teaching, third edition*, New York: Macmillan.

COPELAND, W.D. (1991) 'The reflective practitioner in teaching'. Paper presented at the American Educational Research Association annual meeting, Chicago, 1991.

ELLIOTT, J. (1980) 'Implications of classroom research for professional development', in HOYLE, E. and MEGARRY, J. (Eds) *World Yearbook of Education, 1980*, London: Kogan Page.

FENSTERMACHER (1986) 'Philosophy of research on teaching: three aspects', in WITTROCK, M.C. (Ed.) *Handbook of Research on Teaching, third edition*, New York: Macmillan.

FLODEN, R.E. and KLINZING, H.G. (1990) 'What can research on teacher thinking contribute to teacher preparation? A second opinion', *Educational Researcher*, **19**(5), pp. 15–20.

FURLONG, V.J., HIRST, P.H., POCKLINGTON, K. and MILES, S. (1988) *Initial Teacher Training and the Role of the School*, Milton Keynes: Open University Press.

GIBSON, R. (1986) *Critical Theory and Education*, London: Hodder and Stoughton.

KORTHAGEN, F.A.J. (1988) 'The influence of learning orientations on the development of reflective teaching', in CALDERHEAD, J. (Ed.) *Teachers' Professional Learning*, London: Falmer Press.

McCaleb, J., Borko, H. and Arends, R. (1992) 'Reflection, research and repertoire in the Masters certification program', in Valli, L. (Ed.) *Reflective Teacher Education: Cases and Critiques*, New York: SUNY Press.

McCutcheon, G. (1980) 'How do elementary school teachers plan? The nature of planning and influences on it', *The Elementary School Journal*, **81**, pp. 4–23.

— (1981) 'On the interpretation of classroom observation', *Educational Researcher*, **10**(5), pp. 5–10.

McIntyre, D. (1980) 'The contribution of research to quality in teacher education', in Hoyle, E. and Megarry, J. (Eds) *World Yearbook of Education. 1980*, London: Kogan Page.

McNamara, D. (1990) 'Research on teachers' thinking: its contribution to educating student teachers to think critically', *Journal of Education for Teaching*, **16**(2), pp. 147–60.

Ross, D., Johnson, M., and Smith, W. (1992) 'Developing a PROfessional TEACHer', in Valli, L. (Ed.) *Reflective Teacher Education: Cases and Critiques*, New York: SUNY Press.

Sardo-Brown, D. (1990) 'Experienced teachers' planning practices: a US survey', *Journal of Education for Teaching*, **16**, pp. 57–71.

Shulman, L. (1986) 'Paradigms and research programs in the study of teaching: a contemporary perspective', in Wittrock, M.C. (Ed.) *Handbook of Research on Teaching, third edition*, New York: Macmillan.

Zeichner, K.M. (1983) 'Alternative paradigms of teacher education', *Journal of Teacher Education*, **34**(3), pp. 3–9.

Chapter 2

Anticipating Teacher Thinking

Maureen Pope

This chapter will consider the anticipatory nature of theory building with a particular focus on teacher thinking research. Consideration will be given to the extent to which research into teacher thinking can be seen to be a progressive research program in the Lakatosian sense. It is perhaps timely for us as reflective practitioners of teacher thinking research that we consider the focus of our work and the protective belt which we may be erecting.

If one peruses the scientific discourse of teacher thinking researchers one can detect particular interpretative perspectives amongst them. Some examples of the language used to describe our craft will be given. Kuhn (1970) pointed to the central role of language in the development of a paradigm. The examples given reflect the teacher thinking paradigm in its current state. Teacher thinking research has evolved as an alternative paradigm to that form of research which aimed to link teacher personality to action in the classroom. One can question whether the language used by different researchers within teacher thinking research is incommensurable.

The area of appropriateness of research methodology within teacher thinking has been addressed and a paradigmatic move towards qualitative research can be detected. In this chapter I will suggest a number of directions that teacher thinking research could take in terms of methodology and areas of focus. In commenting on the future of psychology, Kelly (1969: 17) commented 'In order to survive, psychology must invent as well as discover'. I will argue that this equally applies to teacher thinking research and it is imperative that we anticipate new horizons if the theoretical foundations of our work can be seen as a truly progressive paradigm.

A major proportion of ISATT researchers embrace some form of constructivism in their thinking about knowledge and its development. Many have been particularly influenced by the work of George Kelly (1955) and his philosophy of constructive alternativism. Kelly maintained that knowledge was not developed by collecting 'nuggets of truth' — this he labelled accumulative fragmentalism. Reality exists, but the philosophy of constructive alternativism holds that we do not conceive this directly, rather we place an interpretation on our worlds. Our knowledge is limited by the extent to which we are courageous in our experimentation with alternative constructions of the world.

Kelly maintained that we do not need to be victims of our biography if we accept our responsibility for shaping our future. The constructs we erect as our navigational model of the world have a dual function, that of theory testing and theory building. Our construct system is that with which we *anticipate* future events. Persons are not reactive to their environment but have the potential for constructing new horizons.

The *anticipatory* function of image or constructs should be stressed. Connelly and Clandinin (1984: 147) refer to an image as reaching 'into the past gathering up experiential threads meaningfully connected to the present. And it reaches intentionally into the future. . .'.

In this chapter I do not intend to provide an exhaustive review of research on teacher thinking. The writings of Clark and Peterson (1986) and the selective papers from previous ISATT conferences published in Halkes and Olson (Eds) (1984), Ben-Peretz, Bromme and Halkes (Eds) (1986), Lowyck and Clark (Eds) (1989) and Day, Pope and Denicolo (Eds) (1990) provide a rich source of literature on teacher thinking. In addition, Calderhead (1987) has edited a collection of works by researchers in this field. Such material provides some evidence as to the main assumptions operating within the field of teacher thinking. The 'reflective practitioner' (Schon, 1983) needs to reflect critically on the meaning of his or her thoughts and actions as a route to the enhancement of professional practice. Researchers need to examine some of their fundamental beliefs. Consideration of current constructs does not necessarily imply the need to change, although we may deduce that in some areas we have been limited. We need to be prepared to entertain alternatives.

In analysing the progress of science, Lakatos (1970: 104) made an important distinction between passivist and activist theories of knowledge in that:

> Passivists hold that true knowledge is Nature's imprint on a perfectly inert mind: mental activity can only result in bias and distortion. . . . But revolutionary activists believe that conceptual frameworks can be developed and also replaced by new, better ones; it is we who create our 'prisons' and we can also, critically, demolish them.

This view of knowledge is similar to that of Kelly's constructive alternativism. Kelly referred to the frames we create to interpret our world as a system of personal constructs within which certain of these are core or fundamental in defining our existence. Lakatos (1970) had a similar view when he analysed the progress of science. It might be illuminating to apply Lakatos's notions to the progress of teacher thinking research.

Lakatos's central notion was that of a research program. This he saw as an evolving succession of theories, characterised by a negative heuristic and a positive heuristic. Whilst successive theories evolve, the research program is held together by a set of fundamental assumptions, the 'hard core' of the program. The following could be some of the hard core assumptions of teacher thinking researchers adopting a constructivist perspective:

- the world is real but individuals vary in their perception of it;
- an individual's conception of the real world has integrity for that individual;
- teachers use personally pre-existing theories to explain and plan their teaching;

- teachers test these theories for fruitfulness and modify them in the light of such testing.

This set of assumptions sees the teacher as a reflective practitioner (Schon, 1983). This assumption, being part of the hard core, is not put to the test. Lakatos suggests that the hard core is kept intact through a series of auxiliary hypotheses which function as a 'protective belt'. The research programme can be kept empirically progressive by the operation of these auxiliary hypotheses. Examples of this within teacher thinking research are the many studies into the differences between novice and expert teachers within a number of different subject areas.

A research programme will have distinct aims although the fundamental assumptions are not necessarily articulated in detail. We can perhaps look to Halkes and Olson (1984: 1) for a statement which reflects the fundamental aim of many teacher thinking researchers.

> Looking from a teacher thinking perspective at teaching and learning, one is not so much striving for the disclosure of 'the' effective teacher, but for the explanation and understanding of the teaching processes as they are. After all, it is the teacher's subjective school-related knowledge which determines for the most part what happens in the classroom; whether the teacher can articulate his/her knowledge or not. Instead of reducing the complexities of the teaching learning situations into a few manageable research variables, one tries to find out how teachers cope with these complexities.

Teacher thinking research has adopted a different paradigm from that which has dominated educational research in the past. Consider, for example, the following quote from Kerlinger (1977: 5–6):

> The purpose of scientific research is theory . . . scientific research never has the purpose of solving human or social problems, making decisions, and taking action. The researcher is preoccupied with, and should be preoccupied with, variables and their relations. He should never be required to think about or to spell out the educational implications of what he is doing or has done.

Kerlinger was suggesting a particular methodology not only for educational research but for the purpose to which it is put. Halkes and Olson are suggesting description of teachers' thinking as the major purpose. Lowyck (1990: 86) questions this focus on describing in order to explain and understand teaching and asks 'Can we really be interested in teaching as it is, without any perspective on improvement?'

Adopting a Lakatosian perspective it is possible, within a teacher thinking research programme, for there to be differing aims and methods used, provided these are compatible with the hard core of the negative heuristic. Much of the earlier work on teacher thinking drew upon cognitive psychology, particularly information processing theory, giving rise to metaphors such as 'teacher–as–decision maker' (Shavelson, 1976). However, Clark (1986: 9) noted that:

Table 2.1: *Some Theoretical Concepts in Research on Teacher Thinking*

TEACHERS' UNDERSTANDINGS	– Bussis, Chittenden and Amarel, 1976
TEACHER CONSTRUCTS	– Olson, 1980
DECISION STRATEGIES	– Borko and Caldwell, 1982
METAPHORS/BELIEFS	– Munby, 1982
PRACTICAL KNOWLEDGE	– Elbaz, 1983
TEACHERS' VOICE	– Butt, 1984
PERSONAL INTENTIONS	– Day, 1984
TEACHERS' COGNITION	– Huber and Mandl, 1984
TEACHERS' CONCEPTIONS	– Larsson, 1984
INTUITIVE THEORIES	– Pope and Denicolo, 1984
PERSONAL CONSTRUCTS	– Pope and Scott, 1984
KNOTS/IMPERATIVE COGNITIONS	– Wagner, 1984
TEACHERS' COGNITIVE ACTIVITIES	– Bromme and Brophy, 1985
IMAGE	– Clandinin 1985
PERSONAL PRACTICAL KNOWLEDGE	– Connelly and Clandinin, 1985
TEACHERS' PERSPECTIVES	– Tabachnik and Zeichner, 1985
EXPERT PEDAGOGUE	– Berliner, 1986
PROFESSIONAL CRAFT KNOWLEDGE	– Brown and McIntyre, 1986
SCRIPTS/SCHEMA	– Clark and Peterson, 1986
SUBJECTIVE THEORIES	– Krause, 1986
DILEMMAS	– Lampert, 1986
ROUTINES	– Leinhardt and Greeno, 1986
PLANS	– Clark and Yinger, 1987

The teacher of 1985 is a constructivist who continually builds, elaborates, and tests his or her personal theory of the world . . . we have begun to move away from the cybernetically elegant, internally consistent, but mechanical metaphors that guided our earlier work.

A current core assumption is that teacher thinking researchers are trying to understand and interpret ways in which teachers make sense of and adjust to and create the educational environment within their schools and classrooms. Whilst sharing a focus and ideological commitment to viewing teachers as active agents in the development of educative events, the field of teacher thinking is diverse in terms of theoretical and methodological approaches. Kuhn (1970) would probably assess the field as pre-paradigmatic. He stressed the sociological and psychological aspects of the development of science and suggested that the community of scholars develops a set of premises and language which separates them from a previous paradigm. The language of one paradigm is deemed to be incommensurable with that of a subsequent paradigm. The community of teacher thinking scholars embraces a wide range including psychologists, sociologists, curriculum specialists, anthropologists, philosophers, linguists and a variety of 'subject specialists' e.g. mathematicians and physicists. If one peruses the scientific discourse of teacher thinking researchers, one can detect particular interpretative perspectives amongst them. Table 2.1 gives some examples of the language used to describe our craft.

Given Kuhn's emphasis on language as a determinant that shapes our thinking within a paradigm, one needs to ask to what extent is the different language used by these researchers such that it renders them incommensurable with each other. One advantage of adopting a Lakatosian framework is that it is possible to entertain variants without threatening the core of the program. I would suggest that the above work is a demonstration of the progressiveness of the teacher thinking research programme in building a body of empirical data to support the general premises of the program. The above works are some of the examples of *what* is the focus of teacher thinking research; they may vary in terms of the *purpose* and the 'how' of the research.

Hunt (1987: 54), commenting on 'the enormous increase in research on teacher thinking', suggests that it 'seems to be a sign of accepting and respecting teachers' experienced knowledge', but he advises caution and asks:

> Why are psychological theorists and educational researchers interested in teacher thinking? To develop conceptual models of teacher thinking (Outside in)? To evaluate critically how teachers think (Outside in)? To catalog the different kinds of thinking among different groups of teachers (Outside in)? Or to help the teachers themselves clarify their thinking to form a foundation that enables them to communicate with other teachers and develop and extend their theories (Inside out)?

Teacher thinking researchers should ask themselves this question. I see myself as largely engaged in 'inside out' research. No doubt all four rationales exist in current research. Berliner (1986), for example, uses standardised tasks in laboratory settings. He has been concerned with conceptualisation of teacher thinking in terms of routines, scripts and schema. By comparing novices versus expert teachers, and experienced versus less experienced teachers, particularly in mathematics and science, he has identified 'the troublesome routines or scripts or ill-informed schemata, that are characteristics of less expert/less experienced teachers' (p. 77). Categorising different kinds of thinking exists amongst those whose methodology is not of the 'standardised test' variety. Carlgren (1987) for example, using a phenomenographic approach (Marton, 1981), describes teachers' conceptions of their own innovative work in terms of different categories or thinking modes. There are many examples of what Hunt would categorise as 'Outside in' research. However, the focus of research on teacher thinking and methodology used has shifted. There is much more emphasis on Hunt's fourth rationale.

As in other fields of social enquiry, methodological debates regarding appropriateness of particular paradigms exist within educational research (see, e.g. Popkewitz, T. (1984), *Paradigm and Ideology in Educational Research*). Kemmis (1989) draws on the critical theory tradition of the Frankfurt School and Habermas's categories and summarises some of the major aspects of the positivist, interpretative, and critical research approaches to education science. My own view is that all three forms of research, i.e. positivist, interpretative and critical, can be identified within the field of teacher thinking research.

Within the interpretative model the important features for teacher thinking research are the emphases placed on Verstehen (understanding) of the complexity of situations adopting a more holistic stance towards definition of that to be researched; likewise, the importance of authenticity of material, as opposed to the traditional concepts of validity and reliability, and the interactive mode of engagement with participants offering them bilateral control of the research process with the view that the 'results' of such engagement lie in the utility of the process for informing and changing praxis.

Table 2.2: Assumptions within the Interpretative Form of Research

	KNOWLEDGE AS CONSTRUCTION OF REALITY		
COHERENCE theory of truth			IDIOGRAPHIC
SUBJECTIVITY (objectivity = social agreement)	INTERPRETATIVE FORM OF RESEARCH		SCIENTIFIC VERSTEHEN
REFLEXIVE			
DESCRIPTIVE			AUTHENTICITY
PRAXIS			UTILITY
BILATERAL CONTROL			INTERACTIVE
	HOLISTIC		

In Table 2.2 I suggest a protective belt of assumptions inherent in the interpretative form of research; these are discussed in Pope and Denicolo (1986). I believe that these are consistent with the basis of much of current teacher thinking research. Shifts in individual writers can be noticed, for example, Yinger's (1978) work reflects a search for cognitive structure, whereas his later work, Yinger (1987), is attempting to illuminate the classroom language and interplay between actors in the process of teaching.

Research on teacher thinking has moved beyond the purpose of being 'merely curious about teachers' thought and action' (Clark 1986: 7). Writers such as Day (1984), Connelly and Clandinin (1985), Butt (1984), Yinger (1987) and Elbaz (1988), reflect their concern to enable participants in such research to gain from the experience of reflection and clarification of their thinking in anticipation of further action. Calderhead (1987) discusses the practical contribution of teacher thinking research which includes recognition of the complexity and ambiguity of the professional domain in which teachers work, the role of teacher thinking in the implementation of curriculum innovations and helping us to 'conceptualise the processes of professional development and how these might be enhanced through pre-service and in-service education' (p. 17).

Clark (1986: 4) advocates thinking about research on teaching 'as providing *service* to the practice of teaching'. In order to enhance this a change of relationship between teachers and researchers is developing and the goal of teacher thinking research has become that of 'portraying and understanding good teaching in all of its irreducible complexity and difficulty. Quality portraiture may be of more practical and inspirational value than reductionistic analysis and technical prescriptiveness'.

Clark is suggesting a purpose which is in contradistinction to that indicated by Kerlinger. Adopting a position such as Clark advocates necessitates a rethink of the traditional researcher's role. Just as teacher-as-constructivist needs to experiment with alternative constructions so, too, do researchers on teacher thinking need to reflect and evolve differing research processes to be consistent with a change of focus in the research programme.

Kelly's root metaphor person-the-scientist has been of use in my own theorising. Recently, alongside other personal construct psychologists, I have been exploring the implications of an alternative metaphor, that of person-as-story-teller. This is implicit in much of recent teacher thinking research. One can think, for example, of the work of Elbaz (1990).

Howard (1988) suggests that the model of 'human as storytellers' may assist in the evolution of personal construct psychology as a 'living, viable, intellectual enterprise' (p. 270). The work of Sarbin (1986) and Polkinghorne (1987) on narratives and story analysis and Mair's (1988) article 'Psychology as Storytelling' are important texts which we could reflect upon and ask ourselves: 'If I think about my research in such terms, then what are the ramifications for the anticipated future of my work?'

Mair advocates a 'psychology that shows more care for the *stories we live* and the *stories we can tell*' (p. 130). This will require a shift from much of our conventional training and the stories of the world of psychology we were induced into.

In reflecting on my work within teacher thinking I have noted an evolution in techniques employed — from my earlier work (Pope, 1978) using repertory grids to more recent emphasis on biographical methods, 'snakes' and concept mapping (Denicolo and Pope, 1990). Needless to say, these techniques have allowed different stories to be told regarding teacher thinking. My current inclination is that autobiographies will become increasingly important since they allow more ownership and authorship of the stories to be told by the teachers. The use of Kelly's self characterisation sketch method is worthy of exploration.

Much of teacher craft thinking is tacit — i.e. knowhow gained through experience and not usually articulated. Autobiographies may reveal something of this tacit knowledge *provided* that these are also related to current everyday classroom problems that teachers experience. They should also help reveal what Wagner (1984) terms 'Knots in thinking' — the conflicts faced by teachers in their professional practice. These are not merely intellectual discussions and strategies to be evolved but are 'subjectivity experienced as anger, anxiety or stress' (p. 163).

The telling of and reflection on autobiographic narratives can make conscious for the teacher the images, knots imperatives, core constructs and experiential metaphors forming part of the teachers' professional lore. It can be emancipatory in the sense that the telling of the story liberates an understanding of its power. By making the tacit articulate it can be critically appraised.

If we adopt more autobiographical or biographical methods within our research on teacher thinking, then Elbaz (1990) notes some important problems which need to be addressed, ones similar to those raised by Mair (1988) and by teachers themselves, i.e. *whose story is it anyway?* Elbaz notes that the discourse of teaching and of much educational research has meant that it has been difficult for teachers to voice their concerns. She draws attention to the *non-linearity* of tacit knowledge and suggests that researchers drawing on psychological models of problem-solving or decision-making have usually accounted for this non-linearity in negative terms (e.g. Shavelson and Stern, 1981). She suggests (p. 19) that 'since tacit knowledge is not always coherent and consistent, the teacher's voice ought to be able to speak in several registers at once; teachers' knowledge is not logically sequenced or linear and there are many concerns being entertained at any given moment'.

This poses a number of methodological problems, including the problem of *research reporting on teachers' narrative*. Whilst metaphors such as teacher-as-constructivist can be transformed into teacher-as-storyteller without extensive shift from a constructivist perspective, in so doing we have to recognise that teachers themselves may not identify with some of the stories which may be told — especially if they are not asked to authenticate the tale.

The questioning by teachers of much of traditional research has been well documented (Stenhouse, 1975; Deforges and McNamara, 1979; Elliott and Whitehead, 1980). Jones (1989: 51) puts his view graphically when he says:

> Much research related to education had the cutting edge of a sponge; for a long time I questioned the honesty of much that I read about in some of the academic journals. Don't get me wrong, I'm not suggesting that their authors were anything but sincere and well intentioned. What I am trying to say is that their research did not speak the truth to me. These works seemed more concerned with statistics than sensitivities; rats rather than brats; research rather than the researched.

This lack of identification with the researcher's story has been a prime force behind the teacher-as-researcher movement and fostered an interest in action research by teachers in their own schools. Lomax (1989) is an interesting collection of action research reports which seek to address criticisms such as those lobbied by Jones.

Action research approaches encourage teachers to ground their analysis of educational issues in the evidence they generate from reflection on their own context rather than borrow from or rely on the 'grand' theories from psychology, sociology, philosophy, etc., particularly those positivistic theories suggesting truth statements expressed as nomothetic context-free generalisations. Thus authentic contextual relevance and the empowering of participants both to contribute fully to such research and to apply practically the ongoing results are of paramount importance in such approaches to professional development.

The importance of full participation is one notion held in common by personal construct psychologists and action research theorists, e.g. Grundy and Kemmis (1982). In addition to their emphasis on collaborative participation, action researchers and personal construct psychologists share the following core assumptions consistent with those outlined earlier as those describing a set of assumptions for a teacher thinkers' research programme:

- the person is a responsible agent;
- growth may occur through reflection *on* and *in* action;
- understanding another's perspective requires empathy and a 'conversational' approach;
- the participant's and researcher's account of events may differ and needs to be negotiated;
- human beings are active, meaning seeking, potentially open to change, development, and capable of self-direction.

Linter (1989) gives an account of his action research into his own practice which highlighted 'a number of issues that had been hidden before the research was undertaken' (p. 87). As an initial phase of his research Linter explored what he saw as characteristics of his practice using a repertory grid, and established some of the values he assumed were underlying his practice. He then put these values to the test to see the extent to which they were expressed in practice. Linter also used his pupils as collaborators. He concluded that from his own experience of action research involving reflection on practice it 'is an extremely time consuming experience but is very rewarding' (p. 96).

Despite the time consuming aspect, such research is essential for the teacher who wishes to act as a reflective practitioner. The role of the teacher thinking researcher becomes one of an adviser on research tools and consultant on process.

Tools with this dual purpose include diaries, logs or journals (Warner, 1971); self-narrative auto-ethnography (Elbaz, 1990); auto-biography (Pinar, 1981); illuminative incident analysis (Pope, 1981); biography (Butt, 1984); repertory grids (Diamond, 1985); life history (Woods, 1985); 'snakes' (Denicolo and Pope, 1990). Viney (1989: 9) examines the implications of constructivists' assumptions for social science and anticipates how we should work in the 1990s. She suggests that:

> As researchers we learn to examine our own assumptions more carefully, make appropriate use of the constructivist abilities of our data contributors and collectors, and develop more collaborative data collection interactions. . . . I have recommended employing a greater range of methods and more data analyses using constructivist, theatre related and narrative analyses. These latter suggestions could lead to the use of a wider variety of methods of data collection and more meaning-based methods of data analysis.

The tools suggested above can extend our repertoire of data collection techniques within teacher thinking research. However, it is not simply a case of increasing our kitbag of tools. The implications of a constructivist perspective on research would require us to reconsider our roles as research workers. I commented earlier that there had been a paradigmatic swing towards more qualitative data collection methods within an interpretative approach to research and that action research is a fruitful vehicle for the foreseeable future. Adopting a more consultative role the researcher has to undertake a carefully modulated set of negotiations for such research to be fruitful.

Day (1990) gives an account of five school-initiated and school-based professional and curriculum development projects. Day's role was that of an 'external evaluator' and was designated in a brief provided by the school team as that of a 'sympathetic outsider to tell us what is happening as we go along . . . and later to report our feelings as people, our perceptions as professionals, our achievements as educators'. In order to fulfil such a brief Day needed to 'achieve an evaluation which was derived from the cultural perspectives of the participants . . . to seek insider information and respect indigenous definitions and values' (p. 2). Action research and school-initiated work such as Day describes are consistent with what Clark (1986: 14) suggests is a 'mission of advocacy and service to teachers'. This aspect of our research requires that we pay more attention to 'the volatile and challenging problem areas in our education systems'. For Clark these include

- poverty
- nationalism
- cultural conflict
- racism
- sexism
- discrimination
- massive failure to learn in certain quarters of our educational systems.

Clark points out that most of our work is on teacher planning and decision-making which has been done 'almost exclusively in nice, well organised, upper middle class suburban elementary school classrooms' (p. 16).

Elbaz (1990) has drawn attention to a potential danger within teacher thinking research in addition to those highlighted by Clark. She maintains that much, if not all, of our work is based upon the teacher thinking of articulate teachers. The silent voice of the ordinary teacher is not illuminated in the stories we tell. Within teacher thinking research there are those who are critical of Elbaz's approach. Berliner (1986), for example, admits that 'thinking of ordinary people usually bores me'. However, 'I do not think that it is usually a wise expenditure of our minimal resources to do studies of the thinking of ordinary people. They can so easily mislead us' (pp. 19, 20). Berliner cites the case of his mother who, whilst being articulate and well able to voice her thoughts about planning to cook and her thoughts and decisions while cooking, was nevertheless a terrible cook. As Berliner said 'a record of her thoughts would surely have misled'. However, this is returning to the issue raised by Lowyck. In describing the actual behaviour of teachers we may not be concentrating solely on effectiveness within teaching. I would suggest that within our teacher research programme there is room for both agendas. There is room for Berliner's process-product research with its roots in functionalism alongside qualitative approaches such as action research.

Clark (1986) suggested that we need to avoid narrow parochial attitudes within our research and that this could be the result if we focus too much on the teacher as a source of influence and become 'insensitive to the very powerful forces and constraints that shape and influence schooling'. There is a need for more research on the teachers' thinking about:

- political constraints on education;
- the management of budgets;
- the interpersonal context of teaching;
- the role of classroom dialogue.

We would be advised to take note of teacher thinking research within contexts other than schools. We can perhaps learn much from the theoretical underpinnings and methodology used by, for example, Letiche's (1988) study of polytechnic teachers and also that of Akinsanya (1988) in nurse education. Comparative studies are few. Osborne and Broadfoot of the University of Bristol and Gilly and Paillet of the Université de Provence have compared French and British classrooms. Likewise Pope and Denicolo and Ben-Peretz have compared the attitudes towards their professional role of Israeli and British teachers whilst, in conjunction with de Bernardi, they have made comparisons with Italian teachers.

The future focus of teacher thinking research will be a personal choice of individual researchers. Schon (1983: 43) suggested that in considering options within professional practice:

> there are those who choose the swampy lowlands. They deliberately involve themselves in messy but crucially important problems . . . other professionals opt for the high ground. Hungry for technical rigour.

It is perhaps not so much a matter of which avenues we choose, i.e. whether we choose to inhabit the high ground or get ourselves immersed in the swamps. More important is that we act as reflective practitioners and become aware of our constructs in use and keep them under review — allowing ourselves the opportunity to extend our horizons.

Hampshire (1983: 267–8) argues for the need to become explicit about our choices.

> The more explicit a man (*sic*) is in formulating to himself the end of his action, and the grounds upon which his decisions rest, the more he is aware of himself as having made choices between specific possibilities, choices that are always subject to revision. The more self-conscious he is in his criticism of his own intentions and activities, the more he is aware of the limits of his habits of classification, limits that determine the possibilities open to him.

Reflection on practice and making explicit one's choices is no easy matter. The consultant role recently advocated to aid the teacher has its parallels in the possibilities afforded within international conferences. Personal contact is essential in innovation because it provides the opportunity for dialogue and questioning and the intense form of interaction that can accompany radical changes in attitude. Such personal contacts go beyond mere exchange of information. This should provide the opportunity to develop what Lakatos would call the 'positive heuristic' of our work, i.e. some partially articulated sets of suggestions or hints on how to change and to develop 'refutable variants' of our research program. I invite you to anticipate what some of these might be.

So far I have suggested that our work shows some of the features of a Lakatosian research program. It is certainly progressive in the sense of having spawned a large amount of research under the umbrella of ISATT. At the 1988 conference there were some eighteen countries represented which demonstrates a worldwide interest in the research program.

However, in order for it not to become degenerate, it must not fail to lead to the discovery of novel phenomena. Keeping our choices under review is one way to ensure progression in our work. Failure to do this will lead to a degenerate programme and Kelly (1955) warns us of the dangers of a 'hardening of the categories'. He saw this as a common affliction amongst scientists, which could herald the end of a creative phase of a hitherto distinguished career. The responsibility lies with each of us to avoid such an affliction!

References

AKINSANYA, J. (1988) 'Teacher Research Methods in Nursing: A Demystifying Approach'. Paper presented at the 4th International Conference of ISATT, Nottingham, September 1988.

BEN-PERETZ, M., BROMME, R. and HALKES, R. (Eds) (1986) *Advances of Research on Teacher Thinking*, Lisse, Netherlands: Swets and Zeitlinger.

BERLINER, D.C. (1986) 'In pursuit of the expert pedagogue', *Educational Researcher*, 15(7), pp. 5–13.

— (1986) 'The Place of Process Product Research in Developing an Agenda for Research on Teacher Thinking', invited address 3rd Conference on Teacher Thinking and Professional Action, Leuven University, Leuven, October 1986.

BORKO, H. and CALDWELL, J. (1982) 'Individual differences in teachers' decision strategies: an investigation of classroom organisation and management decisions', *Journal of Educational Psychology*, 74(4), pp. 598–610.

BROMME, R. and BROPHY, J.E. (1985) 'Teachers' cognitive activities', in CHRISTIANSEN, B. (Ed.) *Perspectives in Mathematical Education*, Dordrect: Reidel.

BROWN, S. and McINTYRE, D. (1986) 'How do teachers think about their craft?', in BEN-PERETZ, M., BROMME, R. and HALKES, R. (Eds) *Advances of Research on Teacher Thinking*, Lisse, Netherlands: Swets and Zeitlinger.

BUSSIS, A. CHITTENDEN, E. and AMAREL, M. (1976) *Beyond Surface Curriculum*, Boulder: Westview Press.

BUTT, R.L. (1984) 'Arguments for using biography in understanding teacher thinking', in HALKES, R. and OLSON, J.K. (Eds) *Teacher Thinking*, Lisse, Netherlands: Swets and Zeitlinger.

CALDERHEAD, J. (1987) *Exploring Teacher Thinking*, London: Cassell Education.

CARLGREN, I. (1987) 'School-centred innovations and teacher rationality', in STROMMES, A.L. and SOVIK, N. (Eds) *Teachers' Thinking*, Trondheim: Tapir.

CLANDININ, D.J. (1985) *Classroom Practices: Teacher Images in Action*, Lewes: Falmer Press.

CLARK, C.M. (1986) 'Ten years of conceptual development in research on teacher thinking', in BEN-PERETZ, M., BROMME, R. and HALKES, R. (Eds) *Advances of Research on Teacher Thinking*, Lisse, Netherlands: Swets and Zeitlinger.

CLARK, C.M. and PETERSON, P.L. (1986) 'Teachers' thought processes', in WITTROCK, M.C. (Ed.) *Handbook of Research on Teaching* (3rd Edition), New York: Macmillan.

CLARK, C.M. and YINGER, R.J. (1987) 'Teacher planning', in CALDERHEAD, J. *Exploring Teachers' Thinking*, London: Cassell Educational.

CONNELLY, F.M. and CLANDININ, D.J. (1984) 'Personal practical knowledge at Bay St School: ritual, personal philosophy and image', in HALKES, R. and OLSON, J.K. (Eds) *Teacher Thinking*, Lisse, Netherlands: Swets and Zeitlinger.

— (1985) 'Personal practical knowledge and the modes of knowing: relevance for teaching and learning', *NSSE Year-book*, 84(2), pp. 174–98.

DAY, C. (1984) 'Teachers' thinking — intentions and practice: an action research perspective', in HALKES, R. and OLSON, J.K. (Eds) *Teacher Thinking*, Lisse, Netherlands: Swets and Zeitlinger.

— (1990) 'The Developments of Teacher Personal Practical Knowledge Through School-based Curriculum Development Projects', in DAY, C., POPE, M.L., DENICOLO, P.M. *Insights into Teachers' Thinking and Practice*, Lewes: Falmer Press.

— (1990) 'Conditions for the Management of Professional Development: the Impact on Teachers' Thinking of Involvement in School-based Curriculum Development Projects', in DAY, C., POPE, M.L., DENICOLO, P.M. *Insight into Teachers' Thinking and Practice*, Lewes: Falmer Press.

DAY, D., POPE, M.L., and DENICOLO, P.M. (Eds) (1990) *Insights into Teachers' Thinking and Practice*, Lewes: Falmer Press.

DEFORGES, C. and MCNAMARA, D. (1979) 'Theory and practice: methodological procedures for the objectification of craft knowledge', *British Journal of Teacher Education*, (2), pp. 145–52.

DENICOLO, P. and POPE, M. (1990) 'Adults Learning — Teachers Thinking', in DAY, C., POPE, M.L. and DENICOLO, P.M. *op.cit.*

DIAMOND, C.T.P. (1985) 'Becoming a Teacher: An Altering Eye', in BANNISTER, D. (Ed.) *Issues and Approaches to Personal Construct Theory*, London: Academic Press.

ELBAZ, F. (1983) *Teacher Thinking: A Study of Practical Knowledge*, New York: Croom Helm.

— (1988) 'Knowledge and Discourse: the Evolution of Research on Teacher Thinking', in DAY, C., POPE, M.L. and DENICOLO, P.M. (Eds) *Insights into Teachers' Thinking and Practice*, Lewes: Falmer Press.

— (1990) 'Knowledge and Discourse: The Evolution of Research on Teacher Thinking', in DAY, C., POPE, M. and DENICOLO, P. (Eds) *Insights into Teachers' Thinking and Practice*, Lewes: Falmer Press.

ELLIOTT, J. and WHITEHEAD, D. (Eds) (1980) *Action Research for Professional Development and Improvement of Schooling*, Cambridge: CARN Publications.

GRUNDY, S. and KEMMIS, S. (1982) 'Educational Action Research in Australia: the state of the art', in KEMMIS, S. (Ed.) *The Action Research Reader*, Victoria: Deakin University Press, pp. 83–97.

HALKES, R. and OLSON, J.K. (Eds) (1984) *Teacher Thinking: a New Perspective on Persisting Problems in Education*, Lisse, Netherlands: Swets and Zeitlinger.

HAMPSHIRE, S. (1983) *Thought and Action*, Notre Dame, University of Notre Dame Press.

HOWARD, G.S. (1988) 'Kelly's thoughts at age thirty-three: suggestions for conceptual and methodological refinements', *International Journal of Personal Construct Psychology*, **1**, pp. 263–72.

HUBER, G.L. and MANDL, H. (1984) 'Access to teacher cognition — problems of assessment and analysis', in HALKES, R. and OLSON, J.K. (Eds) *Teacher Thinking: a New Perspective on Persisting Problems in Education*, Lisse, Netherlands: Swets and Zeitlinger.

HUNT, D.E. (1987) *Beginning with Ourselves*, Cambridge, Mass.: Brookline Books.

JONES, B. (1989) 'In conversations with myself: becoming an action researcher', in LOMAX, P. (Ed.) *The Management of Change*, BERA Dialogue No. 1, Multilingual Matters Ltd.

KELLY, G.A. (1955) *The Psychology of Personal Constructs*, Vols 1 and 2, New York: W.W. Norton and Co.

KEMMIS, S. (1989) 'Metatheory and Metapractice in Educational Theorising and Research'. Paper presented to first International Conference on Action Research in Higher Education, Industry and Government, Brisbane, Australia.

KERLINGER, F. (1977) 'The Influence of Research in Education Practice', *Educational Researcher*, **6**(8), pp, 5–12.

KRAUSE, F. (1986) 'Subjective theories of teachers' reconstruction through simulated recall, interview and graphic representation of teacher thinking', in BEN-PERETZ, M. *et al.* (Eds) *Advances of Research in Teacher Thinking*, Lisse, Netherlands: Swets and Zeitlinger.

KUHN, T.S. (1970) *The Structure of Scientific Revolutions*, Chicago: University of Chicago Press.

LAKATOS, I. (1970) 'Falsification and the methodology of research programmes', in LAKATOS, I. and MUSGRAVE, A. (Eds) *Criticism and Growth of Knowledge*, Cambridge University Press.

LAMPERT, M. (1986) 'Teachers' strategies for understanding and managing classroom dilemmas', in BEN-PERETZ, M. *et al.* (Eds) *Advances of Research in Teacher Thinking*, Lisse, Netherlands: Swets and Zeitlinger.

LARSSON, S. (1984) 'Describing teachers' conceptions of their professional world', in HALKES, R. and OLSON, J.K. (Eds) *Teacher Thinking*, Lisse, Netherlands: Swets and Zeitlinger.

LEINHARDT, G. and GREENO, J.G. (1986) 'The cognitive skill of teaching', *Journal of Educational Psychology*, **78**, pp. 75–95.

LETICHE, H. (1988) 'Development in Polytechnic Instructor Thinking'. Paper presented at Fourth Conference of ISATT, Nottingham, September 1988.

LINTER, R. (1989) 'Improving classroom interaction: an action research study', in LOMAX, P. (Ed.) *The Management of Change*, BERA Dialogue No. 1, Multilingual Matters Ltd.

LOMAX, P. (Ed.) (1989) *The Management of Change*, BERA Dialogue No. 1, Multilingual Matters Ltd.

LOWYCK, J. (1990) 'Teacher Thinking Studies: Bridges between description, prescription and application', in DAY, C., POPE, M.L. and DENICOLO, P.M. *Insight into Teacher Thinking*, Lewes: Falmer Press.

LOWYCK, J. and CLARK, C. (1989) *Teacher Thinking and Professional Action*, Leuven University Press.

MAIR, J.M.M. (1988) 'Psychology as story-telling', *International Journal of Personal Construct Psychology*, **1**(1), pp. 125–37.

MARTON, F. (1981) 'Phenomonology — Describing Conceptions of the World Around Us', *Instructional Science*, **10**, pp. 177–200.

MUNBY, H. (1982) 'The place of teachers: beliefs in research on teacher thinking and decision-making', *Instructional Science*, **11**, pp. 201–235.

OLSON, J. (1980) 'Teacher constructs and curriculum changes', *Journal of Curriculum Studies*, **12**(1), pp. 1–11.

PINAR, W.F. (1981) ' "Whole, Bright, Deep with Understanding": Issues in Qualitative Research and Autobiographical Method', *Journal of Curriculum Studies*, **13**, pp. 173–88.

POLKINGHORNE, D. (1987) *Narrative Approaches in Psychology*, Albany State: University of New York Press.

POPE, M.L. (1978) 'Monitoring and reflecting in teacher training', in FRANSELLA, F. (Ed.) *Personal Construct Psychology*, London: Academic Press.

— (1981) 'In True Spirit: Constructive Alternativism in Educational Research'. Paper presented at Fourth International Congress on Personal Construct Psychology, Brock University, St Catherines, Canada.

POPE, M.L. and DENICOLO, P. (1986) 'Intuitive theories — a researcher's dilemma', *British Educational Research Journal*, **12**(2), pp. 153–65.

POPE, M.L. and SCOTT, E. (1984) 'Teachers' epistemology and practice', in HALKES, R. and OLSON, J. (Eds) *Teaching Thinking*, Lisse, Netherlands: Swets and Zeitlinger.

POPKEWITZ, T. (1984) *Paradigm and Ideology in Educational Research*, London: Falmer Press.

SARBIN, T.R. (Ed.) (1986) *Narrative Psychology: the Storied Nature of Human Conduct*, New York: Praeger.

SCHON, D.A. (1983) *The Reflective Practitioner: How Professions Think in Action*, New York: Basic Books.

SHAVELSON, R.J. (1976) 'Teacher's decision-making', in GAGE, N.L. (Ed.) *The Psychology of Teaching Methods*, Chicago: University of Chicago Press.

SHAVELSON, R.J. and STERN, P. (1981) 'Research on teachers' pedagogical thoughts, judgements, decisions and behaviour', *Review of Educational Research*, **51**(4), pp. 455–98.

STENHOUSE, L. (1975) *An Introduction to Curriculum Research and Development*, London: Heinemann.

TABACHNICK, K.M. and ZEICHNER, R.B. (1985) 'The impact of student teaching experience on the development of teacher perspectives', *Journal of Teacher Education*, **35**(6), pp. 28–36.

VINEY, L.L. (1988) 'Which data collection methods are appropriate for a constructivist psychology?' *International Journal of Personal Construct Psychology*, **1**, pp. 191–203.

WAGNER, A.C. (1984) 'Conflicts in consciousness: imperative cognitions can lead to knots in thinking', in HALKES, R. and OLSON, J.K. (Eds) *Teacher Thinking*, Lisse, Netherlands: Swets and Zeitlinger.

WARNER, J.W. (1971) 'The journal of introspection and its place in the graduate elementary teacher education program', *Journal of Teacher Education*, **22**, pp. 287–90.

WOODS, P. (1985) 'Conversations with Teachers: Some Aspects of Life History Method', *British Educational Research Journal*, **11**, pp. 13–25.

YINGER, R.J. (1978) 'A study of teacher planning: description and a model of preactive decision-making', *Research Series 18*, East Lansing: Michigan State University.

— (1987) 'Learning the language of practice', *Curriculum Enquiry*, **17**(3), pp. 293–318.

Chapter 3

Changing Minds: The Dissemination of Research and its Effects on Practice and Theory

Michael Huberman

The dissemination of research brings us directly into the arena connecting theory to practice. In so doing, it sets off a debate which has been more rhetorical than informed. There are, however, lines of inquiry dealing seriously with this issue. This chapter lays out the parameters of one of these lines of inquiry: research on the 'dissemination and utilisation of knowledge (D&U).'

Within the D&U perspective, the construct of 'sustained interactivity' has emerged recently. This is really less a construct than a cluster of variables, all having to do with the ways in which researchers bring their findings to the worlds practitioners live in. While the construct features the more interactive relationships between researchers and practitioners during or after a study, it has other aspects: contextually grounding research findings, working with intermediaries, mixing written and in-person contacts, focusing on 'alterable' variables, etc.

The classic 'D&U' perspective has been criticised for its hyper-rationality, and justly so. But it can be stretched conceptually to include other versions of the ways practitioners interact with researchers. The result is a more transactional, sometimes conflictual, perspective, in which researchers defend their findings and some practitioners dismiss them, transform them, or use them selectively and strategically in their own settings.

In the findings reported in this chapter, research teams engaging in 'sustained interactivity' with practitioners produced changes in practitioners' ideas, under-standings and practices. This finding held even in settings where practitioners were initially sceptical or hostile to social science theory.

The next question to ask is this: what does sustained interactivity do to researchers? In the same study, the findings point to effects on teaching and consulting activities, and suggest that initial apprehensions about working with practitioners are assuaged. Beyond this, however, is the hypothesis that research-ers may also change their research agenda — may actually change their ways of conceptualising their field of inquiry. If this is the case, there would be a high conceptual payoff for research teams to engage interactively and over time with groups of experienced practitioners.

Introduction

To talk about the dissemination of research, as I am about to do, is to talk about the relationship between theory and practice. I have argued elsewhere (Huberman, 1990) that much of the literature on this topic has been of a rhetorical nature. We find it periodically in keynote speeches or occasional papers or in the report of a blue-ribbon commission addressing the 'two communities' problem: the difference in norms, rewards and working arrangements between researchers and practitioners.

There are, however, bodies of knowledge that bear on this issue. For example the process of dissemination of research can be seen as a particular instance of more general constructs derived from the sociology of knowledge (Berger and Luckman, 1967). Work in communications, in person perception, in social influence, also inform this field. Action research addresses directly the theory-practice relationship as well.

There is, however, a specific and fairly elaborate body of literature pertaining to this area. One can trace its roots back 50 or 60 years, to the seminal work of Kurt Lewin, Ronald Lippett and Paul Lazarsfeld. Gradually, a body of empirical and conceptual knowledge has accumulated in an area which has come to be known as 'the dissemination and utilisation of scientific knowledge' (hereafter 'D&U').

Basically, this work relates to the ways in which research knowledge becomes practice knowledge, and with the transformations undergone in the process of transfer from one realm to the other. Over the years, empirical studies have explored, then sought to replicate the main findings from earlier work. In fact, if one reviews the most recent syntheses of this literature (e.g., Glaser *et al.*, 1983; Beyer and Trice, 1982; Thayer and Wolf, 1984; Huberman, 1987), a strong case can be made that few, if any, fundamental conceptual changes have been forthcoming since the earlier 'landmark' studies (e.g., Havelock, 1969; Rogers and Shoemaker, 1971; Glaser *et al.*, 1976). One should be aware, however, that most of the work in D&U has been in the neo-positivist vein, and that its basic objective has been to derive a 'soft technology' for getting knowledge which is produced in centres of research into the hands of practitioners.

It might be useful, at this point of the paper, to represent the problem in a schematic form (see Figure 3.1) In the logic of D&U research, there are two ways in which researchers and 'users' can interact. The first path runs along the top of the figure (1 → 2 → 3). Research is generated in a 'scientific' universe, with the aim of contributing to a specific body of knowledge, then it is transferred to practitioners. The bulk of research in the D&U community has to do with the transfer process and the conditions under which it can be accelerated, without resulting in an undue amount of 'distortion' on the part of users. The bottom path of the figure puts us more clearly in the action-research tradition: the practitioners define the type of knowledge they require, and the research community frames its next raft of studies around those needs. Typically, a research community will divide its work between the two paths of the figure, by generating some knowledge in response to user needs and other scientific work to more purely conceptual issues.

Figure 3.1: Relationship between diffuser and user

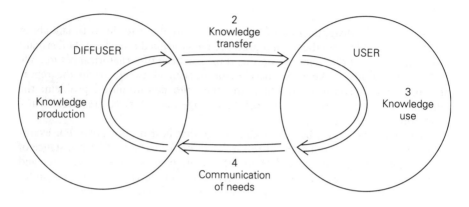

Robust Findings: The Construct of 'Sustained Interactivity'

Figure 3.1 suggests that researchers and practitioners will interact at two points: as the knowledge base is transferred, and as practitioners communicate their needs to researchers. For the remainder of this chapter, I shall centre on the dynamics regulating the process of transfer, i.e., on the 'classic' flow of knowledge from research centres to schools and teachers.

One of the more robust findings in the research utilisation literature has to do with the strong relationship between the *type or intensity of dissemination of research findings* and the measured *effects on a target public of 'users'*. In particular, in studies in which researchers have used an approach to the dissemination of their results which can be characterised as 'sustained interactivity', the impact of the study on users and user organisations is pronounced. This is as much the case for educational research as in other domains, from vocational rehabilitation to waste management (e.g., Muthard and Felice, 1982; Johnson, 1985; Yin and Moore, 1985; Cohen, Sargent and Sechrest, 1986). It is also worth noting that the same construct has figured prominently in the evaluation utilisation literature (cf. Cousins and Leithwood, 1986; Marsh and Glassick, 1987).

What is 'sustained interactivity?' Basically, it involves multiple exchanges between researchers and potential 'users' of that research at different phases of the study. For example, exchanges initiated by researchers *prior to the actual conduct of the study* typically have two functions: (a) identifying the points of convergence between the scope of the study and the 'priorities' or 'interests' of the target publics; and (b) recruiting one or more key actors in the target public to follow the study and to help carry it into the user organisation.

Exchanges initiated *during the conduct of the study* usually include the following: (a) creating a mechanism for including members of the target public in the review and analysis of intermediate findings; (b) identifying the data sets of greatest potential interest or use to the target public; (c) envisaging the ways in which these data can be compiled in forms most likely to flow smoothly in internal channels of communication and decision-making (internal newsletters, training facilities, study groups, planning councils); (d) leaving 'slack' time for more informal exchanges.

Next, 'sustained interactivity' usually includes the following exchanges during the *analysis and write-up phase of a study*: (a) specification of a dissemination plan, including the roles to be played by researchers and users who have followed the study; (b) negotiating for the allotment of time and other resources required to bring the study to the users' setting; (c) discussing in depth the findings most likely to challenge local norms, objectives and working arrangements, and sorting out the superficial from the real sources of discrepancy.

In most instances, there is, at best, modest activity at any one of these phases. The pace picks up, however, during the following phase, during which *the study findings are brought directly to the user organisation*. In many instances, in fact, this is how the dissemination of research is often construed: as something one does more or less energetically once a study is completed. The 'sustained interactivity' construct, by contrast, dictates a larger number of transactions over a longer period of time. It also conceives this last phase more as an ongoing 'conversation' between researchers and practitioners around the import of the study than as a straightforward extrapolation from the findings to the local setting.

The list of interventions and exchanges during this ultimate phase is a long one. Combining some of the items allows for some economy:

- translating findings into contextually grounded, semi-operational forms, e.g., alternative ideas of what study results can mean locally, of what can be 'done' with them;
- 'nourishing' intermediaries, i.e., providing inputs and advice to local actors recruited earlier in the process to bring the study into the host setting;
- mixing 'readable' written products with in-person interventions on the part of the research team;
- staying with the user setting over time, typically to the point where internal discussion, training and decision-making mechanisms have engaged actively with the findings;
- focusing on 'alterable' variables, i.e., on connections between the study's findings and policies or practices within the user environment that are judged amenable to change;
- scouting out and taking into account local susceptibilities;
- going beyond the study, i.e., engaging with users on issues of local significance or controversy for which the study has no specific answers but in which the researcher has conceptual or practical expertise.

If one reads this catalogue closely, stripping away some of the 'meliorist' turns of phrase and remembering that this is a researchers' eye view, one can see that the construct is less 'technological' than it might appear at first. Users are not construed simply as 'targets' but as actors who will transform the knowledge base in line with their own representations of the problem. Also, the process of knowledge transfer is seen as a series of transactions, in which study findings are 'negotiated' between the two parties.

For example, several items assume an idiosyncratic understanding of the study's frame or of its findings on the part of potential users. The length of time given to contacts before, during and after the study is also an acknowledgment of the fact that there will be cognitive accommodations on both sides. Users will gradually be 'educated' to the meaning and import of the study, and researchers will come to understand how non-researchers make sense of the findings and, as the researcher interacts in the local context, which findings are meaningful. More generally, there is an implicit assumption that researchers and users will be negotiating the meaning of the study and the validity of its findings. During and immediately after the study, this transactional space will be dominated by the researcher. Later on, the researcher will venture into a universe of practice with which she or he is unfamiliar, which is far more complex than the settings likely to be arrayed in the study design. In these settings, practitioners will 'talk back' — i.e., will toss up counter-examples or qualifications to the main findings, or simply dismiss them. What happens to researchers when practitioners 'talk back' is also a focus of this chapter.

'Sustained interactivity' contains another premise: in the final phase of dissemination, the researcher will be trading on his or her expertise to legitimate his or her claims against truth, claims made by other actors trading on their formal status, on their experience, on their access to other sources of information, on their informal influence, etc. Put in a slightly different way, the model acknowledges the micro-politics of information use in social settings. Both the researchers and their findings are likely to be pawns in other negotiations taking place in the settings in which they venture: negotiations having essentially to do with influence and power. This means that there will be attempts locally to transform, to distort, to make illegitimate inferences from the findings of a given study for 'strategic' reasons. In fact, a prime reason for the researchers remaining active in the setting after completion of the study is to attenuate these effects by advocating *their* interpretation of the findings.

Research showing the effects of 'sustained activity' typically centre on practitioners or 'users' in different settings. In the following sections, I shall try to illustrate such effects. At the same time, there is the other side of the coin: *what does 'sustained interactivity' do to researchers*? Does it have an effect on their next piece of research, on their conceptual frames, on their teaching, on their attitude towards dissemination? The latter part of the chapter will take up this issue.

An Illustration: Research Utilisation in Vocational Training

To illustrate some of the dynamics we have just reviewed, I shall be drawing on a recent study in the field of vocational training. Since the descriptive information is available elsewhere (Huberman and Gather Thurler, 1991), I shall take some short-cuts. I shall cut back on methodological details.

Approximately fifteen years ago, the Swiss National Research Council created a series of 'national' programs of applied research. In the first wave, for example, were integrated programs in preventive medicine, water purification, social integration and energy. In the next series were programs in micro-electronics, health policy, vocational training and regional development. Each program has contained roughly twenty-five to thirty distinct studies; budgets for each range from $3.5 to $10 million. The total budget to date is roughly $280 million.

Up to now there has been no systematic assessment of the degree to which these national programs have, in fact, been 'applied'. Implicitly, the definition has been restrictive; 'applied' means 'problem-centred' rather than the extrapolation of findings to contexts of use. Several programs, however, have taken a more aggressive stance toward dissemination, notably the one in vocational education, in which 10 per cent of the program funds were set aside explicitly for dissemination work outside the scientific community. Projects including a dissemination design could qualify for funding, but applicants had to specify dissemination objectives, target publics, even message types and timelines. For most, it was the first foray either outside the scientific community or beyond an *ad hoc* approach to dissemination of their findings to practitioners.

This research program, entitled EVA (*Education et Vie active*), itself consisted of some twenty-five projects, divided thematically into studies of: (a) future apprentices' personality development, scholastic and technical performance and vocational maturity; and (b) characteristics of schools and teacher-training institutions. The median project lasted three to four years, was conducted by an experienced principal investigator housed in a university institute and cost about $160,000.

Figure 3.2 lays out the general model for the study and indicates that more specific models were derived for variable sets relating to researchers, users and attempts to disseminate the findings of the studies. The variables in these models derive from the D&U literature reviewed earlier. As the general model shows, organisational and contextual variables in both the researcher and user universes determine the shape and extent of linkage, both generally (in terms of interdependencies preceding the study) and in the case of the specific study being disseminated. Degree of linkage is then presumed to determine the variable sets on which we shall be concentrating first: the dissemination *'effort'* and the *predictors of use within the practitioner's environment* (e.g., time and resources committed to the study, relationship between the main findings of the study and the unit's major objectives or working arrangements). These variable sets, in turn, mediate the outcomes. The primary outcomes are multiple (scope, relative influence of the study, degree of local transformation of findings, etc.), but we shall be addressing only changes in levels of knowledge, understanding or attitude (*'conceptual' use*) and, tangentially, changes in behaviours and practices ('instrumental' use). The study also measured a raft of second-order effects, as shown in Figure 3.2.

While the dissemination study as a whole addressed a host of research questions within and across these variable sets, I shall take up here the questions relating specifically to the first-order outcomes (conceptual and instrumental use) and to their immediate predictors.

Methodologically, the EVA study was designed as a multiple-case, 'tracer' study. We picked up a sample of projects near the end of the research phase, preceding by several months the post-study dissemination activities, and followed each for about 18 months. By identifying target publics with whom research or dissemination staff interacted, we followed the traces of the study until they petered out, measuring the various impacts along the way and recycling periodically to see whether the initial degree of impact grew or waned over time.

Twelve of the twenty-six program projects were selected for study. All twelve constituted a 'major' research project (>$150,000) and contained an explicit dissemination component. Variation was sought in geographical location and in the institutional 'nesting' of the research team (university, independent institute, cantonal research service). In the course of study, one project was dropped due to lack of cooperation on the part of the principal investigator.

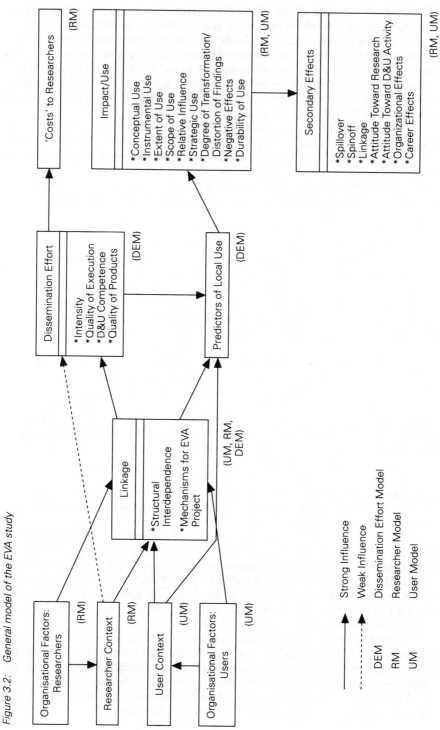

Figure 3.2: General model of the EVA study

40

For each of the remaining eleven projects, principal investigators were asked to identify two 'target publics' who were, or would be, affected by the dissemination being envisaged. This allowed for the study of the 'strongest cases', i.e., instances in which effects of the dissemination were theoretically the greatest. But we assumed as well that differential efforts to disseminate the findings to these publics would provide enough variation in outcomes to drive the analysis. This assumption was borne out.

The strategy for data collection and analysis was derived from several sources, but above all from Miles and Huberman (1984). It consisted of a multiple-case field study of a largely 'investigative' nature. In line with this approach, field data were collected in several 'waves', with successive sequences of analysis that re-oriented or differentiated the next round of data collection. Such an iterative mode of data collection allows for interview questions, observations and retrieval of documents or products to shift over time. Researchers then focus progressively on those mediator and outcome variables emerging from each successive 'pass' at the field as critical indices or determinants.

Measures of Conceptual Effects

Now for a closer look at the outcome having to do with effects of the EVA research projects on practitioners' knowledge, understanding, perceptions and ideas. The general line of inquiry followed in the interviews was the following: did the findings of the EVA study have any measurable effect on users' understanding of the phenomenon under study and on its pertinence in their context? Did they, for example, construe their own work situation differently (as trainer, journeyman, head of personnel, vocational counsellor) and, if so, what was the precise relationship between the findings of the study and this new perception? Did they derive new ideas or become more aware of their own behaviour or of phenomena around them to which they had been oblivious? Alternatively, were they more perplexed than before?

Prior to these questions, some open-ended and others nested in scales, informants were probed carefully as to their understanding of the study and its findings. They were asked, at various moments, to resumé the main findings, to identify the problem area which the study addressed, to illustrate the import of the findings by connecting them to their own work and to their organisations. When conceptual effects were claimed, informants were asked to justify them, usually by giving examples, but also by connecting them to more 'instrumental' effects (changes in tools or methods of daily work; changes in policies or practices at a more institutional level). In the cases of claims of particularly strong effects, we checked for corroboration from colleagues and/or conducted on-site observations.

Several measures were derived from these data. One, testing conceptual mastery of the study and its import locally, ranked each informant (n = 103) on an ordinal scale, running from 'no effect' to 'sensitisation' to 'basic assimilation' to 'strong understanding' and finally to 'integrated understanding'. Instances of 'strong understanding' required clear conceptual connections between the main findings of the study and the informants' work situation. Such, in fact, was the modal case, forty-one of the informants (40 per cent) fell into this category. These are, to be sure, unusually strong effects in the research utilisation literature, and

Table 3.1: Conceptual Effects: Summary of Scale Items (n = 95)

This study: . . .	Yes	Somewhat	No
Helped me to understand better the problem area generally	56	23	16
Made me aware of some important things I didn't know about	36	31	28
Helped me to better understand my own work environment	29	23	37
Gave me some new ideas	53	23	37
Made me look at things differently, from another perspective	29	31	33
Made me aware of some things I shouldn't be doing	25	19	49
Has contributed to changing my ideas about my work in the future	24	30	39
Totals (652)	252	180	220
Relative %	39%	27%	34%

are explained largely by the fact that *all members of the sample were the target of a more or less intensive dissemination of the findings on the part of the respective research teams.* The general drift of informants' comments is that they have come to a 'deeper' understanding of the meaning of such findings in their work environment, they see it in a more differentiated, precise, self-conscious yet also 'de-centred' way, 'as if someone shone a light in a dark room I walk around in all the time'. Again, claims such as these were subjected to stiff cross-examination.

If we look beyond the modal effect at the individual level to the distribution across the twenty-three cases, with each individual aggregated to case level, the 'mean' coefficient is at the 'global assimilation' level, one understands the import of the study and can identify correctly its ramifications locally, but at a more general level. Here, then, at the 'mean', the cases of 'no effect' (19 per cent) and of 'sensitisation' (12 per cent) begin to take their toll. But the aggregated data also show a clear and fascinating within-case trend: *levels of conceptual mastery are far higher among informants associated earlier with the study (as members of an advisory panel, for example) or associated more intensively (as intermediaries) in the local dissemination.* This is the case as much for instances in which the host organisation was receptive to the findings of the study as for unreceptive units. These levels are also higher, as we shall see, in instances of more intensive dissemination on the part of the research team.

A second, more general, cognitive scale was generated from the same data sources. This one ranked informants ordinally from 'no/minor conceptual effect' (34 per cent of the cases), 'demonstrable awareness' (34 per cent), 'moderate changes as perspective' (22 per cent) and 'new conception — multiple changes of perspective' (10 per cent). Here again, remember that, for the majority of informants, this was the first time since post-secondary studies that they had come to grips with a research project in such detail and that, in many instances, practitioners in the area of vocational training were initially hostile to social scientific research in their field ('half common sense, half nonsense', said one during an initial interview). With one-third of the respondents rated at 'moderate/multiple changes of perspective', we are in the universe of strong effects.

We also extracted items relating to conceptual effects and derived from the scales administered to informants. Table 3.1 is a summary. Although these are self-report data, they were collected in face-to-face interactions by researchers who had come to know the local surroundings and who asked these practitioners for details which were then checked out. Moreover, in this particular study, there was no strategic reason for practitioners to inflate their judgments.

These judgments are fairly 'positive': 40 per cent of the users claiming un-equivocal conceptual effects, over half the users claiming strong effects at the levels of 'better understanding' and 'new ideas'. If we pool the 'yes' and 'some-what' responses, most items show conceptual effects for more than half the sample. This is all the more striking when one considers that, up to now, the research community and the vocational training community in Switzerland had had virtu-ally no prior relationships. Furthermore, initial measures of practitioners' attitudes toward social science research and researchers ranged generally from 'sceptical' to 'hostile'. For field researchers as well, it was difficult to attribute these conceptual effects to other factors than to the dissemination effort on the part of several research teams. More on this shortly.

The self-report data were combined with the two other measures of concep-tual use to produce a weighted score for individuals ($W = 61$, $p < .01$) and for units ($W = .57$, $p < .01$), then ranked. It is with these unit-level rankings that we will be working shortly.

A Note on Instrumental Effects

There is too little space to develop these findings, beyond reporting that, in many instances, what we called 'instrumental' effects (changes in tools or methods of daily work; changes in policies or practices at a more institutional level) were also prominent. For example, 27 per cent of the informants ($n = 73$) named clear in-stances in which the EVA study findings had pushed them to action in an arena in which, up to now, they had hesitated entering. Some 20 per cent documented instances of the findings having resolved a particular problem at work. Some 13 per cent attributed changes in ongoing activities to the influence of the EVA study with which they had come into contact.

In addition, many of these effects transcended the individual level. From interviews and observations, we estimated that, in 14 per cent of the cases ($n = 99$), the EVA study had accelerated the formulation of a policy; in 8 per cent, the study had contributed to the adoption of a policy decision. In 25 per cent of the cases, the study had acted to change the profile of ongoing institutional activities in a modest way (e.g., new programmes, changes in apprenticeship training, new orientation batteries), and in 17 per cent of the cases, these changes affected the core or principal activities of the institution. In the remaining 36 per cent of the cases, no institutional effects were found. Here again, we have unusually strong effects, especially when one considers the social and epistemological distance sepa-rating practitioners from researchers in the field of vocational education, be it in Switzerland or elsewhere.

Predictors of Conceptual Effects

How does one get such strong effects? Which variables discriminate between cases of high conceptual or instrumental use and cases leaving little or no traces among practitioners?

Lacking space here to describe the full set of variables in play, let us move to the final, most integrative analysis. Here, we were essentially trying to 'predict' the level of conceptual effects from: (a) the kinds and intensity of dissemination undertaken by the various research teams, and (b) the response of informants' units to the dissemination. It is important to note that, in terms of the 'sustained interactivity' construct discussed earlier, we shall only be looking at variables in play during the *last phase* of the dissemination process, when the study findings are brought directly to the practitioner setting. Having both scale scores and ranks for the level of conceptual effects, the task was then to determine which 'dissemination' and 'response' variables discriminated between cases with higher and lower levels of conceptual effects. With a sample of twenty-three cases, we resorted mainly, but not exclusively, to qualitative analyses.

In this analysis, covering twenty cases with a complete data set, the field researcher worked only with those variables shown to have exerted a 'determinative' influence in the case. In other words, from the full set of variables posited in the conceptual framework or emerging gradually after successive 'waves' of data collection and analysis, the researcher gradually winnows the list to a small number which exert, unambiguously, a directional influence on another variable — for our purposes here, on an outcome variable. Typically, this judgment is made from the progressive analysis of scales, observations and interview data, and is tested independently by a colleague (cf. Miles and Huberman, 1984; Guba and Lincoln, 1985).

Unlike the corresponding statistical analyses (e.g., regression, discriminant analysis), we are working here with a smaller set of cases, ones in which the variables of interest have 'passed' a preliminary, qualitative test of significance. So we have sacrificed degrees of freedom by throwing away cases for which we had a measure but decided, upon gradual examination of its local workings, that it added little light to the analysis of the case. Next, each of the surviving variables is rated (low, moderate, high), and the 'moderate' cases are discarded, mainly to facilitate the use of basic qualitative tools, i.e., comparison and contrast. We are thus left with variables judged as exerting a determining influence on another predictor or on the outcome, and judged as 'high' in instances of strong outcomes and 'low' in instances of weak outcomes'.

How does this play out in the case of 'dissemination effort', 'predictors of local use' and 'conceptual effects?' Let us examine a simplified chart (Figure 3.3) which displays only those variables present in 30 per cent of the cases. This is a busy figure, but it repays a close reading. Globally, these are the 'surviving' variables, the ones that predict different levels of outcome. To facilitate a closer reading, let us illustrate with a highly 'significant' variable, 'targeted products'. In eight out of ten cases of strong conceptual outcomes, use of dissemination products tailored specifically to the target public (as opposed to omnibus reports, monographs, workshops, etc.) was associated directly with one or more of the predictors and/or associated with high conceptual outcomes. Conversely, in six out of ten cases where targeted products were *not* used and were judged as affecting adversely, say, time and resources invested locally, this leads in turn to null or low conceptual effects.

Whereas in each case-level analysis, the analysis explicates specific links between distinct variables, before moving to 'families' of cases with similar paths, Figure 3.3 regroups the variable into blocks. It does, however, plot fairly well the

Figure 3.3: Conceptual effects: Explanatory model

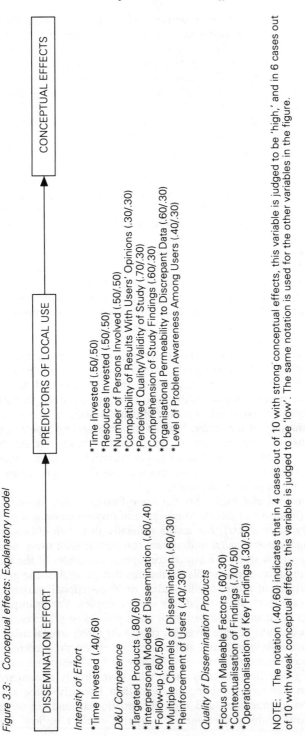

DISSEMINATION EFFORT

Intensity of Effort

*Time Invested (.40/.60)

D&U Competence

*Targeted Products (.80/.60)
*Interpersonal Modes of Dissemination (.60/.40)
*Follow-up (.60/.50)
*Multiple Channels of Dissemination (.60/.30)
*Reinforcement of Users (.40/.30)

Quality of Dissemination Products

*Focus on Malleable Factors (.60/.30)
*Contextualisation of Findings (.70/.50)
*Operationalisation of Key Findings (.30/.50)

PREDICTORS OF LOCAL USE

*Time Invested (.50/.50)
*Resources Invested (.50/.50)
*Number of Persons Involved (.50/.50)
*Compatibility of Results With Users' Opinions (.30/.30)
*Perceived Quality/Validity of Study (.70/.30)
*Comprehension of Study Findings (.60/.30)
*Organisational Permeability to Discrepant Data (.60/.30)
*Level of Problem Awareness Among Users (.40/.30)

CONCEPTUAL EFFECTS

NOTE: The notation (.40/.60) indicates that in 4 cases out of 10 with strong conceptual effects, this variable is judged to be 'high,' and in 6 cases out of 10 with weak conceptual effects, this variable is judged to be 'low'. The same notation is used for the other variables in the figure.

factors which variously turn on or turn off the power among practitioner units and, from there, which heighten or lower the conceptual impact of the study locally. It also suggests that the *presence* of certain factors can matter more in increasing conceptual effects than their *absence* can lead to null or low effects. This is the case, for example, with 'multiple channels of dissemination' (print, visual, in-person), for the focus on 'malleable' factors in the setting, for the perceived quality or validity of the study, for the comprehension of findings, etc. Higher levels 'help' more than lower levels 'hurt'. The inverse case is less frequent. For example, not 'operationalising' study findings in the local context and investing little time in the dissemination activity are associated, directly or indirectly, with lower conceptual effects on target publics.

Taken together, the figure tells a story, with a few subplots. It says that the most promising dissemination strategy for obtaining conceptual effects on a target public implies a consequential time investment, especially when study findings become available, including a follow-up period, and personal contacts in addition to reports and other media, with some concern for users' motivation (reinforcement). The products of that dissemination are put in context, trained on factors that *can* be influenced and connected to ongoing operations. Very likely, the 'follow-up' variable is crucial; researchers who spend time in the setting come to learn its ground rules, see its malleable features, figure out where the findings are most relevant, reinforce their writings with personal interventions, identify key actors and reinforce them, etc. This is, in effect, the 'sustained' component of 'sustained interactivity'.

The dissemination strategy just described acts to improve the level of understanding of the findings among practitioners, to increase the perception of their validity in the setting and, in response to the time invested by researchers, to increase the corresponding investment (in time, in resources, in numbers of persons or services involved). The product of that investment, seen linearly, is strong conceptual mastery of the study, both of its more general aspects and of its local significance. If we turn the same variables on their heads, we see that little time invested, no follow-up, etc. lead to lower comprehension and minimal investment in the study's findings among practitioners for whom, under questioning, the study is a remote memory trace.

The other subplot highlights the same factors in the 'dissemination effort' variable set (intensity of effort, competence in dissemination and utilisation strategies, quality of products), but insists generally that such efforts will not automatically engage users, *unless* findings are compatible with users' opinions, unless people bring to the study a minimal conceptual awareness of the factors at stake and the organisation is permeable to findings that go against the grain. These are good illustrations of more 'conflict-laden' or 'transactional' variables in action.

At the case level, these trends are more complex. For example, when users treat findings as incompatible with their basic policies or practices, some researchers lower the amount of time invested, reduce the interpersonal modes of dissemination, reduce follow-up, etc., and conceptual effects drop correspondingly. In other instances, however, low compatibility or local resistance *stimulates* the investment of researchers, notably those who have already committed themselves over time to this target public, and who then intensify some aspects of their dissemination 'competence' and turn the situation around. In other words, instances of low problem awareness or internal conflict or low comprehension of the study's findings do not necessarily weaken or stymie sustained modes of dissemination, especially in the case of more professional ('D&U users') or more committed research teams.

As supporting evidence, partial correlations (Kendall Tau) were run on these variable sets. The effects of 'intensity of effort' and of 'D&U competence' clearly overrode the variables associated with the local setting ('predictors of local use' on Figure 3.3). In other words, what researchers do or don't do, along with the investment they make, counts more than do the features of the practitioner environment they engage with.

In effect, the engagement of the researcher in the user's setting changes many of the cards being played. When researchers essentially hand over a study to a set of practitioners, low levels of 'problem awareness' and low 'permeability to unwelcome findings' usually spell instant oblivion for the study, however valid and well-packaged its findings. When, on the other hand, researcher teams remain active in the setting over time, and negotiate their presence carefully, we are likely to get an upward shift in the level of problem awareness and a far clearer sense of which findings are, in fact, discrepant with local objectives and mores. Among the cases in this study are instances of both types. On the other hand, researchers reacting this way are brought more clearly into the micro-politics of the setting. The various transactions between reseachers and practitioners in the setting highlight the 'interactivity' component of the 'sustained interactivity' construct.

By way of an intermediate summary, we should note that those variables listed on Figure 3.3 under 'dissemination effort' — the ones that discriminate most clearly among instances of high and low conceptual use of research findings — are, in all cases, components of what we listed as 'sustained interactivity' earlier in this chapter. These components imply, to be sure, deliberate, skilled and effortful activity on the part of researchers, but they also assume a transactional frame of reference. As it passes into the practitioner community, research knowledge is not 'communicated'; it is negotiated and, invariably, it is re-elaborated to fit the body of prior knowledge and frames of meaning which users bring to any new piece of information. It is, in fact, the very activity and tension inherent in that process of negotiated re-elaboration which assures a higher level of retention and use at the individual level. Without it, we have non-existent or ephemeral effects among practitioners or, alternatively, a raft of distortions and simplifications relative to the original findings.

The Effects of Dissemination on Researchers

Up to now, I have tried to make the case that certain kinds of dissemination of research, and above all, of kinds that entail sustained interactions between researchers and practitioners, can have measurably strong effects on those practitioners. In other words, there are ways to bridge the gap between theory and practice, even in settings that are initially hostile to theorists.

What I now want to address is a cognate question, and one for which the data base is thinner: *what effects does sustained interaction have on researchers?* Surprisingly, this is a question which is virtually absent in the D&U literature.

Some initial hints appear in the interviews in which researchers (n = 35) were asked about the impact of their study on other aspects of their work. Predictably, virtually all respondents evoked a greater conceptual and empirical mastery of the domain represented in their project. When asked to explain themselves a bit more, roughly 15 per cent of this group said spontaneously that dissemination component was an important factor in their obtaining greater conceptual mastery of the field under study. As one principal investigator put it whimsically: 'When you have to discuss, explain and illustrate your study, then answer to their (practitioners') criticisms, you end up understanding more about your study than you did when you wrote the report'. This is, I think, a telling remark and I shall come back to it in a slightly different form.

Some more hints appear when researchers are asked about effects on their teaching or professional practice. Here again, two-thirds of the researchers reported that they had already transposed conceptual frames, illustrations, segments of their data base into their teaching or their work with clients. Again, there appeared, here and there, the spontaneous remark that having to convert these materials into forms more suitable to non-specialists during the dissemination of the study, rendered the materials far more user-friendly, less didactic in nature. In a third of the cases, researchers claimed that their 'stance' toward teaching had changed as a result of the dissemination component of EVA. The gist of their remarks was that they were now more sensitised to the characteristics of the students or clients with whom they dealt — more aware of the ways in which these people represented in their own minds the questions or content at hand. The stock phrase here was 'more centred on the learner than before', often as a result of having to 'de-centre' from their own perspectives and formulations when explicating their study with various practitioner groups.

Not surprisingly, 89 per cent of the researchers considered themselves better than before at disseminating their findings to non-specialists. More interesting, perhaps, are the data bearing on the evolution of researchers' feelings about the dissemination component in their work. In the initial phase of the study, when researchers were still collecting or analyzing data, they were administered a scale (Kendall's: $W = .76$) of nine statements and asked about their agreement with each. Generally, these statements had to do with eventual 'problems' arising from work with practitioners during or after a study, e.g., that time and energy would be diverted from the study, that non-specialists would simplify or distort findings, that researchers would be drawn into a political arena, that researchers were not competent in matters of dissemination, that practitioners were looking for 'magical' solutions.

The same scale was administered eighteen months later, when the dissemination component was completed or nearly completed. There was a significant shift in the direction of a lesser apprehension (Sandler's: $A = .153$, 8df, p. <005), both about what practitioners would do with research findings and about the perils of researchers' committing time and energy to such tasks. It is noteworthy that the sharpest changes come from research teams with the least experience in dissemination outside the scientific community. Here again, the gist of researchers' remarks during the second administration of the scale was that non-specialists were often far more knowledgeable than researchers had imagined, and that there had been less 'distortion' than they had feared. This was especially the case for teams which had designed the dissemination component as a series of encounters over time with the same target publics.

An Hypothesis

Because our study was more measurement-sensitive to the effects of dissemination efforts on practitioners, we paid less attention to what was happening to researchers during these encounters over time with non-researchers or non-specialists. But there are several indicators that something was happening to people in the research teams who had invested the most in 'sustained interactivity'. We see it in their remarks about the conceptual enrichment resulting from their study, about the transposition of materials from their studies to their teaching and consulting and in the shift of attitudes about work with practitioners more generally.

My hypothesis is fairly straightforward. The fact of having to reframe one's findings in different ways for different publics, and of having to address counter-examples, qualifications and outright challenges on the part of practitioners testing the research findings against their own experience and local context, appears to trigger a decentring process among researchers. The field talks back, both more strongly and in a different way than, say, a replication or a set of generalisability coefficients typically provide to a study.

Let me run through an example. Suppose that a research team, on completion of a study on career choices of adolescents, engages for a year in a fairly intensive discussion with a dozen experienced vocational counsellors. Two things, I think, would start happening after the first two to three sessions. First, the practitioners would gradually submit a barrage of counter-examples, of reservations, of important factors not included in the study, of contextual factors underweighted in the study, perhaps even of constructs that run against the conceptual grain of the study. After all, these are experienced people. Some would have tested or interviewed hundreds of adolescents and derived their own ideas about the key determinants of career choice. Even if there are sharp differences, even contradictions, between the counsellors, we can safely assume that the research team will be struck by some of the remarks made and by the drift of the discussion over time. This over-time aspect is crucial; it obliges both parties to continue their debate or their dialogue over a period long enough for reciprocal influences to be exerted.

The second thing that occurs, I think, is that the researchers are obliged, early on, to go *outside* the particular study at hand in order to respond to the practitioners. This entails their marshalling many of the key concepts they trade on when a study is mounted, concepts having to do with adolescent development, with career choice, with tests of vocational maturity, etc. In many ways, in fact, the *real* confrontation occurs at this level, where both sides have staked their understanding of the underlying determinants.

As we saw earlier, when researchers resorted to a long and interactive mode of dissemination, there were consequential conceptual changes among the target publics: new understandings, new ideas, different ways of thinking about their work, and the like. There were even instrumental effects: changes in patterns of monitoring or teaching apprentices. There are enough compelling data from the EVA study to safely assume that much of this was due to the kinds of exchanges we have just created in our fictitious example. Conversely, there is good reason to think that these interactions would have a reciprocal effect on the researchers engaged in them, unless these researchers dominated the exchanges. Our observations indicate that they did not. The question remains: *how exactly are such effects obtained?*

49

On the face of it, this scenario looks like a classic instance of what cognitive psychologists call 'socio-cognitive conflict' (Doise and Mugny, 1981). Let us run through the scenario briefly, using the principal investigator as our subject. In interacting with a group of experienced practitioners, she will first become aware of the fact that some legitimate criticisms of her study are being made, and that those criticisms derive from other ways of viewing the same phenomena she has studied. Since these criticisms and alternative conceptions do not come from the scientific community, where she is already well armed, she may at first be disconcerted. At this point, she may decide to dismiss these 'alternative' views. But she may also choose to listen more carefully, to ask more probing questions to members of the group and to take a harder look at her data or at her conceptual framework. The further exchanges in the group may then bring her gradually to integrate this discrepant information into her own conceptual schemata — typically at a higher level of abstraction — or even to begin changing some of the ways she looks at the kind of research questions addressed in her study. As she goes back to some of her source material, she may find herself reading it in a different way. This 'different way' is then brought to bear on the next discussions with the group of counsellors. It produces some new, unexpected, unsettling information, since the structure of her new way of representing the phenomena is not stabilised; it feels like a series of uncoordinated conceptual strands. The same cycle then repeats itself, several times. At a later point in these encounters, she will have worked her way through to a conception of the problem which satisfies most of the qualifications and counter-examples put out by members of the group and, at the same time, is conceptually conciliable with at least some lines of inquiry in her professional community. In simple words, she will have changed her mind. Cognitive theory suggests that this change will be for the better — that her new set of conceptualisations will be more integrated and differentiated than her prior set (Piaget, 1975).

The key here, for both parties, is probably the fact that they do not function at the same level of conceptualisation, nor in the same settings, but they both contend with the same phenomena. As a result, once they get beyond the initial discomfort of defining common meanings and of working out the social dynamics of their encounters, each party is bound to be surprised or annoyed or even shaken by some of the information and the reasoning put forth by the other party. Both bodies of knowledge are 'valid', albeit on different grounds, and both are contending for salience and prominence. Were the researchers and the counsellors to remain among themselves, there would probably be far fewer instances of cognitive shifts. Each side will have worked out its 'stance' toward its referent community, and will not be going out of its way to put it into question.

My hypothesis, then, is that such a sustained conversation results in measurable shifts in the ways people construe the issues on the table, and derives from attempts to reconcile the conflicting versions of what those issues mean. The result, for many practitioners, is what we called 'conceptual effects'. On the face of it, as noted earlier, there should also be a corresponding change among members of a research team.

The problem is that I have only scraps of data to support the thesis of a corresponding change among researchers. The one scrap to be added to the pile comes from a question posed to principal investigators (n = 11) about their future research. Here, researchers with the least amount of prior experience in dissemination outside the scientific community, but who had invested heavily in interactions with different practitioner groups, were far more likely to report that they were now designing studies of a different scope and nature than was the case in their earlier work. In some, but not in all, cases, they attributed this shift to new insights gained during the dissemination process.

I think that this view of things, were it confirmed, has important implications. Up to now, mainstream researchers in education have often avoided dissemination like the plague. Working with practitioners has been seen as a distraction from their priorities and, in some cases, as a real handicap to professional advancement. Similarly, members of the research community who have devoted blocks of time to 'the field' have defined that activity as social activism, or as altruism, or as a gesture of good faith toward the profession at large.

What we see now is that sustained, interactive dissemination is of as much value to researchers as to practitioners, but of value in a different way for each, according to the community in which they look for professional intelligibility and satisfaction. The value to practitioners has always been obvious: access to new, potentially powerful ideas and tools. The value to researchers has been less clear. If it turns out, however, that interactive modes of dissemination are a booster to conceptual progression, as depicted in my fictitious example, the 'payoff' within the research community may be far greater. One would then work through one's findings with a group of experienced practitioners not for reasons of altruism nor of activism, but rather to empower or to refine the conceptual tools with which we researchers ply our trade. Doing it this way, in fact, may often be more beneficial than replicating a study or engaging with colleagues at professional meetings. One might, literally, change one's mind. In other words, if we researchers are interested in changing our minds, we need to take our findings out into the field and observe very carefully how they hold up under duress.

References

BERGER, P. and LUCKMANN, T. (1966) *The social construction of reality*, New York: Doubleday.

BEYER, J. and TRICE, H. (1982) 'The utilization process: a conceptual framework and synthesis of empirical findings', *Administrative Science Quarterly*, **27** (December), pp. 591–622.

COHEN, L., SARGENT, M. and SECHREST, L. (1986) 'Use of psychotherapy research by professional psychologists', *American Psychologist*, **41**(2), pp. 198–206.

COUSINS, B. and LEITHWOOD, K. (1986) 'Current empirical research on evaluation', *Review of Educational Research*, **56**, 3, pp. 331–64.

DOISE, W. and MUGNY, G. (1981) *Le Developpement social de l'intelligence*, Paris: Inter-Editions.

GLASER, E. *et al.* (Human Interaction Research Institute) (1976). *Putting knowledge to use: A distillation of the literature regarding knowledge transfer and change*, Los Angeles, CA.: HIRI.

GLASER, E., ABELSON, H. and GARRISON, K. (1983) *Putting knowledge to use*, San Francisco, CA.: Jossey-Bass.

HAVELOCK, R. (1969) *Planning for innovation through the dissemination and utilization of knowledge*, Ann Arbor, Mich.: CRUSK, Institute for Social Research.

HUBERMAN, M. (1987) 'Steps toward an integrated model of research utilization', *Knowledge*, **8**, 4, pp. 586–611.

— (1990) 'Linkage between researchers and practitioners: A qualitative study', *American Educational Research Journal*, **27**, 2, pp. 363–91.

HUBERMAN, M. and GATHER THURLER, M. (1991) *De la recherche la pratique*, Berne: P. Lang.

HUBERMAN, M. and MILES, M. (1988) 'Assessing local causality in qualitative research', in BERG, D. and SMITH, K. (Eds) *The Self in social inquiry*, Newbury Park, CA.: Sage, pp. 351–82.

JOHNSON, K. (1985) 'Research influence in decision-making to control and prevent violence', *Knowledge*, **7**, 2, pp. 161–89.

LINCOLN, Y. and GUBA, E. (1985) *Naturalistic inquiry*, London: Sage.

MARSH, D. and GLASSICK, J. (1987) 'Knowledge utilization in evaluation efforts', *Knowledge*, **9**, 3, pp. 323–41.

MILES, M. and HUBERMAN, M. (1984) *Qualitative data analysis*, Beverly Hills, CA.: Sage.

MUTHARD, J. and FELICE, K. (1982) 'Assessing activities for the utilization of rehabilitation research', *Knowledge*, **4**, 2, pp. 309–28.

PIAGET, J. (1975) *L'equilibration des structures cognitives*, Paris: Presses universitaires de France.

ROGERS, E. and SHOEMAKER, F. (1971) *The communication of innovations*, Glencoe, N.Y.: Free Press.

THAYER, W. and WOLF, W. (1984) 'The generalizability of selected knowledge diffusion/utilization know-how: the case of educational practice', *Knowledge*, **5**, 4, pp. 447–67.

YIN, R. and MOORE, G. (1985) *The Utilization of research: Lessons from the natural hazards field*, Washington, D.C.: Cosmos Corp.

Chapter 4

Deconstructing Control and Consent

Hugo Letiche

Within the theme of 'Teacher Thinking and Subject Knowledge' I wish to de-construct a conflict between two Dutch exchange students and their British lecturers. The sociotexts of the students and lecturers conflicted; two different concepts of the social organisation of knowledge were revealed. The postmodern assumption to be made here is that subject matter mastery veils prescribed models for manipulating sociotext. Normally the legitimacy of the text and/or the manipulation is, more or less, unconditionally accepted. But international exchange programmes, such as Erasmus, threaten the symbiosis of power and subject knowledge. Exchange students are confronted with situations wherein their sociotext fails them and lecturers are faced with students who will have no truck with prevailing discourse. Following discussion on the theory of teacher thinking, I will examine a specific case of the social enactment of academic power.

Teacher Thinking/Teacher Self-reflexivity and Postmodern Thought

Questions and Artefacts

Has it been assumed by its research proponents that *teacher thinking* is something *out there*, demanding to be studied? Is research into teacher thinking characterised by a positivist epistemology? What is the epistemological status of researcher claims about teacher thinking? Is teacher in-class, with colleague, interview, diary, essay text simply, uncritically to be repeated? Do researchers have some sort of blind trust in teacher reflexivity, i.e. *What teachers say about themselves is not self-serving, clichéd, defensive or manipulative*? Whose teacher thinking — the teacher's or the researchers' — actually gets into print?

Admitting that the text of teacher thinking is an artefact of the research process, we must acknowledge that it is not an innocent or inevitable outcome of teaching.[1] The division into *thinking* and *non-thinking*, assumed by the concept of teacher thinking, implies priorities. The version(s) of teacher thought with which we are presented are organised around themes chosen by researchers such as: tacit knowledge, empowerment, career history, social status, entitlement. All sorts of alternative themes are, *de facto*, being suppressed by the researchers. Investigation into teacher thinking is paradoxical: at once it claims to refer to what lecturers plan, conceptualise, and say; but it centres on what teachers think about themselves. Inevitably it also refers to researchers' preoccupations, values and thoughts. In the textual framework of teacher thinking, researcher reflexivity ascribes educational meaning (and non-meaning), purpose (and non-purpose), as well as correctness (and incorrectness) to teacher self-awareness. What principles of inclusion (exclusion) are articulated? What is (is not) practitioner thought?

Authorial Voice

Education normally takes place in an arena of pretended certainty; participants seem to know and accept their texts (roles). The decision has been made to stop doubting: a body of knowledge (supposedly) exists to be taught, learned and examined. In the exchange of students described below, the suspension of disbelief failed. Different parties doubted the wrong things at the wrong moments. The illusion of a stable, meaningful reality became impossible. Instruction was precarious; no agreement over the correct (pedagogic) form of behaviour was forthcoming. Implicit agreement on who should do what, when and why, was lacking. Confusion, instability and paradox resulted; a carnivalesque scene was created. Roles were reversed. Authority was unclear. Cause and effect were transposed. A carnivalesque parody of canonised educative genres resulted: research was done wherein the faculty supervisor did the data collection; exams were written wherefore the students did not read the required literature; an in-company project was agreed to without company say-so; theses were written without any significant link to the research already done; students interviewed lecturers to see if they were acceptable to study under.[2] This disconcerting burlesque created ambiguity. In this chapter I examine the tension between expectation and event. I use the gap between what I can present as having happened, and what could be reasonably assumed ought to have happened, to generate my authorial voice. Because I can make it seem as if there was an educational mess, I can write an article. The seeming inability of the instructors and students to find common ground, permits me to offer my perspective on what happened. My rendering of *teacher and student thinking* imposes a perspective on events; events which refused to accept such limits. A battle ground of perspectives has occurred wherein no one point of view predominated. No single definition of reality succeeded in imposing itself. Differing stories remained in unresolved competition with each other. The different texts did not reach closure. A series of artefacts (essays, interviews, observations) are at my disposal. No stable order has been agreed to: the players interpreted events, assigned meaning, drew conclusions, differently. Every educational act, to be successful, needs to presuppose some postulates about education which it doesn't doubt further. Such postulates include assumptions about the discourse structure of teaching (who speaks when/how discussion is orchestrated); and the distribution of rights, responsibilities and authority in teaching (who prepares what/who is responsible for keeping order/who gets paid [better]/who grades who). In the case described the players' assumptions contradict one another. The role of my authorial voice is to distrust all the perspectives: I have assumed the task of deconstructing each of them.

Theory and Carnivalesque

Research into the in-class social organisation of knowledge needs artefacts (exams, essays, classroom transcripts to form data) and theory (concepts of teacher/pupil interaction, learning, socialisation). When the lecturers (British and Dutch) and exchange students (again British and Dutch) were confronted with one another, role negotiation resulted. My goal is to describe the belief structure(s) i.e. the basic proposition(s), underpinning the interactions. To portray this process, a vocabulary for the formulation and reconstruction of the interacts is needed. On two levels there was a crisis in order/disorder:

- the students and lecturers weren't able to define effectively their educational situation, i.e. to decide what to do, determine how to do it, and actually to get anything done;
- my authorial *I* doesn't know with any certainty how to describe the players and their actions; i.e. what vocabulary, perspective, norms should be used?

What is to be determined is: the *structures of reflexivity* underpinning the educational interaction.

The search for the actors' (lecturers' and graduate students') grounds for action, amounts to an effort at deconstructing their teaching behaviour. I believe that the concept of *teacher reflexivity* is theoretically more powerful and empirically more manageable in this effort, than that of *teacher thinking*, because it refers to a much more specific and definable variable. Actor *reflexivity* pertains to the position the subject accords him or herself in his or her theory-in-practice of action; i.e. the functioning of the *I*, the ascriptions to the *me*, the experiencing of the *Other*. I assume that:

- almost no human social action occurs without *a theory of action*; but that,
- *in-practice theories of action* are partial and incomplete.

The student and teacher statements about the student exchange and in-company field work, which form the empirical background to this chapter, presuppose different assumptions about the nature of education and about one's role therein. The participants in the student exchange posited that their own assumptions were valid and that their judgments based on them were legitimate. Thus I abandon the very broad terminology of teacher thinking, which includes whatever thought (conscious or unconscious/individual or collective) influences, determines, accompanies teaching; and I choose for a more narrow focus on teacher reflexivity which focuses on the logic of participant assumptions and interactions. Much teacher thinking research has, in fact, concentrated on teacher reflexivity, i.e. has discussed teacher voice, teacher self-understanding, teacher awareness, tacit knowledge. By redefining the research goal to make teacher reflexivity the focal point, attention is riveted on practitioner labelling or metaphorisation of practice, i.e. to the practitioner's linguistic structuring of social action, wherein self and world are generated.

Labels are also the most unobtrusive means of control; it takes a great deal of self-reflectiveness to become suspicious of a classification or of a name. 'What's in a name?' asks Juliet, 'That which we call a rose, By any other name would smell as sweet' (*Romeo and Juliet*, Act II, Scene 2). But Romeo knows better and points out that the name one has, can decide one's fate. . . .[3]

The naming of actions, players and situations such as: mastery teaching, change consultants, decentralisation, constitutes in-service reality and posits the self's position in that reality. The verbal inventions of educational theorists and researchers, i.e. labels like: the teacher as researcher, self-evaluation, emancipatory education, influence teacher self-image and steer professional action. Obviously these thoughts owe a great deal to Bruner (symbolic interactionalism), Goffman (the presentation of self), Lacan (*Le moi c'est l'autre*) and Weick (frames). In the present chapter I follow their leads and examine lecturer/graduate student verbal inventions-in-use via a postmodern ethnography of teacher/student reflexivity. I add, at this stage, the qualifier postmodern to make the assumption explicit that practitioner statements of educational practice are grounded in assumptions about teaching which are both necessary to keep professional activity going and hidden so that practitioner discourse is not revealed to be paradoxical. Much educational in-practice interaction is paradoxical: the lecture posits that dialogue is essential, that the assumption is *not* dialogical; the pedagogue premises emancipatory education, i.e. those to be freed are *not* free to choose the terms of practice, the instructor tells students how to do research, i.e. research is *not* independent investigation. The terminology used to describe practice — the labels of professional interaction — mirror the non-reflective norms of the conventionalised forms of practice. The tacit agreement about what sort of performance university teaching and learning demands is maintained. Denying the belief that *self* will be the same as *role*, assuming that *text* is a contrived inscription of order, positing that students and lecturers stage meaning effects not grounded in personal commitment, fearing that nothing guarantees meaning, sense-making or purposiveness, makes the point of view taken here postmodern. Universities are part of the representation industry. Just like the TV news, fictionalised documentaries and political image builders, academics defend the public against disorder and unreality by offering a text imbued in order and reality. But in Holland the truth effects of at least undergraduate university teaching have broken down. Lectures are interrupted by the flight of paper airplanes; the undivided attention of students is often to the newspaper before them, and not directed towards the teacher; the noise level in the lecture hall often makes it impossible to hear what the instructor is saying, despite microphones. The persuasion and seduction of teaching does not carry the day. In contradistinction, the outward signs of instructional authority are intact in Britain. The hierarchy of the educational performance has been sustained. The subversion and corruption of education hierarchy, which has led to near anarchy in the Dutch lecture halls, has not touched the authority and privilege of British lecturers. The boundary of who speaks and who listens, who sets norms and who obeys, whose text is *canonical* and whose is to be criticized, has not been breached in the UK. The radical unbinding of the educational process has only occurred on the Dutch side of the channel.

Two interdependent and oppositional postmodern criticisms of teacher thinking are operative in this article. The first examines how the self-reflexivity of the practitioner disguises the contradictions between the teacher's (student's) text and his or her background assumptions. It examines the hidden propositions of practitioner logic with which prioritised positions such as lecturing as permanence, teaching as self-empowerment, research as truth, are defended; even though the logic of that defence is paradoxical. Lecturing doesn't present the last word but a transient, often loosely structured, narrative; teacher narcissism is only to be matched by student derision; research is either driven by radical doubt or it is mere ideological rhetoric.

The second criticism reveals the *carnivalesque* in the discourse of teaching or studying, i.e. the postmodern society achieving the zero degree of learning:

> We may think of zero degree essentially as a state — if this word can be properly applied to such a dynamic concept — of no specific order, organisation or direction, a process of undecidability that pervades all social organisation. Zero degree is always conceived of as an excess to order or meaning, it is always 'more than', it is the over-abundance of the signifier in contrast to the 'reduction' contained in the signified.[4]

Without ontological necessity, epistemological clarity or social ethical purpose, managerial science, organisational behaviour, managerial informatics, etc., threaten to degenerate into mindless cynicism. Teaching and learning only retain whatever value one is able to ascribe to them. There's no fixed orientation to thought, automatic criteria of accomplishment or certain focus to application. Performativity reigns; there are no privileged organising principles to knowledge. Any value ascribed to analytical skills is the subject's own. To each his or her own meta-text, each teacher or student must organise the behavioural repertoires as best they can. An over-abundance of possible meanings confronts a poverty of reductions, i.e. the ideas, theories, concepts at one's disposal do not clarify, simplify or reduce complexity. Since the teacher or student cannot find any coherent system of order in the elements of knowledge at their disposal, they are forced to construct an improvised structure of action-principles. Knowledge and skills are governed by make-shift protocols which have proven to be able to deliver short-term results. Learning is not oriented to any transcendent goal; technical know-how is not balanced by social philosophy; leadership capacity is not tempered by responsibility. How one uses what one learns is solely one's own matter; the *meta-structure* of learning is indeterminate. One organises, explains, justifies the use of one's learning (*meta-text*) as best one can.

The first strand is used to reveal paradoxes in practitioner self-reflexivity (assumptions) and the second to disclose the *ad hoc* assignation of meaning (*meta-text*) to carnivalesque circumstances. Both assume the impossibility of establishing a stable or trustworthy epistemology, i.e. way of learning, grounded in social or historical *truth* and able to give teaching a firm identity or purpose. The first centres on the paradoxical acts of the *self* as it tries to maintain, justify and assert its role in interaction with Others; the second portrays the *self*, defending a minimal territory, battered about by carnivalesque absurdity, no longer able or almost unable to transcend egocentric performativity.

Teachers and Students

Carnivalesque mis-meaning forces Dutch students to improvise fixed nubs of significance for themselves. The educational institution, rather than foreclosing on questions such as: Why study? What is worth learning and why?, and thereby privileging order hierarchy and concentration, continually confronts the student with crises in meaning. No meta-structure of educative legitimacy seems to be on offer. Students have to generate improvised inscriptions of order pretty much on an *ad hoc* basis. Is the resulting educative meta-text sufficiently stable?

British teaching seems to offer heroic lecturer monologues, which seek to maintain rather than compromise accepted disciplinary boundaries. The creativity and challenge of persistent doubt may be sacrificed to the stability of totalisation, to the rigour of academic exactness and to the safety of professionalism. Teaching and learning do not have to be fun, they are produced and consumed as standard products. My assumption is that the educational mess which occurred between the Dutch (staff/students) and British (staff/students) resulted from inadvertent mutual revelations of paradoxical structures of activity. A postmodern deconstruction of the interaction will, I submit, be illuminative. The inescapable tension between the parties involved was linked to unachieved teacher and student reflexivity. Neither identity nor thinking was stable. The logic of teacher thinking research assumes that the researcher knows who the teacher is and can identify the processes involved in his or her thinking. The theory used to describe educational thinking determines the sort of thinking that will be discovered. The logic of the study of teacher thinking is both positive and circular. The concept of teacher thinking assumes knowledge of behaviour and introspection and the ability to link the two meaningfully. Since teacher thinking is at once action, for example, the teacher teaching, a social role, a concrete activity, a form of interpersonal interaction and reflection, involving thinking, consciousness, intuition, self-reflexiveness, no clear differentiation between foreground and background is retained. The concept of teacher thinking results in a semiotic crisis. Nouns such as teacher are normally used to describe verbs such as thinking, and vice versa; otherwise definitions become endless chains of synonyms. Objects are defined by telling how they are used, i.e. by describing potential action; and activity is defined by determining who does what and with what results, i.e. what states of existence are produced. Teacher Thinking is a statement of cause and effect; action is presumably guided by thought otherwise teacher thinking does not exist or it is irrelevant. Only a theory of *social cognitive causation*, explaining how thought influences action, could successfully link the two terms in some sort of philosophical idealism. Without such a connection teacher thinking research degenerates into mindless behaviourism, or loses itself in the unicity of introspection. But in the contemporary world, no theory of the relationship of thought to action has succeeded; postmodernism has been born just from the failure to achieve epistemological, ethical, thought, action, closure.

The perspective of teacher reflexivity avoids the demand for any isomorphism between self and world, thought and action, purpose and history, by focusing on the role of the subject's assumptions in his or her own discourse. The study of teacher reflexivity is a form of semiotic investigation. The study of teacher thinking focuses on the social psychology and legitimacy of a specific professional practice.

Control and Consent

If we assume that so-called subject matter mastery is met by repeating, using and manipulating prescribed texts, then graduate education is where the novice gains an active knowledge of this sociotext. The legitimacy of the sociotext, and/or of its manipulation, is normally more or less unconditionally accepted. But international student exchanges can threaten the symbiosis of power and subject matter. The exchange student can be confronted with a situation wherein their sociotext fails to function. And lecturers can be faced with students who will have no truck with the prevailing discourse. It is a Goffman commonplace that the effortless common management of backstage is crucial to lecturers and graduate students maintaining their power positions. Expert use of the prevailing sociotext is a crucial means for maintaining lecturer, and developing graduate student, control. It is a postmodern observation that the symbolic structures of academic legitimatisation are often endangered. The stability of the university order is threatened by the devalorisation of its text. Backstage becomes messy. In the rest of this chapter I will examine a specific case of the social enactment of academic power. The fact that the graduate students and the lecturers did not share a common sociotext permitted conflicting interacts to become pronounced. The students were M.Sc. candidates from the Management School of a Dutch university and M.A. candidates from the Behaviour in Organisation Programme at a British university; the staff were members of faculty in the same two universities. Commitment to the culture of one's own institution brought the parties into conflict. The symbolic interaction required by the Other, threatened to de-legitimate the *self's* point of view.

Since teaching, assigning and grading are manifestations of discursive power that serve as gateways to economic, organisational power, the appropriate discursive codes are highly valorised throughout a 'successful' educational career. The codes are thoroughly internalised by staff and students alike; deviants who would challenge the socio-code are effectively banished. Challenges to the power exercised by the discursive code are more or less automatically repulsed. Positing that control is the central problem of advanced administrative organisation, and that graduate-level management school training leads to relatively privileged positions within such organisations, I assume that a challenge to the educational code becomes, inevitably, an attack on the discursive politics of the meso-society. The university will ensure that its text predominates, since loss of control would devalorise the management school as gatekeeper.

In the case to be discussed, the Dutch students had internalised the socio-code of their lecturers, and were not prepared to abandon that code. The prescribed ways of dealing with, i.e. of symbolising, social power came into conflict. Of course the institution (the university) prevailed, but it was forced to reveal more of its hidden propositions than it would normally choose to do. While difference was encapsulated in academic garb such as exams, criteria, grades, etc., the institutional codes of control were in effect challenged. Ultimately, conflict in higher education is almost always about consent; for consent is the principal mode of control in postmodern society, i.e. in the contemporary labour process. Educational discourse functions as an initiation into the prevailing structures of consent; its social grammar is, I submit, isomorphic to the structures of consent and control in the dominant formal organisations. The Dutch student/British lecturer conflict was enacted within the university discourse of teaching/assigning/grading, where the structures of control and consent dominate the meaning system. I will examine how each side: (1) tried to play the discursive game, (2) justified its sets, and (3) colluded with the other side to keep the power dimension hidden.

Hugo Letiche

Narrative

Postmodern commentary reveals the hidden propositions which undermine the subject's consistency in relationship to his or her text, and/or discloses the subject's flawed effort to justify that text as an instance of social, historical and ethical responsibility.

First Narration

Story:

A Monday morning, 10.00 am, in November: the first meeting of the Dutch exchange students Arian (age 26) and Maurits (24), Patrick (24) who is enrolled at the British institution but is currently an exchange student in Holland, and Lawrence (45) a British university lecturer.[5] Patrick, after completing a summer of in-company research, has gone to Holland to study. Arian and Maurits are due to come to Britain in January to carry on the in-company research project begun by Patrick under Lawrence's supervision. Arian is tall, blond, athletic and very muscularly built. He looks the sportsman and physical education instructor that he is. After completing his polytechnic degree in physical education he decided to earn a graduate degree in Bus.Ad.; he finances his study by working part-time (substituting for colleagues on vacation). He wears khaki pants and a wool sweater. Maurits, after leaving school, had worked for a couple of years, been drafted into the army and thereafter had begun his university study. Maurits is thin, dark and intense. He wears old levis and a blue sweater. Patrick did a politics degree at an Irish university. Having been faced with near non-existent career possibilities, he decided to do a graduate business degree in Britain. He has sandy-red hair, a light complexion and looks just as unhealthy as Arian looks (excessively) healthy. Lawrence is small, balding, a bit over weight. He bustles about his office, making the visitors welcome. Piles of papers have to be removed from chairs to create enough sitting space. He is friendly, seems a bit shy and exudes academic-other-worldliness. He is dressed in blue twill pants, a white shirt and wears a wool wind-breaker. After Lawrence offers everyone coffee, Arian begins the conversation.

'We want to determine if the in-company project has been well arranged, and if so what is expected of us. Will the company cover our costs; how large a budget do we have?'

Lawrence explains that he has had lots of experience in doing projects in the company, and that he is confident that his contacts will come through with a research project. He steers the conversation towards a discussion of the first phase of research, which Patrick had been responsible for.

Arian interrupts: 'Can we be sure of the company's cooperation? It's worthless starting out on a project when management isn't interested in cooperating. You can better invest your time in something that is better organised.'

Lawrence explains that British companies are never eager to see students. They see in-company projects as a favour to the student and university. Companies take their time to say yes, so they don't have to pay too much in expenses such as travel costs, and so that the university will feel who is dependent on whom. The company — having recently become a Dutch subsidiary — ought to grab this research chance with two hands. By involving Dutch management students in a project, the British managers can gain insight into Dutch management and comprehend Dutch practices a bit better. But the managers insist on seeing students as a chore; students have to be thought about as people without practical knowhow who will probably get in the way. If you scratch below the surface you discover that British managers are unsure of their intellectual capabilities and thus fear contact with students.

Arian: 'No wonder mis-management is at the root of the sale to the new Dutch owners. What can we learn from them?'

Lawrence describes the company's qualities: highly skilled labour, well designed products, a whole industrial tradition, which has, however, been sacrificed to Thatcherist monetarism and to the City's interests. Only by investing like the Germans do, can one defend one's industrial capacity, i.e. make it productive.

Arian again: 'But what will the company want us to do?'

Lawrence: 'Two teams of British workers have been sent over to Holland. The first cohort was a great success. The workers were told they were redundant but if they went for several months to Holland, and did their work well in the factory there, a job would be found for them on their return. Patrick and I have been interviewing them to hear what they thought of their experience of working under the very different conditions in Holland.'

Arian: 'Yeah, but Patrick has made it clear to us that the company gave no support to that work. You've had to interview the people at home, not even being permitted to do so on the boss's time, and there's no managerial interest in the project. Why do it then?'

Lawrence spelled out the differences between the company's English management and the Dutch mother company's approach. He was convinced that the British factory was the more modern of the two, but that in Holland they got maximum results out of their production potential. In Britain the results were far below what ought to be possible. The distance between management and labour was much smaller in Holland; managers were accessible, and workers identified with the company. The English workers had a history of going on strike, knowing full well that the company couldn't afford to pay their present wages let alone to talk about any raise. But the attitude was *That's their problem; we want our money.* The British who had been over to Holland showed that they were far more flexible in their attitudes than was commonly assumed. They had adapted to Dutch corporatism and seemingly had valued it.

Arian: 'Our Professors have taught us that organisational change cannot be successfully initiated without the commitment of top management; what's then the worth of interviewing all sorts of workers?'

Aftermath:

Soon after this Arian quit the project; he never came to Britain to study. He saw no purpose, as a management student, in interviewing a bunch of workers. It was so much sociological hanky-panky as far as he was concerned.

Since Patrick was supposed to complete a further set of ten interviews with Arian and Maurits, as a way of introducing them to the project, and he was not motivated to do the work, the confused conversation served his purpose. The discussion of aims and goals blocked all concrete planning. No decisions were taken, the group separated with future plans up-in-the-air. Maurits was distressed. Loyalty to a friend (Arian) was in conflict with what needed to be done to make the exchange work. Lawrence called Leon the next day to inquire about Arian 'What sort of Fascist did you send me?'

De-constructs:

- Arian had acted as an aggressive sceptic who had little trust in either British companies or universities. Though everyone present later agreed to this characterisation, Arian was neither aware that he had played a dominant role (Maurits and Patrick said next to nothing) nor that he had attacked Lawrence's position of authority. Arian claimed that he had tried to give an up-front and in-charge performance. He had intended to display business-like competence. His comments were meant to confirm the planning, organising, controlling ethos of management. But he had no real business experience. His dismissal of workers as irrelevant to management, voiced his belief that managers shouldn't share profits, decision-making, prestige or work planning with labour. In his avowal of consulting, as organisational change done for top management, he outed his rejection of sharing prestige, privilege or power. But in reality, he belonged to the excluded; neither in his background nor life experience had he ever been a member of the privileged groups. His unconditional belief in management would, logically, exclude him — the inexperienced student and son of a working class father — from taking action or initiating change.
- Lawrence had expected to receive a group of enthusiastic students, whom he would initiate into doing research. He was nonplussed by the inquisition let loose on him. He was already troubled by the arrogance of the Dutch managers who he knew found the company's British direction to be bureaucratic, reactive and ineffective. Lawrence feared a mentality of blind maximalisation which would see the British subsidiary as so many muscled machines or radio-directed tools, only good to execute foreign orders. Here, right in front of him, he was confronted by the blind ignorance he dreaded. But his attachment to bottom-up research was just as dubious as was Arian's. If the goal of management research was engendering the reproduction of power, then the study of workers' attitudes wasn't a logical route to achievement. The Dutch experience showed that the English workers could break the old mould, and work much more collectively with management. But did middle management want to be confronted with this challenge to its usefulness? Did top management want to face any such questioning of established practice? Was Lawrence committed to fighting any of these wars? In his heart, he agreed with Arian's critique; but his own political and intellectual legitimacy would be threatened by admitting as much. What should be the role of the intellectual in management research? Defence of management's unlimited confidence in technical solutions such as automatisation and robotics, touting vulgar fashions in organisational structuration, i.e. divisionalisation, project management, etc., becoming an apologist for miraculous solutions, for example, organisational culture, quality circles, etc., was all too clearly kitsch to be academically respectable.

Story:
Tuesday morning, 9.00 am in late July. Lawrence and Leon have an appointment (9.00 to 10.00 am) and are scheduled to be joined by Emil and Maurits at ten. Leon (age 45) lectures at the Dutch School of Management. He is taller and heavier than Lawrence; he also has more hair. He is dressed in twill trousers and a tweed jacket (it's rather cold outside). Emil (23) has taken Arian's place. He is younger and somewhat more flexible than Maurits, but he is academically less distinguished. Lawrence has arranged for the meeting because he is concerned about the two exchange students' exam results.

Lawrence begins the conversation, after having offered the expected cup of coffee. He voices his concern about Emil and Maurits' grades. It is not clear that they will pass their courses. Lawrence explains that the students had given Dutch university answers to British university questions, which was not looked upon favourably by the examiners. While some sources were favoured in Holland, exam questions were written to be answered out of particular assigned books, and the exchange students had not revealed knowledge of those books in their answers. Lawrence is obviously uncomfortable with his role of delivering bad news. He explains that exams in Britain are a ritual; you don't just give any intellectually defensible answer, but you prove you've read required readings. Emil and Maurits wrote down their own answers to the questions, instead of repeating what the lecturers wanted to hear. Lawrence showed Leon some past exams to illustrate how they should be written.

Leon had already realised that something must be wrong, so he had eaten dinner the evening before with the students. To his inquiry 'What could be wrong?' they'd answered that they had written the exams without having read all the required readings. To his exasperated 'WHY!?!' they answered, 'Because we were spending all our time interviewing managers at the company, and hadn't had time to prepare better.'

Lawrence went on to explain that he was worried about the two Dutch students. He'd been in an argument with them for months about money. They wanted the company to pay them for the research they did. Lawrence found the idea absurd — the company sees it as a favour to the students that they are being allowed to do field work. Only when the students threatened to talk directly to the company's Personnel Office about payment, had Lawrence accepted to broach the issue. He had tried, half-heartedly, to get an advantageous expense remuneration. The company promised to judge the quality of the final report, and on that basis to study the merits of upping their contribution to travel costs. Maurits and Emil had correctly surmised that this 'Yes' was fairly worthless, and had wanted to make more demands. Maurits and Emil threatened not to submit their findings to the company unless it agreed to pay. Lawrence saw his good relationship with the company going up in smoke and got worried. While Lawrence had supervised many research projects in this company, he shared the company's doubt in the professional value of the results. He was convinced that he could better spend his own time writing theoretical articles on paradigm incommensurability. Empirical investigation was thankless; there were no credos in work floor research, and it was fantastically time consuming. Lawrence, to win peace and quiet, finally guaranteed Emil and Maurits's travel expenses out of his own research budget. To

Lawrence's amazement, the quality of Emil and Maurits's work turned out not to have suffered from what he'd termed: 'All that pissing about.' While Patrick never conducted one interview alone (Lawrence constantly had to go along), these boys had collected their data professionally and thoroughly. Thus Lawrence was irritated with them, and respected them. He didn't really want them to fail. Also he feared that if they failed, the principle which was dear to him of Europeanising the program might come into disrepute.

Leon had known about the money chicanery and had advised Maurits and Emil to lay off. Soon thereafter Lawrence had come up with his compromise. The good exams Leon was shown were fairly stereotyped; the candidates voiced no opinion of their own but had written: X states that . . . , Y has argued that . . . , Z maintains that. . . . If he was honest with himself, he did not think the exams were really very good, but he did not want to defend his students, who had not done their homework. Also he surmised that if he defended Emil and Maurits, Lawrence would criticise them all the more; but if he just listened politely, Lawrence would quickly run out of steam.

Lawrence obviously did not have much more to say; he began to repeat his story of how irritated he'd been with Emil at their first meeting which had been in Holland. Emil had been proposed as a substitute for Arian. Emil wanted to know what Lawrence would expect of him and what they would be doing. Emil had explained that he needed to talk to Lawrence, think the whole matter over, and would give his answer whether he'd come to Britain or not within a week. Lawrence felt that he was offering to teach Emil how to do qualitative management research and that he should be grateful at the opportunity. He found Emil's attitude denigrating — he felt treated like a piece of steak which a housewife wasn't sure if she did, or did not, want to buy.

Leon had explained that Emil's attitude had been typically Dutch. Emil did not want to feel that he had rushed into anything, or that he had to be pressured into doing something. Emil wanted to go to Britain certain that he was committed to the task at hand. There was no disrespect meant, but a norm had to be respected; one should only take decisions which one has thought a lot about.

It was 10.00 am; Emil and Maurits knocked. Everyone took a cup of coffee and Lawrence then introduced the subject of the conversation. He explained that the exams had not gone as well as one would have liked, though no definite results were available. He divulged the rules for re-sits. Then he introduced the issue that needed discussing: the MA thesis. Lawrence prefaced his enunciation of the required standards and grading practices with his favourite story about the Dutch students. The first week they'd been in Britain they'd discovered that they only had class one day per week. They'd come to Lawrence in disbelief and asked him: 'What are we supposed to do all day?' Lawrence had been as amazed by the question as they'd been by the schedule. For Lawrence it was self-evident that MA students spent most of their time in the library reading up on themes developed in the classroom. Emil and Maurits had never done any such thing. Lawrence explained that in the thesis one had to prove theoretical competence by linking a fieldwork experience to the theoretical cadres that had been taught in the course.

Leon wondered if the two students would find it difficult to meet the theoretical standards. He realised that while both institutions called themselves Management Schools, there were big differences. The Dutch program emphasised practical know-how, business reality and developing a repertoire of concrete social skills; the British program was concerned with labour process theory, distinguishing between organisational theory and behaviour and discussing the sociology of work. Could Emil and Maurits write theses that would fit-in? Would they understand that, after the debacle of the exams, they had to conform?

Maurits knew that his exam results were better than Emil's. At worst one re-sit hung above his head. Maurits had learned from the problems he'd had in Holland in the autumn. Arian, Patrick and he had been assigned to do research into the strategic background to Dutch take-overs of the British companies. Patrick was totally demotivated, submerged in personal problems. Arian saw himself as a doer — a manager whose aptitude to command would only lessen if shut up in a library. Arian wasn't a thinker — waste, stress and pollution wouldn't get tackled by his style of management; he was out to make up for lost time and to climb the status ladder. Maurits had suffered humiliation when he had to present the results of the first semester's work to the Dutch staff and students. He had analyzed his idealism, his belief in reflective management and its failure to effect change (i.e. to get Arian and Patrick to do any work). He had explored his inability to carry the task further as a soloist, and how that was coupled to his need to work in a group. While Leon and Clemens {a second lecturer in Holland} had been supportive and had passed him — arguing that a flopped research project can produce a valuable learning experience and a worthwhile report, fellow students had insisted that he should have failed.

Maurits wanted to write his thesis on the cultural differences that he'd discovered between the UK and Holland during the in-company project. The workfloor interviews had revealed management issues such as low worker motivation, insufficient quality control, ineffective middle management giving little leadership to the production line. However unforthcoming and difficult the company may have been in its negotiations with Lawrence, the managers had been open and responsive in their interviews with Maurits and Emil. The bottom-up research approach had worked; it had led from daily work practices, to issues of work supervision, to questions of authority, to problems of proactiveness and synergy. Maurits preferred to discuss thesis proposals and to talk about the project. Lawrence had never been enthusiastic about the extension of the project to include management ramifications. He had refused to believe that the company could be interested in what a couple of students had to say. To refight that issue could only serve to lower their grades! Also Maurits wanted to tread softly, to keep his chances open of later becoming Leon's teaching assistant. He'd figured out how high staff costs were for one course. Knowing that Leon taught more than his share, he was betting on becoming a TA and raking in a substantial salary.

Emil, like Maurits, originated from the Catholic South of Holland. He'd uprooted himself to escape the provincialism of his upbringing. The next step in his study would be a semester in South America. Emil liked Lawrence. He found Lawrence's interest in him warm and genuine. He had decided to look at the socio-technical background to the company's change strategy in his thesis. His hope was that it would be a pretty straightforward subject.

Leon listened to the thesis ideas. He made a few comments, but did not want to get drawn into the conversation. He did not want to take any responsibility for the theses. Furthermore, he wanted to avoid discussing the future with Maurits. While Leon had been interested in Maurits' offer to become a TA, which could lighten his heavy teaching load by one course, he had lost all interest on seeing

Maurits's salary request. Of course Maurits, if taken on, would only be paid the standard rate; but by asking four times that Maurits looked foolish. Leon recalled Lawrence's money problems with the students and decided not to risk a repetition.

De-constructs:

- Maurits' discourse balanced incoherently between material opportunism and intellectual idealism. His attitude jumped between two irreconcilable opposites, as if the contradiction just wasn't there. In Maurits and Emil's eyes the bottom-up research strategy had only served to justify the project to the outside world (to Lawrence, perhaps to the company). Lawrence clearly preferred that they ignore the management significance of the research. No one in the company had asked them to hold a mirror up to management. All they had to do, to get the job done, was to interview the workers and write a report. But Maurits opposed doing any such mindless fieldwork. The research would be valuable because it revealed something about doing business and did not just blindly report worker attitudes. For Maurits, managers had to be self-reflective and understand their causal role in events. Worker attitudes could only be understood in the context of management interacts, and should not be approached as facts unto themselves. Maurits had consistently defended the holistic approach against Lawrence and the company's indifference; they obviously just did not want to know. While Maurits opposed management's blind spot, he remained a victim to his own. He did not see that he had alienated Leon and Lawrence over money matters. A mystical, holistic strand of sentiment and an immediate short-term desire for gain, ran through his thinking. Maurits' vision of management, as a complex form of social and environmental ecology, drove him to expose the multifold, intertwined interacts of management practice. The goal led him to do a lot more work than he really had to do. But sometimes, out of laxness and indifference, he did a lot less than was required of him, for example, in the exams. In his approach to his graduate study, he acted as if he was only responsible to himself. But on a content level, he argued that organisational existence was characterised by complex patterns of shared responsibility. What he intellectually espoused, he avoided in his attitude to himself.
- Lawrence's relationship to the students resembles the police's relationship to criminals: he is at once opponent and social accomplice. While Lawrence assigns, supervises and grades, he also counsels, advises and gives support. It remains unclear for Emil and Maurits which side he is on. Does Lawrence identify with the student duo; does he see them as the underdogs in need of defenders? Or is Lawrence simply trying to do his job with as little effort and conflict as he can get away with? Is his teaching style that of a friendly nurturer, or one of an impersonal professional? Emil and Maurits were convinced that Lawrence was, in some sense, a friend. After their period of study in Lancaster they continued to call him, even from South America, to tell him what was happening to them. While Lawrence resented Maurits' and Emil's insistence on payment, he was ambiguous in his attitude to the research they were doing. If all the

intellectual kudos are reserved for theoretical gymnastics, then why do intensive, time-consuming empirical work? A possible answer: to earn consulting money. But then Maurits' and Emil's demand to be better paid, is consistent with the work being done. What did Maurits and Emil learn from the fieldwork? Was there good academic justification for the time spent in the company, or were they merely cheap, or even worse, unwanted labour? Lawrence never clarified the *raison d'etre* of the project. Were Emil and Maurits doing spade work for a future project, a comparison of several European companies? Or were they merely doing a, possibly stupid, assignment needed to get a degree? Were they unwanted management consultants? While all these options had been mentioned, no clarity was forthcoming. Leon was just as much in the dark as the students were. He had proposed to Lawrence the idea of sponsoring a series of MA student in-company projects and to later write a series of ethnographic monographs on international mergers and acquisitions making use of the data collected. Lawrence had not committed himself to this plan. Lawrence wasn't really interested in focusing on the nitty-gritty of business practice, but he was reluctant to reveal his hand all too clearly.

- Leon avoided commitment by listening. He didn't say what he thought about the exams; abstained from offering commentary on the theses; held back from discussing his position to the company project; refrained from clarifying his relationships to the others. *Self* was held up to the others in denial of itself; he was *present* as *not-present*. He had concluded that the in-company project was a burden. The interdependence and mutual critical support you needed to make a project work was not forthcoming. Rather than ask whose guilt it was, he chose to ask nothing. He assumed everyone's opinion was incomplete, chaotic, untrustworthy and uncertain. The network of instructors and students had failed. The participants didn't depend on one another, when working together. Interaction was limited to goal setting, followed by disputing the responsibility for not meeting obvious obligations. The strong social bond, needed to make a research network function, wasn't there. Without commitment, there wasn't enough self-discipline or social control to make the group function successfully. There was no way to determine if Leon's attitude was cause, or effect, to the network's failure. His self-reflexivity was ambivalent.

- Emil was more acted upon, than he was an actor. His need to think about the project, before committing himself to it, had been an unappreciated bit of carnivalesque behaviour. He was much too inexperienced in research to have been able to form any idea of whether or not the project proposal was good. He knew far too little about himself, as a researcher, to be able to infer what he would find difficult or rewarding, frustrating or fun. Emil had become an exchange student to escape the impersonality of the Dutch institution; Lawrence evidently was willing to pay more attention to him than anyone did at home.

Analysing the Narratives

The narratives were produced to show postmodern self-reflexivity at work in, what could be called, teacher thinking. Many critical incidents mentioned in the research interviews have been included.[6] I now wish to consume the narratives; to see what they can tell us about the struggle for educational control.

Two concepts of teaching can be constructed from the narratives: a dominant *paternal* one and a (much weaker) *negotiated* one. Lawrence represents the paternal mind set. His reflexivity is:

> ... characterised by symbolic violence leading to voluntary submission. The authority is a prescribing power, who is construed to be legitimate, s/he most often is autocratic and hierarchical, but it is sometimes charismatic or inspiring.
>
> The inequality between teacher and student forms a difference which is legitimately transformed by authority, negating interdependence, into producing a one-way dependence. The authority tends to paper over or mask the difference. S/he refuses to acknowledge conflicts in interest because his/her legitimacy rests on claiming to represent the general good (academic rigour, scientific exactness). S/he is thus irreconcilable with a negotiated order.
>
> Crozier would undoubtedly say that this was an 'un-compensated dissymmetrical relationship,' but legitimate. Pages or Mendel could call it a *paternal form* of power. Authority privileges the homogeneity of activity and assures the ontological security of knowledge.
>
> Arbitration, or the principles of jurisprudence, are a variation on this theme.
>
> A contemporary form of this type of regulation — though not really new at all, since it has always been practiced by the church — is mastery (learning) which is a soft form of violence, an insidious and diffuse sort of power. A *maternal* sort of power or one of a social psychological nature which bears on unconscious identification and introjection.[7]

Lawrence's stance met many of these characteristics. It led to the, more or less, voluntary submission of Emil and Maurits, who continued to protest a bit, but had agreed by July to play the game by Lawrence's rules. Though Leon didn't value Emil and Maurits' exams (too much opinion, too little learning), he also didn't think much of the *correct* exams. But there was no question for him of fighting authority. The hierarchy of the university was accepted. The authority of the exam readers' judgments were based on their position, and not on an open debate over content.

Though Lawrence's relationship to the in-company project was dubious, the status of inequality meant that his role was incomparable to that of the students. They needed him to complete their work; he did not need them for anything. While an explicit style of social comradery was developed, the actual differences in position were extreme. Lawrence can doubt the value of empirical field work; Emil and Maurits have no such rights. Lawrence can see interviewing as a hardship with little career value; Emil and Maurits aren't to doubt its usefulness. Lawrence thought of himself as representing good academic practice to the students. His reification of academic norms, into social (hierarchical) behaviour, was posited as if it was self-evident. Lawrence represented *unquestionable academic authority* and the students were dependent personalities. Thanks to Lawrence's psychological dominance, the students could ill afford to doubt what he told them. Emil and Maurits were forced to accept that a body of knowledge existed in the books assigned, which they would have to master. This basic submission to academic authority, which they utterly lacked on their arrival, was established. But since they were very recent converts to the conventional academic belief structure, it was difficult for them to write theses based upon its rules. They had, in Britain, become inoculated with conventional academic dependency, but they had not yet mastered the rituals of their new point of view.

Furthermore, Lawrence assumed a semi-legalistic relationship to the students. He explained things such as how they could overcome a negative judgment of their exams (re-sits), and what criteria they were supposed to meet in their theses. Again, there was no discussion of content but an interaction focused on how to get along with established, academic authority.

The lecturer/student relationship to which they were being initiated, revolved about *mastery learning*. The person of Lawrence was not an ideal object for the students; command of the academic field, familiarity with professional literature, and skill in management research played that role. Identification with the afore-mentioned *reified qualities*, was to lead to the necessary imitative behaviour.

The *negotiated* concept of teaching:

> . . . is characterised by the restraints it puts on violence. It is a no-lose game.
> It recognises that common interest and interdependence go hand in hand with conflicts in interest and power relationships. It assumes paradox and contradiction. It implies that education knows *compensated dis-symetrical relationships* and *negotiated power*.
> The collective action re-constructs itself continually by means of the com-promises made between individuals or groups concerning their divergent interests or contradictory desires.
> While a negotiated order respects heterogeneity, it doesn't collapse into soporific security.
> This is the privileged form for regulating democratic systems. Appeal is made to no other form of legitimacy (or consensus) than that of democ-racy itself. It is, thus, incompatible with a system of authority founded on ideological or charismatic legitimacy.[8]

Leon's concept of research and learning approximated to this point of view. His crisis in effectiveness, the co-control over the company project that had escaped him, and the co-leadership in guiding Emil and Maurits' work that had evaded him, was grounded in the group's lack of interdependence. Socially *negotiated order* is powerful because it marshals and virtually ensures commitment; but it is weak if key players refuse to take part. The process of organising the company project was inevitably complex: two universities, five students, six lecturers, two national cultures, a complex bureaucratic company were all involved.[9] Constructing an effective research, learning, teaching network encompassing all the divergences would unavoidably be demanding. The functional unit of work would have had to include upwards of ten persons, at any given moment. How should one form and run this fairly large interdependent network? How should the cooperation change, evolve and develop?

What happened was that a narrow definition of responsibility prevailed so that one player (Lawrence) became the identified authority. Mutual interaction between the players and the organisations died. Leon and the company had no influence on one another; Lawrence and Leon had little impact on each other; the students and the company had almost no hold on one another; contact was virtually severed between Leon and the students; between previous and future student researchers there was no add-on effect. The strong network needed to make such a large-scale project effective was lacking. Without interdependence everyone stayed in or retreated into, their own hole, and didn't budge. A mutually interactive community of diverse persons was required to make the project work. Without such a network the two students were left to complete a required fieldwork assignment. In effect, there was NO in-company project. The parties involved acknowledged no interdependence: they refused to commit themselves to co-operate. The social choice to work together, and to learn from the experience, was not made. The *project* was not run by open consultation and compromise. The company, according to Lawrence, had never accepted the principle of overt, shared decision-making. The company brought internal conflicts between levels of hierarchy, management and workers, different divisions, the British plant versus the Dutch home office, to the project. Furthermore, in Britain, graduate students were not considered to be mature research partners. Students were rarely co-researchers; staff dialogue and student/staff interaction were separate. In addition, the Dutch students were used to doing everything themselves, alone, without staff support. In the Department from which they came, almost everything was possible; very little was required. Staff attention for students was non-existent. In Holland there was *divergence* without *integration*. Either Leon did not have the symbolic power, the research ideas, intellectual thrust, philosophical commitment, to empower the others, or he was so immersed in structuralist qualifiers, the small margins of the subject and the rejection of overburdened political/philosophical expectancies, that he never tried. The strategy of participatory consulation, wherein everyone had to manoeuvre through the network of interested parties to find a course of action which met group needs, was never attempted. The participants never mastered the complex negotiating process needed to make such a network succeed. When key players refuse to participate fully enough in a network, the system collapses. All the actors with an interest in the project would have to participate actively in the network if they were to get attuned to one another.

While the integration of key players into a network is always a complex matter, in this case it would have demanded exceptional energy. Before the players could recognise that they had connected interests, and could learn to manage these, they would have had to accept that working in a complex totality was a better idea than sticking to one's own segmented part. The multi-actor, differentiated network would have been very rich, but exceptionally complex. Integrating the differentiation would have been difficult, but it would have provided a tremendous research potential. By leaving themselves to fight out their interaction on a basis of *the strongest decide*, the actors abandoned integration for the violence of micro-political stride. Each party defended his or her own terrain; they did not commit themselves to set up, and make effective, a network of interaction. The emotive sharing of a common project, which gives the network momentum and cohesion, never got off the ground. The integrative glue of *interactive self-reflexivity* got unstuck right at the beginning.

Credo

Teacher reflexivity can boost changing, complex configurations of interdependence, wherein different persons, situations and needs, try to achieve interactive understanding. Instead of bringing about such an open and realist negotiation of variety, the lecturers and graduate students described here, produced micropolitical violence, leading to control and consent. The philosophical rigour of postmodernism has confronted us with contradictions in lecturer reflexivity, which dis-enable independent learning.

Notes

1 Linstead, S. and Grafton, R. (1990) 'Small Theory as Artefact: Artefacts as Theory', in Gagliardi, P. (Ed.) *Symbols and Artefacts*, Berlin: de Gruyter.
2 Jeffcutt, P. (1991) 'Styles of Representation in Organisational Analysis', *Proceedings SCOS-8*, Copenhagen, June 1991.
3 Czarniawska-Joerges, B., Joerges, B. (1990) 'Linguistic Artefacts at Service of Organizational Control', in Gagliardi, P. (Ed.) *Symbols and Artefacts*, Berlin: de Gruyter, p. 341.
4 Cooper, R. (1990) 'Organization/Disorganization', in Pym, J.D. (Ed.) *The Theory and Philosophy of Organisations*, London: Routledge, p. 182.
5 All names have been changed.
6 Several researchers were involved in the interviewing of the project members. Some of these had, and some hadn't, played a role in the in-company project. The data were collected long before I conceived of this article. Any ethnography is so-called, subjective; this text is not much more so than others.
7 Paraphrased from: van den Hove, D. (1991) 'Vers un management negocier', *Les Dejeuners d'Archimede*, 18 February 1991, H.E.C. Montreal.
8 *Ibid.*
9 Many players were omitted from the narration to keep the data as clearly arranged as possible.

Part 2 Exploring Teachers' Knowledge and Beliefs

Chapter 5

Teachers' Professional Responsibility and Development

Rosa Laffitte

The project discussed in this chapter aims at investigating the kind of professional responsibility assumed by teachers towards different aspects of their teaching activities, and the effect that the perspectives of accountability existing around them may have on them. One of the aspects considered in the study is an analysis of the legitimacy of power and authority within institutional structures, together with the degree of responsibility conferred on and assumed by different groups within the system: inspectors, parents, teachers, etc. and the effect they may have on teachers' conceptions of themselves and their work.

The study also takes into account teachers' implicit theories, values, beliefs, ideological traditions and their situation, i.e. resources, external circumstances, administrative limitations, etc. It takes as its starting-point a number of different research projects carried out in Great Britain in this field.

Background to the Study

This study is part of a broader research project on systems of teacher evaluation for professional development appropriate to the Spanish and Catalan cultural and institutional context.

The aim of this part of the project was to discover the opinions of teachers in the Barcelona area on the degree of responsibility assumed towards different aspects of their teaching activities. Who do they feel responsible to and what do they feel responsible for? The study also aimed to find out which aspects of their teaching activities are of most importance to them and most influence their values and beliefs in their daily work, since although they are experienced individually, they are within the cultural traditions of the profession.

The interaction between values and feelings or affect is critical because people's actions are based on a connection between how they think they ought to behave and what they ought to aim towards, to how they feel about themselves and what they want. (Kogan, 1988: 94)

Rosa Laffitte

Perspectives of Teachers' Accountability

Accountability is in itself a complex concept that tends to be present implicitly or explicitly in every social context. It can be used to refer to a wide range of mechanisms controlling the relationships between the state administration, public institutions, the organs of government within these institutions, the individuals who work in them and society in general. Nevertheless, the concept of accountability in education tends to be identified with a classical perspective, based on unilateral control according to a narrow definition of efficiency — input-output. When this perspective is applied to the social services in a country, it can interfere inappropriately with the service instead of making it really more efficient.

As a subject for study within the educational field, it implies the need to consider the structures of institutions and therefore to look at questions of power, authority, ideology, values and responsibility. As Gibson suggests (1981), structures develop gradually and are rooted in history and culture, so that although they are based on power relationships and the legitimacy of this power, they also represent forms of thought and of feeling. When we speak of 'the school' or 'the students', 'the teachers' or 'the administration', we are accepting or recognising the presence and the strength of different social structures; these structures are closely interrelated and have a powerful influence on each other and on individuals, since they tend to be the basis on which individuals construct their own concept of reality. Therefore in the study of perspectives of teachers' accountability we also need to try to understand the structures of feeling (Gibson, 1981) which encompass individual values, ways of seeing, interpreting and valuing the world within a historical and cultural context. They are basically emotional states that allow us to consider what must and what must not be, and are found in all human activity:

> Whether we name or try to unravel their complexities in words such as ideology, beliefs, attitudes (or, less familiarly *zeitgeist*, spirit) it is always clear that every individual moves within, embodies and expresses such affective states. (Gibson, 1981: 62)

In the study I am referring to, the aim has been to try to detect the values and beliefs that make up the 'structures of feeling' of teachers with regard to their perspective of accountability; these structures of feeling are no doubt influenced by the institutional structure imposed on the teachers and by the historical and cultural context in which they have developed and are developing.

Research Methodology

The research design of the study involves a combination of quantitative and qualitative methods in two basic stages. The first phase was an analytical one of gathering data on the formal macro and micro organisation structures of the country. Primary sources were used for this, such as official documents (the laws, bills and publications of the educational administration), as well as secondary sources — descriptive studies already published, the literature relating to the subject, articles, reports and various work study documents. These data have also been used for comparison and contrast with in-depth interviews with teachers, parents and professionals working in the administration.

The second phase involved developing a questionnaire based on one used in a comparative study made by Broadfoot and Osborn (1987) *Teachers' conceptions of their professional responsibility in England and France (1984–1987)*, and on the questionnaire on attitudes of the Tennessee Self-Concept Scale, adapted to the Spanish context by Garanto (1984). The questionnaire was answered by a sample of 232 teachers teaching in the Barcelona area at different levels within primary education, which up to now has covered ages from six to thirteen.

Before commenting on the results obtained so far, I would briefly like to indicate the basic characteristics of the Spanish educational system according to the 1990 Act, and the organisation of schools at present, especially in so far as these are relevant to the study and in so far as they differ from the structure in England and Wales.

Main Features of the Spanish Educational System

After winning the election in October 1982, the new Socialist government began a reform of the educational system and in 1985 passed the Organic Law of Educational Rights (LODE). The law aims at ensuring everyone's right to education within the existing network of public and private schools, and at laying down the norms for a system based on the participation of all those involved in running educational establishments financed by public money.

The new law of Organisation of the Spanish Educational System (LOGSE), passed in 1990, establishes the organisation of schools on similar lines to that of any other European country. This replaces the old General Law of Education (LGE) of 1970, which previously determined the structure of the school system in its basic levels. With the advent of democracy and the new political structure of autonomous communities, the old law no longer reflected the real situation in the country.

Evaluation of students is continuous (global in primary school, according to subjects in secondary school) and it is necessary for students to reach the standards laid down for each level in order to pass to a higher class (Figure 5.1). It must be remembered in this context that there are no nationally organised state examinations at these levels. A student who does not reach the standard required may remain a further year in the same class and in this way it is possible to continue in basic education up to the age of 18.

Structure and Organisation of Educational Centres

As already stated, the LODE of 1985 made a substantial alteration to the previous model in establishing that the structure and functioning of educational centres was to be based on the concept of participation in educational administration, expressed by the Constitution, article 27.7. This lays down that parents, and in given circumstance students, should take part in the control and organisation of all centres financed by the government. To this end a new administrative body was established for all schools, the *Consejo Escolar* (Governing Body), on which all members of the school community are represented. As a result all schools in

Figure 5.1: The Spanish educational system

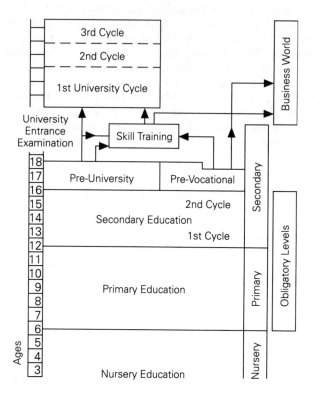

SPANISH EDUCATIONAL SYSTEM

the Spanish public educational system and those in the private system which receive government grants belong to a democratic, participatory structure composed of the following elements.

Consejo Escolar (Governing Body).

The *Consejo Escolar* is composed of representatives of the parents, teachers, other school employees, and of students in the upper levels, together with representatives of the local government authority, and with the participation of the Head and Director of Studies. In all, including the Head and Director of Studies, the teaching staff make up 50 per cent of the *Consejo*. Governing bodies vary in size according to the number of students involved. The *Consejo* is renewed by means of elections every two years and is responsible, among other things, for policy-making, selecting the Head, and approving the budget.

Head.

In public and state-supported schools the Head is elected for a period of three years by the *Consejo* from among the full-time teaching staff of the school with three or more years' experience. He or she is responsible for choosing the Director of Studies and Secretary, subject to the approval of the governing body.

Teachers.
All the teachers in the school belong to an organ of participation called the *Claustro*, chaired by the Head, which is responsible for establishing the criteria of evaluation and for syllabus coordination. Public sector teachers are civil servants, divided into two categories, those who have graduated from a teachers' training college and university graduates.

Findings of the Study: Development of the Questionnaire and Findings

As already stated, the questionnaire used was based on the questionnaire developed for the comparative study of teachers' conceptions of professional responsibility in England and France (Broadfoot and Osborn, 1987), although the majority of the sections were altered and extended.

In developing the questionnaire a number of variables were taken into account, such as sex, age, the level at which the teacher was teaching, as well as whether or not the teacher had held the post of Head or Director of Studies. As previously explained, in Spain posts of authority such as Head Teacher are held for a period of three years, and he or she is democratically elected by the representatives of the school community. Consequently, it is not possible to speak of an educational career consisting of different stages depending on promotion. For this reason, those who have held the post of Head or Director of Studies were asked to state whether they held it now or had held it previously, since those who have held it subsequently revert to being members of the teaching staff.

The points picked out for attention in this chapter coincide to the greatest extent with the comparative study previously referred to although it must be remembered that that study dates from 1985 and the levels/ages of primary education in England and Spain do not coincide absolutely, so that a precise comparison is not possible. Mention will also be made of any other items that have proved particularly significant.

The questionnaire consists of six sections, containing 71 items in all, with a rating scale of one to five.

Section A: Responsibility/Accountability — 'I am responsible to . . .'

This section contains twelve items, four more than those in the original questionnaire. Its aim is to detect the dominant model of accountability (bureaucratic-contractual, moral and professional, Becher, Eraut and Knight, 1981; Kogan, 1988) (Figure 5.2).

The Spanish teachers in the sample, although they rated the first question high (myself, my own conscience) at 4.54 had a lower average than their English and French colleagues (4.98 and 4.95 respectively). The same is true of the second question, my pupils. They coincide more with the French in the degree of responsibility felt towards parents (French 3.37, Spanish 3.76, English 4.31) and towards

80

Figure 5.2: Section A: *Responsibility/accountability*

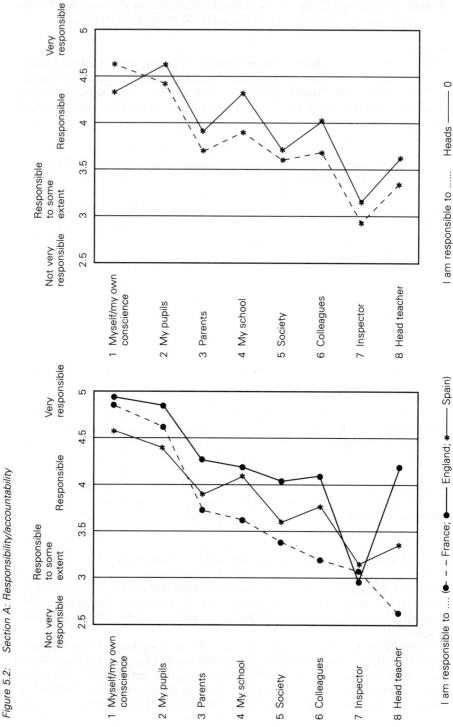

I am responsible to .... (●− − France; ●——— England; ✳——— Spain)

I am responsible to ...... Heads ———— 0

society (French 3.41, Spanish 3.59, English 4.03). The Spanish teachers are closer to the English with reference to the school (French 3.59, Spanish 4.09, English 4.16) and towards their colleagues (French 3.24, Spanish 3.81, English 4.04). As regards their responsibility towards the Head they are in between (French 2.61, Spanish 3.46, English 4.19). The four items added to the questionnaire (not shown in Figure 5.2) relate to the structure, with the aim of determining the level of bureaucratic-contractual responsibility. The results were very low, from which we could hazard the assumption that the teachers in this sample are responsively accountable within the professional accountability model (Kogan, 1988) rather than a bureaucratic-contractual one. This is not surprising in a system in which a democratic collegiate structure exists.

It is also interesting to note significant differences in the averages obtained by different groups according to the variables mentioned. In the first place, teachers who had had a post of responsibility answered every one of the twelve items more positively than those who had not, except for Item I (myself, my own conscience). Apart from that, there were significant differences according to age, since teachers over 35 had higher averages. It appears from this that one's personal sense of responsibility increases with age and also if one has occupied a responsible position.

Section B: Models of Professionality: 'I am responsible for . . .'

This section has thirteen items. It aims at determining which aspects of teaching activity teachers feel most responsible for. In drawing up this section, the attempt was made to distinguish between two models of teaching based on a wider (Model A) and narrower (Model B) view of the teaching-learning process. These are close to what Hoyle (1980) calls extended and restricted professionality. The items marked with an asterisk relate to Model B, the others to Model A (Figure 5.3).

The results indicate that the two perspectives are both present, although the items that relate more to Model B obtain more extreme scores, ranging from the average of 4.50 for Item I, the student's learning, to 3.13 for Item 10, achieving predetermined standards. The range of the Model A items is not so great. The highest average score is 4.29, the student's interest in learning, and the lowest 3.43, information given to parents.

In general in this section there were more significant differences according to the variables, above all in connection with age and teaching level. Teachers in middle levels scored lower than those in lower and in upper levels. In so far as age is concerned, the group of teachers aged between 31 and 35 scored lower on all items than their colleagues. There were no significant differences in this section between those who had held posts of responsibility and those who had not.

In the course of interviews with teachers, the two models have also been recognisably present, although when they are talking about their work teachers appear closer to Model A than to Model B. If we consider the historical and cultural context of the country, it is not surprising to find teachers astride the two models. On the one hand they have been working within a curricular tradition which is centralised but subject to relatively little control, and as a result do not appear to believe that they lack autonomy; on the other, although they have been within a closed curriculum tradition, they seem more concerned by the broader

Figure 5.3: Section B: Models of professionality

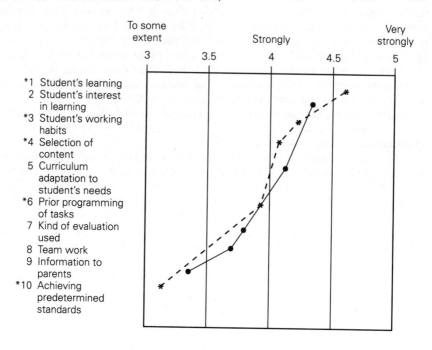

	To some extent		Strongly		Very strongly
	3	3.5	4	4.5	5

*1 Student's learning
 2 Student's interest in learning
*3 Student's working habits
*4 Selection of content
 5 Curriculum adaptation to student's needs
*6 Prior programming of tasks
 7 Kind of evaluation used
 8 Team work
 9 Information to parents
*10 Achieving predetermined standards

I am responsible for ....

needs of the students than by the need to achieve predetermined standards laid down by the authorities.

Section C: Influences on Teaching Practice

This section has fourteen items aimed at determining which contextual aspects affect teachers most in practice. Of these 14 items, nine were adapted from the comparative study of Broadfoot and Osborn (1987) (Figure 5.4).

If we compare the results for the three nationalities, we can see that they all consider themselves most influenced by their own experience (English 4.70, French 4.70, Spanish 4.63). The Spanish resemble the French in estimating the extent to which they are influenced by (a) The Head Teacher — (French 2.75, Spanish 2.85, English 4.19); (b) initial training — (French 3.62, Spanish 3.53, English 3.25); (c) parents — (French 3.00, Spanish 2.72, English 3.25); and (d) inspectors — (French 2.39, Spanish 2.30, English 3.24). The two aspects Spanish teachers appear to consider more influential than teachers in England and France are (a) their colleagues (French 3.24, Spanish 3.83, English 3.55) and (b) in-service training (French 3.17, Spanish 4.10, English 3.52).

The five items introduced to find out teachers' opinions on the influence of formal structure on teaching practice all scored rather low averages (under 3) once

Figure 5.4: Section C: Influences on teaching practice

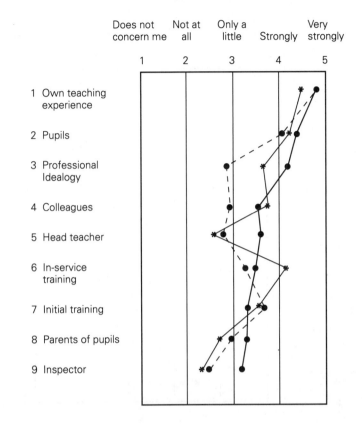

Influences on teaching practice............
(●– –France; ●— England; ✱—Spain)

more. In general there are few significant differences relating to the variables. It is only possible to indicate that the youngest teachers (those between 20 and 25) say that pupils and their parents influence them more in their teaching, and that those who are at present holding the post of Head Teacher or Director of Studies are slightly more influenced by inspectors.

As a general observation, one could say that it seems as if teachers believe their practice is influenced by those aspects that they feel are closest to them. It is also evident that the Head appears to have less influence than the rest of their colleagues, but this is not surprising in a system that is not hierarchical.

Section D: Parent-Teacher Contact

This section has eight items aimed at deciding on the level of contact parents have with teachers. In general, the scores here are very low, ranging from 1.50 to 2.50

Figure 5.5:   Section E: Perceptions on the nature of teaching

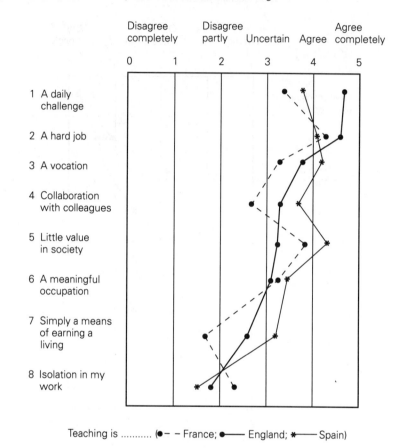

Teaching is .... (●– – France; ●——— England; ✱——Spain)

(that is to say between 'Never' and 'Once a month') although those with respon-sibility seem to score a little higher than the rest. In fact there seems to be a problem in parent-teacher relationships which is also confirmed by the interviews conducted with parents and teachers. This may be due to the system of evaluation and promotion from one class to the next which has been applied up to now. Teachers in this situation have a weighty influence when the moment arrives to distribute final marks and decide which students are to go up or not from one class to another; parents are aware of this and consequently try to put pressure on teachers.

Section E: Perceptions of the Nature of Teaching: Teaching is . . .

This section contains thirteen items expressing different opinions on teaching, some positive, some negative (Figure 5.5). Of these, eight are retained from the original comparative study. The international comparison here reveals that

Spanish teachers obtain an average between the English and French on the question of teaching being a daily challenge (French 3.40, Spanish 3.78, English 4.70) and score a little lower on the question of its being a hard job (French 4.17, Spanish 4.06, English 4.62).

On the other hand, they value more highly the idea that it is a matter of collaborating with colleagues (French 2.63, Spanish 3.60, English 3.27) and a meaningful occupation (French 2.26, Spanish 4.21, English 3.14). They also consider it to a greater extent as a means of earning a living (French 1.74, Spanish 3.16, English 2.58). They coincide more with the English than the French in not considering it isolated (French 2.31, Spanish 1.76, English 1.86) and in general seem to be fairly favourable to the idea that it is a satisfying job.

In this section, the variables that are most significant are age and level. In item nine, a satisfying job, (not included in the chart) teachers who have previously had a responsible post score higher and those who teach in the lower levels also do so. As far as age is concerned, the youngest (under 25) and the oldest (over 35) appear more satisfied than those in between.

As a conclusion to this section, we could say that teachers in the sample, although they consider that their work is insufficiently valued by society, have a fairly positive attitude towards it, and this is confirmed by the scores obtained in the last section (eleven items based on the Tennessee Self-concept Scale developed by Fitts (1965) and adapted to the Spanish context by Garanto (1984)) and by the views expressed in the interviews.

Issues arising

The research project is not yet concluded but perhaps it could be said at this stage that although teaching has the same generic problems everywhere — teachers show similar patterns in valuing the aspects mentioned — their perceptions of their professional responsibility are affected by formal structures and the pressures these exact on them in their context. Pressures related to the mechanisms of accountability implicit or explicit in the structure are probably those that affect them most and are most likely to alter their perspective of a model of professionality and the ways in which evaluation and appraisal are understood and accepted. In this way, for example, although we have not yet formally established a system of accountability is Spain that can be readily defined, it is clear that the pressures exerted by parents anxious that their children will obtain standards good enough to allow them to go to pre-university levels have a greater effect on teachers than any they receive from the inspectorate or the Head. How far this affects their teaching is still not clear, although it appears to relate to it in terms of action or reaction.

References

BECHER, T., ERAUT, M. and KNIGHT, J. (1981) *Policies for Educational Accountability*, London: Heinemann.

BROADFOOT, P. and OSBORN, M.J. (1987) 'Teachers' conceptions of their professional responsibility: some international comparisons', *Comparative Education*, **Volume 23**, No. 3.

— (1988) 'What professional responsibility means to teacher: national contexts and classroom constants', *British Journal of Sociology of Education*, **Volume 9**, No. 3.

FITTS, W. H. (1965) *Tennessee Self Concept Scale Manuals*, Nashville, Tennessee: Counselor Recordings and Tests.

GARANTO ALOS, G. (1984) *Las actitudes hacia si mismo y su medicion*, BARCELONA: E.U.

GIBSON, R. (1981) 'Teacher-parent communication', in *The Cambridge Accountability Project: the self-accounting school*, London: Grant McIntyre Ltd.

— (1981) 'Structures of accountability', in ELLIOTT (Ed.) *School Accountability*, London: Grant McIntyre Ltd.

HOYLE, E. (1980) 'Professionalisation and deprofessionalisation in education', in HOYLE, E. and MEGARRY, J. (Eds) *World Yearbook of Education, 1980: Professional Development of Teachers*, London: Kogan Page.

KOGAN, M. (1988) *Education accountability; an analytic overview*, London: Hutchinson.

Chapter 6

Think You Can: The Influence of Culture on Beliefs

Mary Lynn Hamilton

While the number of studies on teachers' beliefs has grown exponentially in recent years, much of this work has examined individual experience. Group or cultural connections have not often been examined. In a case study of one Midwestern school, this chapter claims that the study of beliefs within the context of culture is essential to understanding teachers' actions and choices in the classroom. Explorations of cultural factors provides a means of more fully understanding the teacher's decision-making processes and the motives behind certain beliefs and actions. A greater awareness amongst teachers of cultural factors may also facilitate reflection upon practice.

Although much of the work on teacher beliefs has focused on the individual (for example Connelly and Clandinin, 1984; Clandinin and Connelly, 1987) and case studies of a teacher's experience (Munby, 1983) or several teachers' experiences (Russell, 1987) have been described, cultural connections have rarely been examined. In contrast, Olson (1988) contends that 'what teachers tell us about their practice is, most fundamentally, a reflection of their culture, and cannot be properly understood without reference to that culture' (1988: 69). Teacher knowledge, then, is constructed from an individual's understanding of shared knowledge about the world. While the study of beliefs is important to the understandings that influence teachers' actions and choices in the classroom, it should be studied within a framework that recognises the influence of culture.

A central problem in research on teacher thinking is how to get 'inside teachers' heads' to describe their knowledge, beliefs, and values (Feiman-Nemser and Floden, 1986). Finding evidence of culture and cultural knowledge can be an additional problem. Using the recent work in cognitive anthropology as a guide, this chapter analyzes teachers' talk and experience for what it discloses about the cultural knowledge used in classroom settings. This analysis attempts to identify the effects of cultural knowledge on teachers' professional knowledge and professional practice. Understanding why and how teachers think and practice in classrooms is essential to understanding teaching. To explore these issues, first, culture will be defined. Second, the role of beliefs will be explored. Third, the use of cultural models will be presented as a way to probe the influence of culture on beliefs. Finally, a case study of one school, New Bradley School, will be presented to elucidate the information discussed.

Culture

Culture structures general guidelines by which people ought to live which, in turn, affect individuals' behaviours, their interactions with kin and friends, and even their approaches to education. An examination of culture exemplifies an effort to understand the various ways people construct their lives as they live them (Geertz, 1973). Furthermore, it can be defined as 'those collective interpretations of social and material experience that are more or less shared by members of a group.' (Elsenhart, 1990: 22). Unquestionably culture is the screen through which we view our lives, and interpret the world around us. This knowledge is implicit, learned through advice, correction, and non-verbal interaction through others (Quinn and Holland, 1987) and can best be conceived of as a complex of ideas utilised according to peoples' needs and motives (Price, 1987).

The importance of social context (Dewey, 1904), cultural setting (Philips, 1983), and social construction (Berger and Luckman, 1966) in schools has been recognised for some time, and much research since that time (for example, Page, 1988; Guilfoyle, 1988) has supported it. Educational anthropologists have emphasised its importance by elaborating on the various aspects of the culture of the school. For example, Wolcott (1973) describes the intricacies of school through the eyes of a school principal; Erickson and Shultz (1982) discuss the role of a counsellor within a school culture; Erickson and Mohatt (1984) address the cultural organisation of Indian students' classroom and participation; McDermott (1976) investigates the social relations between teachers and students in the development of learning environments in the classroom; and Heath (1983) observes the distinctions between home and school. This work contrasts with the work of Lieberman (1988) and Miller (1988), and others who do not add the larger dimension to their examination of school culture.

The school culture addressed in this chapter is the culture of a school that both shapes teachers' understanding of their actions (Feiman-Nemser and Floden, 1986; Lortie, 1975; Sarason, 1982; Metz, 1983, 1986; Rutter, Maughan, Mortimore and Oston, 1979) and their students (Tyler, 1987) and is grounded in faculty members' shared definitions (Page, 1988). It is linked to the larger social order by staff members' shared perceptions of the social class of the school's typical student and to the educational demands of the community. Although typically teachers work in isolation (Feiman-Nemser and Floden, 1986; Fuchs, 1969; Goodlad, 1983; Sarason, 1982) the school culture cuts through that isolation in ways not completely understood. While the beliefs are often tacit and regarded as self-evident by members of the culture, they nevertheless provide a powerful foundation for members' understanding of the way they and the organisation operate.

Beliefs

Among the social sciences there are varied definitions of beliefs from non-existent (Stich, 1983), to personal construction (Kelly, 1955), to ambiguous (Quine, 1978), to a social construction (Berger and Luckman, 1966) which filters information through personal ideas and experience. Anthropological studies reveal that beliefs are a division of things self/non-self (Wallace, 1970); are propositions that are accepted as true and fit into three categories: *private* beliefs, accepted as true irrespective of the beliefs of others; *declared* beliefs, accepted in public behaviour and cited in argument to justify action, and *public* beliefs accepted by group members as their common declared beliefs (Goodenough, 1971). In contrast, Stromberg (1986) suggests that beliefs simply assent to something. Most recently, cognitive anthropologists discuss a view of culture that includes socially constituted understandings of the world. This view suggests what people must know in order to act as they do, and that how they interpret their experience encompasses both personal beliefs and those beliefs about customs, oral traditions and artifacts held by other members (Quinn and Holland, 1987).

While many education studies represent beliefs as commonsensical and generally understood (for example, Hargreaves, 1984; Hollingsworth, 1987; Munby, 1983), some researchers do offer definitions. There are *perspectives*, a coordinated set of ideas and actions a person uses in dealing with a situation that relates to a person's ordinary way of thinking and acting on a situation (Wodlinger, 1985); *understandings*, internal mental processes that are underlying determinants of behaviour and of environments people create (Bussis, Chittenden, and Amarel, 1976); *ground*, which is composed of beliefs, reality judgments about what knowledge is relevant (knowing that), and intentions, value judgments about what courses of action are possible and desirable (Oberg, 1987); and *visions*, images that people have about the way things should be (Barth, 1986). Furthermore, extending the view of beliefs into knowledge, researchers endeavour to clarify teachers' mental processes used to understand and process information (Clark and Peterson, 1986). For instance, Clandinin and Connelly (1987) and Elbaz (1981) consider teacher knowledge to be personal and social; Richardson (1989) and Tobin (1990), identify teachers' beliefs as socially constructed; and Richardson (1990), Russell (1987) and Zeichner (1989) label teachers' knowledge as reflective.

Nisbett and Ross (1980) suggest that aspects of knowledge have a schematic, cognitive structure. Other aspects of this knowledge are represented by beliefs or theories which are 'reasonably explicit "propositions" about the characteristics of objects or object classes' (p. 28). They further propose that a 'rich store of general knowledge of objects, people, events and their characteristic relationships' affects 'people's understanding of the rapid flow of continuing social events' (p. 28). This is culture.

Cultural Models

Cultural knowledge has sometimes been examined combining work on mental scripts (Schank and Abelson, 1977) as they reflect our impressions of our world with analysis of language and its meanings (Holland, 1985). Scripts, gleaned from daily routine, are standardised sequences of events that fill in our understanding of frequently recurring experiences (Schank, 1975). They are learned and help people act appropriately (Schank, 1988). Cultural knowledge has also been studied by looking at cultural patterns in ones' life history (Langness, 1965; Mandelbaum, 1973; Agar, 1973), and has been characterised in terms of 'events' (Agar, 1973). Some theorists have been concerned with the relationship between language and culture that tend to share a cognitive paradigm, in which culture is perceived as a set of 'complexly rational mental phenomena' (Dougherty, 1985: 3). Others such as Keesing (1973), Crick (1976), Hutchins (1980) and D'Andrade (1984), seem to concur that these 'mental phenomena' are a hierarchy of rules for the construction of propositions. These propositions may be very far-reaching and are likely to be a part of implicit understandings which may be explicitly represented in their language and actions. Beliefs are important aspects of the hierarchy.

The acquisition of a culture involves coming to terms with one's cultural models which represent 'culturally shared knowledge [that] is organised into proto-typical event sequences enacted in simplified worlds' (Quinn and Holland, 1987: 24). This is a way to examine the influence of cultural knowledge of peoples' experience and their interpretations of it. A cultural model, a taken-for-granted model of the world that is shared by members of society, sometimes serves

> to set goals for action, sometimes to plan the attainment of said goals, sometimes to direct the actualisation of these goals, sometimes to make sense of the actions and fathom the goals of others, and sometimes to produce verbalisations that may play various parts in all these projects as well as in the subsequent interpretation of what has happened (Quinn and Holland, 1987: 6–7).

In other words, a cultural model is the expected, the unspoken, the taken-for-granted aspects of the world. It is 'shared implicit knowledge' (Holland and Skinner, 1987: 79). It involves the process of identifying the fundamental versus surface elements of the complex of beliefs and knowledge (Holland and Skinner, 1987). An example would be the terminology used by the informants in Holland and Skinner's (1987) study to identify males and females. On the surface the inform-ants use terms like 'jock', 'playboy', 'woman' and 'doll' to identify people with whom they have come in contact. When asked to expound upon those terms a deeper, more fundamental set of beliefs and knowledge becomes apparent. Much of it remains implicit until informants define the labels.

In light of the Holland and Skinner study (1987) as well as other studies by cognitive anthropologists, it seemed evident that the exploration of culture and cultural models could inform educational research. Without doubt in schools, a construct where our cultural knowledge is implicitly and explicitly expressed, evidence for cultural models can be found.

Methodology

The data examined in this chapter have been collected and are being collected as a part of a qualitative study, begun in 1990, of one school's restructuring process. To gather data, many hours of classroom observation have been conducted in classrooms and school staff development programs; on-going field notes have been written after each visit; and eight hours of formal interviews have been conducted with each of the twelve focus teacher/staff throughout the study. These focus teachers/staff selected from each teaching/support level represent the vast experience and diversity in the school. Informal interviews have been conducted with all teachers. Concentration has been focused on the interaction of culture with teachers' beliefs and theories about teaching and learning.

These interviews adapt the Elicitation Heuristic Technique developed by an-thropologists to determine belief systems in groups of people (Black, 1969; Black and Metzger, 1969; Kay and Metzger, 1973; and Metzger, 1973). Within this framework, beliefs consist of sets of assertions held by informants and spoken as declarative sentences. This methodology uses both open-ended questions to construct the informants' propositions about the world and closed-ended questions to establish the interviewer's understanding of the response (Agar, 1973). Although the formal elicitation procedure reveals only general beliefs, the open-endedness of the questions brings forth more specific information. These techniques better serve to conceptualise cultural knowledge than a deterministic grid (Price, 1987). The data are examined to reveal the cultural models underlying the teachers' reasoning (Holland and Quinn, 1987). What the teachers discuss and elaborate upon have been considered as well as possible omissions in information (Price, 1987). This paper presents one detailed case study that attempts to identify the effects of cultural influence on teachers' professional knowledge and practice.

New Bradley School

At first glance New Bradley appears to be an ordinary school from any urban setting. Situated on a busy street in a residential area, New Bradley serves as an historical marker. Pleasant-looking multicoloured houses surrounded by grassy yards dot the tree-lined thoroughfare. While not an upcoming neighbourhood, many of the houses are cared-for, sometimes appearing polished. There are four churches within a five-block radius implicitly signalling a neighbourhood interest. The shopping area, while not central to the school neighbourhoods, is not far away.

Historically this area was populated with Hispanic families hired by the nearby Santa Fe Railroad. Still serving the Santa Fe workers, the recent recession and its persuant loss of jobs brought in other community members. Now there is a mixed-bag of ethnicities, economic statuses, and interests both in the neighbourhood and at the school. Yet this is a long-standing neighbourhood where people have lived for a long time. Some are even New Bradley alumni.

The school itself represents history. Originally built in 1913 and complimented by a 1960s addition, New Bradley sits on a large lot surrounded by macadam and, in extreme contrast, a very small patch of greenery with trees, flowers and grass. Its red brick and white concrete facade stands sturdy against passing time. To one side the multipurpose room addition intrudes upon its strength. On the other side stand portable classrooms, somewhat hidden from view, and austere in structure.

Looking beyond a superficial glance certain clues belie first impressions. The dilapidated condition of the roads, proximity of the houses, the number of people filling the houses, the graffiti on the walls, and the Projects up the hill contradict its middle-class facade. At second glance a complex configuration becomes apparent.

Once inside the school, its antiquated but open design becomes conspicuous. Looking up the stairway a well-organised open office area and staff welcome all who enter the school. Actually the school suggests contradictions in space. While tall ceilings and wide hallways suggest open space, artificial barriers, extra furniture, and office equipment impose upon that space. Complimenting the secretary's friendly face is the low din of children at work. There are three floors in the building, each housing classrooms and necessary offices. Each floor is colourcoded with current popular shades — an attempt to update the building. As you enter any classroom you immediately notice the drone of air-conditioners — another attempt at modernisation — as well as the decorated bulletin boards inviting everyone into the room.

The student body of New Bradley represents Laotian, 6 per cent, Hispanic, 24 per cent, black, 29 per cent and white, 41 per cent. Of the 360 students, kindergarten through to fifth grade, 76 per cent participate in the free or reduced lunch program. They are all neighbourhood students bussed from the surrounding area.

New Bradley Faculty/Staff

The thirty-two faculty/staff working at New Bradley School are 92 per cent female, 8 per cent male with an ethnic mix of 13 per cent black, 5 per cent Hispanic, and 82 per cent white and a mean age is 38. They have an average of eleven years of experience and are in their first few years of teaching at New Bradley School.

The teachers of New Bradley School are a select and highly motivated group. They have vast experience, and are willing to try new ideas and new strategies with students and for themselves. They are also a well-trained group of teachers having attended numerous workshops/inservices to improve their practice and their classrooms and having taken many advanced courses at various neighbourhood universities and colleges. Prior to their tenure at New Bradley School most teachers worked at other inner-city schools.

New Bradley School Culture

The culture at New Bradley School is deliberate. Over a year ago, after receiving funds for a restructuring project written by members of the central district office, New Bradley School hired many new (to this school) teachers and voluntarily transferred anyone not interested in the project. According to the outline of the project proposal the teachers hired have to be committed to similar beliefs — students, positive change, teamwork — and be willing to work long hours. They also have to be articulate about their experiences and their views because the district — its administrators and its teachers — are scrupulously watching for successes and failures.

The New Bradley staff have had the opportunity to build a school culture together. It has been intentional and in-depth while not necessarily being planned by the teachers. Many teachers have the attitude that they should follow the dictates of the proposal. Yet they quickly discovered that that was not enough. Although not a conscious undertaking, their teamwork (each grade level has three teachers who work together) and the collaborative nature of the school encourage the creation of a strong culture. They work together every day after school which contributes to the development of a shared language and strong collegial bond. Moreover, the staff selected for positions at New Bradley are leaders — outspoken and committed to students and change. Consequently, the strong, positive nature of the school quickly became visible.

From the beginning of the project the teachers had a similar language about schooling and students. Evidently their commitment to students came before their introduction to the project. When each person responded to a query about the purpose of the school they used similar words and the same meaning — all children can learn. For example, one teacher said 'we believe in children here. All kids can learn if they have confidence in themselves and if they put forth effort.' Another teacher responded that 'Every child will succeed. The idea of failure should be non-existent.' While another teacher stated that 'all children can learn, given time and support, our staff has the power to help students become active participants in their learning.' Most teachers have a high level of commitment to that purpose.

Once the staff was selected, they participated and adopted a particular staff development program entitled *The Efficacy Seminar.* All teachers and staff, including custodians, attended the five-day seminar which reinforced the beliefs that the teachers brought to the school. More than any other component, this training affected the culture of the school. The Efficacy Seminar provides participants with an operational model for managing student development. An essential element that equates success with a combination of effort and ability. Based on the learned helplessness work of Dweck and others, it focuses on students' attributions of success and failure. One stated assumption is that 'there is no need for you to *prove* you have the brains to be smart in school. We already know that. The objective is to *improve* your intelligence through hard work to get smart. Smart is not something that you are, smart is something you can get. The program appears to be a wake-up call, particularly for white teachers, who might inadvertently reinforce learned helplessness in ethnic minority students. They underscore the 'massive failure' by schools 'to develop the potentials of our children.' The 'Bottom line — we must analyze and dismantle the psychological barriers to the development of our children, and to our own development as educators. . . . We must take responsibility for development, and accept nothing but the best for and from our kids. We must mobilize our resources, overcome feelings of helplessness and, by our example, create a powerful expectation of mastery for all our children' (From the *Efficacy Training Manual*).

The fundamental assumption of the program is that student development is critical to the well-being and the continued prosperity of students and the society. 'It is both a *means* (a pool of developed people is a central ingredient to solving the problems of people of colour, and to advancing group interests), and an *end* (providing for the development of succeeding generations is the central unifying objective for all successful groups)' (From the *Efficacy Training Manual*).

The program comes complete with a shared language, for example: ZOD — zone of development; FOHGICB — finding out how good I can be; POD — process of development. Upon program completion the teachers are encouraged to share their ideas with students, using the ascribed language. In fact, many staff members practised sharing the language, talking about students' POD's and ZOD's and asking each other if they were 'FOHGICB'. For further encouragement, they designed FOHGICB buttons for the students and themselves.

According to the program, designed by Jeff Howard, the American model of development equates ability with development and promotes a helplessness response. In turn, this inhibits people's potentials. On the other hand, the efficacy model of development, which equates confidence and effective effort with development, endorses a mastery response. Significantly the program addresses two American cultural models: *able people succeed* and *work hard to achieve rewards.*

Certainly the later model represents the protestant work ethic — if you apply considerable and worthwhile effort to a particular task, you reap rewards. In the classroom, for example, you might expect to get an A if you work hard enough.

Interested in the psychology of performance, the Efficacy Seminar promotes an 'intellectual work ethic' that will develop strong positive attitudes to intellectual competition. Additionally, it wants to encourage students to attribute intellectual successes to ability and attribute their failures to lack of effort. It calls for the need to address the problems of performance and development of African-Americans and other ethnic minorities (Howard and Hammond, 1985).

New Bradley School culture, consequently, is built upon a program promoting hard-working, confident students who are taught by strong, confident teachers, in a school designed to address the needs of students. Further, this culture appears to reinforce certain cultural models.

Example 1: Is it working hard, or hardly working?
A cultural model around which New Bradley works is *work hard to achieve rewards*. This manifests itself in the language of the teachers when they say 'put out your best effort' and 'try hard'. It also reveals itself in their practice as they schedule drills and re-teaching for students who miss the initial lesson. The teachers of New Bradley believe that all students can learn, but that varied efforts must be put forth to attain mastery of the academic agenda. Consequently, classroom planning and school activities revolve around the notions of working hard. When students fail to attend to a lesson, they are questioned about their willingness to work hard. When they succeed, they are praised for their hard work. If the students make a mistake — it is simply feedback to propel their learning.

According to the teachers, this feedback and encouragement will raise the level of students' self-esteem. New Bradley teachers believe that if a student feels good about her or him self, if a student knows he or she will have the opportunity to achieve in the learning process, if a student recognises that he or she can participate in the learning process, then the students will succeed. And, in fact, as a result of the school culture developed over the past year and the teachers' reinforcement of that culture — through slogans, language and action — the students' interest in school has greatly increased. At one parent tea which the school holds monthly, the parents discussed the students' achievements and interest in school. 'My children used to hate school, now they play school all the time . . . they even talk about working hard . . .' one parent said. Another parent confirmed that her children 'loved to come to school . . . and they were learning alot.' The culture of the school has followed the students home.

The *work hard* model also manifests itself in teacher self-focused discussions and expectations. The teachers discuss among themselves who works hard and who does not. If a teacher is not participating and putting forth her or his best effort, the teacher is criticised, sometimes directly. The teachers will ask why a certain colleague is not working hard, or, in private conversation, the teachers complain that a colleague is not 'doing their share.' The teachers look at their colleagues and their participation in the school and state that those teachers are not 'taking responsibility for the work,' or they 'haven't bought into the extra work.' Some teachers 'talk the talk, but don't walk the walk.' To the teachers this means that, although the colleagues use the language of the school, and appear to participate in the school agenda, in fact, they are not supporting the program, not ascribing to the beliefs or the culture of the school. This indicates that the teachers have a script for successful teaching at New Bradley School.

To be a successful student at New Bradley you must work hard. To be a successful teacher at New Bradley you must also work hard. If you slip in either category you are not following the expectations of the culture. The question becomes 'what cultural knowledge is expected or implicit in this setting?' Assuming that verbal discussion represents explicit information, is the implicit model, that teachers and students typically do not work hard and are not smart? If this is true, it is not simply true, because what is apparent is that the culture is working, at least for the students. They are succeeding and surpassing all work expectations.

Example 2: 'If you believe, If you really believe . . .' The Tinkerbell tenet of teaching. New Bradley School has derived a culture conducive to success and innovations. From the beginning the teachers and staff were willing to foster success in all students and to promote that success. These teachers believe that the students could find success in their educational experience, even though many students had never before experienced success in school. In fact, the culture of the school supports the teachers' notions of success. When asked about the ways that they could or would support their students, several teachers talked about believing that the students could succeed. One teacher discussed the 'honest belief that all kids can and should be on grade level.' Another teacher referred to experimenting 'with how children learn' and 'changing it if it doesn't work.' Yet another stated 'more computers, more planning time, more staff development' would support the students. For them, the simple act of believing was sufficient to guarantee (in their minds) the success of the students. One teacher said, 'If I believe, if I really believe, the students will succeed . . . or I at least have to say I do. . .'. Several other teachers agreed that 'at least looking as if they believed' [in student success] was essential to student success. That statement suggests an ambiguous nature of the setting, alluding back to 'talking the talk but not walking the walk' in Example 1. At once the teacher wants the child/children to succeed, but does not necessarily fully believe that to be possible. Yet, somehow, just like the TV Peter Pan saved Tinkerbell, the teachers' beliefs in student success will pull the students when nothing else will.

Success is the key here. While not a cultural model in itself, there are several important connections made to success for both the teacher and the students. For the teacher, success means the teacher must believe in each child. If a child is not doing well, the teacher must work harder and believe harder to foster the desired results. The true test, however, is whether or not the student succeeds. For the student, success means the student must work hard and believe in her or him self. According to one teacher 'you don't have positive self-esteem in isolation.' A teacher must offer support for the child and demonstrate belief in the child's ability. Importantly, whether the teacher really believes or is simply presenting a facade, most of New Bradley's students appear (at this point in the research) to be experiencing both success and strong self-esteem.

Summary

This case study examines how teachers participate in their school and with students, and how the school views of the teachers and students affects what occurs in the classrooms and the school. Using examples of teachers' interactions with students' and teachers' beliefs about students, the results of this study indicate that dimensions of culture (culture of the teacher and culture of the teacher's workplace) do affect teachers' beliefs. The personal cultural history and the culture of the school affects them as they enact their practice and work with their students.

Implications

Yet, not all questions are answered. Work in this area must continue because recognition of teachers' cultural models can greatly enhance our understanding of classroom processes. Exploring and understanding cultural models impacts both the theoretical and practical levels of education. For the researcher, explorations of cultural models provides a way to understand fully the teachers' decision-making process and the motives behind certain beliefs and choices. For the teacher, awareness of what affects thought and action may facilitate deeper reflection about personal beliefs and practices. Significantly, if a student does not share the same cultural model with the teacher, the child may be perceived as deviant or incompetent. And if the student perceives the teacher as unauthentic in her or his responses, there will be serious consequences.

References

AGAR, M. (1973) *Ripping and running*, New York: Seminar Press.

BARTH, R. (1986) 'On sheep and goats and school reform', *Kappan*, **25**(4), pp. 471–92.

BERGER, P. and LUCKMAN, T. (1966) *The social construction of reality*, Garden City, NJ: Doubleday.

BLACK, M. (1969) 'Belief systems', in HONIGMAN, J.J. (Ed.) *Handbook of social and cultural anthropology*, Chicago: Rand McNally.

BLACK, M. and METZGER, D. (1969) 'Ethnographic description and the study of law', in TYLER, S. (Ed.) *Cognitive anthropology*, New York: Holt, Rinehart and Winston, pp. 137–64.

BUSSIS, A., CHITTENDEN, F. and AMAREL, M. (1976) 'Beyond the surface curriculum', Boulder, Co: Westview Press.

CLANDININ, D.J. and CONNELLY, F.M. (1987) 'Teachers' personal knowledge: what counts as "personal" in studies of the personal', *Journal of Curriculum Studies*, **19**(6), pp. 487–500.

CLARK, C. and PETERSON, P. (1986) 'Teachers' thought processes', in WITTROCK, M. (Ed.) *Handbook of research on teaching* (3rd ed.), New York: MacMillan, pp. 255–96.

CONNELLY, F.M. and CLANDININ, D.J. (1984) 'Personal practical knowledge at Bay Street School: ritual, personal philosophy, and image', in HALKES, R. and OLSON, J.K. (Eds) *Teacher thinking*, Lisse: Swets and Zeitlinger, pp. 134–48.

CRICK, M. (1976) *Explorations of Language and meaning*, New York: Wiley.

D'ANDRADE, R. (1985) 'Cultural meaning systems', in DOUGHERTY, J. (Ed.) *Directions in cognitive anthropology*, Urbana: University of Illinois Press.

DEWEY, J. (1904) 'The relation of theory to practice in education', in *Relation of theory to practice in the education of teachers: Third yearbook, National Society for the Study of Education*, Bloomington, Ind: Public School Publishing Co.

DOUGHERTY, J. (1985) *Directions in cognitive anthropology*, Chicago: University of Illinois Press.

EISENHART, M. (1990) 'Learning to romance: cultural acquisition in college', *Anthropology and Education Quarterly*, **21**(1), pp. 19–40.

ELBAZ, F. (1981) 'The teacher's practical knowledge: report of a case study', *Curriculum Inquiry*, **11**, pp. 43–71.

ERICKSON, F. and MOHATT, G. (1984) 'Cultural organization of participation structures in two classrooms of Indian students', in SPINDLER, G. (Ed.) *Doing the ethnography of schooling*, New York: Holt, Rinehart, and Winston, pp. 132–74.

ERICKSON, F. and SHULTZ, J. (1982) *The counselor as gatekeeper*, New York: Academic Press.

FEIMAN-NEMSER, S. and FLODEN, R. (1986) 'The cultures of teaching', in WITTROCK, M. (Ed.) *Handbook of research on teaching*, (3rd ed.) New York: MacMillan, pp. 505–26.

FUCHS, E. (1969) *Teacher's talk: Views from inside city schools*, New York: Doubleday.

GEERTZ, C. (1973) *The Interpretation of Cultures*, New York: Basic Books.

GOODENOUGH, W. (1971) *Culture, language, and society*, Reading, Ma: Addison Wesley Publishing.

GOODLAD, J.I. (1983) 'The school as workplace', in GRIFFIN, G. (Ed.) *Staff Development*, 82nd Yearbook of NSSE, Chicago: University of Chicago Press.

GUILFOYLE, K. (1989) 'Teaching Indian children: An ethnography of a first grade classroom', unpublished Ph.D. dissertation, University of Arizona, Tucson.

HARGREAVES, A. (1984) 'Experience counts, theory doesn't: How teachers talk about their work', *Sociology of Education*, **84**(57), pp. 244–54.

HEATH, S.B. (1983) *Ways with words*, Cambridge: Cambridge University Press.

HOLLAND, D. (1985) 'From situation to impression: how Americans get to know themselves and one another', in DOUGHERTY, J. (Ed.) *Directions in Cognitive Anthropology*, pp. 389–412.

HOLLAND, D. and SKINNER, D. (1987) 'Prestige and intimacy: the cultural models behind Americans' talk about gender types', in HOLLAND, D. and QUINN, N. (Eds) *Cultural models in thought and language*, Cambridge: Cambridge University Press, pp. 78–111.

HOLLINGSWORTH, S. (1987, April) 'Changes in teachers' views of poor readers', paper presented at American Educational Research Association Conference, Washington, D.C.

HUTCHINS, E. (1980) *Culture and inference: a Tobriand case study*, Cambridge, MA: Harvard University Press.

HOWARD, J. and HAMMOND, R. (1985) 'The Hidden Obstacles to black success — Rumors of inferiority', *New Public*, **193**(11), pp. 17–21.

KAY, P. and METZGER, D. (1973) 'On ethnographic method', in SIVERTS, H. (Ed.) *Drinking patterns in Highland Chiapas*, Norway: Norwegian Research Council, pp. 17–36.

KEESING, R. (1974) 'Linguistic knowledge and cultural knowledge', *American Anthropologist*, **81**, pp. 14–36.

KELLY, G. (1955) *The psychology of personal constructs*, New York: Norton.

LANGNESS, L. (1965) *The life history in anthropological science*, New York: Holt, Rinehart, and Winston.

LIEBERMAN, A. (1988) *Building a professional culture in schools*, New York: Teachers College Press.

LORTIE, D. (1975) *School teacher*, Chicago: University of Chicago Press.

MANDLEBAUM, D. (1973) 'The study of life history', *Current anthropology*, **14**, pp. 177–96.

MCDERMOTT, R. (1976) 'Kids make sense: An ethnographic account of the interactional management of success failure in one first grade classroom', unpublished Ph.D dissertation, Stanford University. Palo Alto, Ca.

METZ, M. (1983) 'Sources of constructive social relationships in an urban magnet school', *American Journal of Education*, **91**, pp. 202–45.

— (1986) *Different by design: Politics, purpose and practice in three magnet schools*, London: Routledge and Kegan Paul.

METZGER, D. (1973) 'Semantic procedures for the study of belief systems', in SIVERTS, H. (Ed.) *Drinking patterns in Highland Chiapas*, Norway: Norwegian Research Council, pp. 37–47.

MILLER, L. (1988) 'Unlikely beginnings: The district office as a starting point for developing a professional culture for teaching', in LIEBERMAN, A. (Ed.) *Building a professional culture in schools*, New York: Teachers College Press, pp. 167–84.

MUNBY, H. (1983, April) 'A qualitative study of teachers' beliefs and principles', paper presented at American Educational Research Association Conference, Montreal.

NISBETT, R. and ROSS, L. (1980) *Human inference: Strategies and shortcomings of social judgment*, Englewood Cliffs, NJ: Prentice-Hall.

OBERG, A. (1987) 'The ground of professional practice', in LOWYCK, J., CLARK, C. and HALKES, M. (Eds) *Teaching thinking and professional action*, Lisse: Swets and Zeitlinger.

OLSON, J.K. (1988) 'Making sense of teaching: cognition v. culture', *Journal of Curriculum Studies*, **20**(2), pp. 167–69.

QUINN, N. and HOLLAND, D. (1987) 'Culture and cognition', in HOLLAND, D. and QUINN, N. (Eds) *Cultural models in language and thought*, Cambridge: Cambridge University Press, pp. 3–42.

QUINE, W.V. (1978) *The web of belief*, New York: Random House.

PAGE, R. (1988) 'Teachers' perceptions of students: A link between classrooms, school cultures, and the social order', *Anthropology and Education Quarterly*, **87**(18), pp. 77–99.

PHILIPS, S. (1983) *Invisible Culture*, New York: Longman.

PRICE, L. (1987) 'Ecuadorian illness stories: cultural knowledge in natural discourse', in HOLLAND, D. and QUINN, N. (Eds) *Cultural models in thought and language*, Cambridge: Cambridge University Press, pp. 313–42.

RICHARDSON, V. (1989) 'Practice and the improvement of research on teaching', paper presented at the American Educational Research Association Conference, San Francisco.

— (1990) 'The evolution of reflective teaching and teacher education', in CLIFT, R., HOUSTON, W.R. and PUGACH, M. (Eds) *Encouraging reflective practice: an examination of issues and exemplars*, New York: Teachers College Press.

RUSSELL, T. (1987) 'Learning the professional knowledge of teaching: views of the relationship between theory and practice', paper presented at American Educational Research Association Conference, Washington, D.C.

RUTTER, M., MAUGHAN, B., MORTIMORE, B. and OSTON, J. (1979) *Fifteen thousand hours: Secondary schools and their effects on children*, Cambridge, MA: Harvard University Press.

SARASON, S. (1982) *The culture of the school and the problem of change*, Boston: Allyn and Bacon.

SCHANK, R. (1975) 'The structures of episodes in memory', in BOBROW, D. and COLLINS, A. (Eds) *Representation and Understanding*, New York: Academic Press, pp. 237–72.

— (1988) *The creative attitude*, New York: MacMillan Publishing Co.

SCHANK, R. and ABELSON, R. (1977) *Scripts, plans, goals, and understanding*, Hillsdale, NJ: LEA.

TOBIN, K. (1990) 'Constructivist perspectives on teacher change', paper presented at the annual meeting of AERA, Boston.

TYLER, R. (1987) 'Education reform', *Kappan*, **69**(4), pp. 277–81.

WALLACE, A. (1970) *Culture and personality*, New York: Random House.

WODLINGER, M. (1985) 'Entry beliefs of first year preservice teachers', *The Alberta Journal of Educational Research*, **XXXI**(1), pp. 54–69.

Wolcott, H. (1973) 'The man in the principal's office', New York: Holt, Rinehart and Winston.
Zeichner, K. (1989) 'Kenneth Zeichner reflecting on reflection', *NCRTE Colloquy*, **3**(2), pp. 15–21.

Chapter 7

Working Knowledge in Teaching

Robert Yinger and Martha Hendricks-Lee

This chapter analyzes the working knowledge of teaching using systemic and holistic notions of learning, knowledge, practice and relationships. A discussion of working knowledge draws upon a review of studies and theories in diverse areas. On the basis of this discussion, ecological intelligence is proposed as a useful conceptual framework with three characteristics: (1) knowledge is inherent and widely dispersed within systems; (2) knowledge becomes available as working knowledge in particular activities and events; (3) working knowledge is constructed jointly by participants and systems in an activity. This view stands in contrast to widely held notions of teacher and student knowledge being solely acquired and applied by an individual.

We begin the discussion by asking some questions. For example, why is it that most graduates of teacher education programs still have most of their learning to do? Why do teachers point to their first few years of teaching as the place where they really learned to teach? Why has the theory-practice split been of such great concern to teacher educators? Why all the recent attention to different types of knowledge that practitioners need?

These questions, among others, have in the past few years led researchers interested in teacher thinking and action to examine more closely what good teachers seem to know, how they know it, and how they make knowledge work for them in instructional situations. This work on knowledge representation and utilisation has suggested new aspects and emphases in teacher education as we have tried to bring instruction about teaching and learning more into line with the nature of practical learning. Our purpose in this chapter is to extend this inquiry into teacher knowledge by examining the nature and characteristics of what we often call 'working knowledge,' that is, knowledge particularly useful to get things accomplished in practical situations.

Our strategy will be more that of lumping than splitting. We are not attempting to distinguish working knowledge from non-working knowledge, common-sense knowledge from scientific knowledge, work from play, or knowledge from action. Working knowledge, for our purposes, is knowledge working (or knowledge at work). Knowledge is working at school, at work, at play, in any theorising, perception, or comprehending, in any making or doing. Bringing intelligence and action to bear on any activity requires working knowledge.

Our argument, simply put, is:

1 Knowledge is not solely a matter of mind and person but one of relationship and place.
2 Learning (becoming knowledgeable) chiefly involves acquiring appropriate conversational abilities and repertoire that allow one to establish and maintain a functional relationship with one's environment.
3 Good teaching creates opportunities for learners to think and act in relation to various aspects of the environment (systems) and models appropriate conversations and relationships.

Technical Intelligence

Our discussion of working knowledge is framed by emerging characterisations of knowledge and thought that diverge and depart from conceptions dominating social science and educational theory for much of this century. Most broadly, these dominant conceptions have been labelled positivistic or Cartesian. In the context of work or practice, they have been referred to as technological thought (Berger, Berger, and Kellner, 1974), as technicist orientation (Bowers and Flinders, 1990), and as technical rationality (Schon, 1983). The term *technical* in each of these descriptions refers to an emphasis on an instrumental orientation emphasising technical problem solving based on specialised scientific knowledge.

Chet Bowers and David Flinders (1990) summarise this technical orientation as possessing three interdependent assumptions.

1 *The rational process is culturally neutral.* Thinking is seen in relation to and describable in terms of objective events and causal relationships. Rationality is separate from other psychological and bodily experiences. Knowing is a mirroring of external reality and the individual knower is free of cultural influence — a perspective referred to by Geertz (1973) as 'I-am-a-camera.' This approach also assumes a naive realism that takes the behaviour of others at face value, free from interpretation or attributed intention or meaning.
2 *Language is a conduit for the transmission of information.* This view holds language to be almost exclusively an exchange of information in a linear sender-receiver relationship. Words are viewed as containers into which information is deposited or seen as corresponding to real objects and relationships. Objectifying the world through language allows 'factual communication' to be established. Communication is a matter of extracting information rather than of constructing meaning, composed of literal meanings rather than metaphorical meanings, and focused on unambiguous verbal messages rather than complexly layered non-verbal, verbal, and contextual interchanges.
3 *Learning is individually centred.* This viewpoint portrays learning as a psychological process controlled by the individual. The mind is the 'inner arena' for thought, and learning is constituted by internal information processing strategies resulting in changes in internal memory stores and cognitive structures. Experience affects an autonomous and contained self

so that the individual thinker or learner becomes the basic unit for understanding thought and action.

The prevalence of this viewpoint in education and the other professions has been due to a complex set of cultural and scientific operating assumptions including technological optimism, individualism, the rise of meritocracy, the nature of industrialised work, and the dominance of psychology in the social sciences. In the past few years a rich body of research and theory has come together to challenge the dominating metaphors related to cognition and action. We are beginning to see emphases and conceptions shifting from the individual to the corporate and communal, from an information focus to an action focus, from mechanistic assumptions to organismic assumptions, from calculation to narrative, from abstracting to situating, from operations to conversations.

The work responsible for these shifts has focused on reconceptualising language, context, social interaction, culture, and practical action. The work of Grice (1975), Garfinkel (1967), Lakoff (1987), Lakoff and Johnson (1980), Johnson (1987), and others have revealed the imaginative, improvisational, metaphorical, and embodied nature of language. Sociolinguists like Erickson (1982), Erickson and Shultz (1982), Cazden (1986) and Mehan (1979) have described the nature of interactional and communicative competence. The importance of context has been highlighted by anthropologists (Geertz, 1973) and psychologists alike (Cronbach, 1975; Campbell, 1978). A re-examination of the philosophy of action (Kerr, 1981; Fenstermacher, 1978) and the influence of Soviet activity theory on American psychology (Vygotsky, 1962, 1978; Leontev, 1972; Scribner, 1984, 1985; Wertsch, 1979) have produced new conceptions of human action and the construction of knowledge. Insights on the nature of complex problems and endeavours have been contributed from the fields of operations research (Ackoff, 1979), systems theory (Bateson, 1972, 1979), architecture (Alexander, 1964), agriculture (Jackson, 1980), education (Doyle, 1986) and curriculum theory (Reid, 1979).

Ecological Intelligence

The above cited work has in the past few years begun to challenge the dominant metaphors and models in cognitive theory. Researchers have wrestled with new monikers to attach to the new work ranging from merely reactive, such as 'post-human information processing' or 'post-cognitive science', to terms attempting to reflect the new conceptions, such as 'constructivist', 'cultural-interactive', or 'situated practical intelligence'.

We propose *ecological intelligence* as a more inclusive term that shifts the focus from individual cognitive processing and technical action to the relationships between the individual and the environment. The field of ecology focuses on the relations between an organism and a habitat or environment, attempting to understand how behaviour and the nature of the organism are constructed in this interaction. Ecological intelligence also allows us to emphasise that intelligence is embedded in social, cultural, and practical interchanges as well as in individuals. In other words, intelligence is not solely a matter of mind and person but also a matter of action and place.

Research on language, culture, and interaction suggests a number of aspects of thought and action in practical situations. Many of these aspects can be grouped under two major characteristics of ecological intelligence: its ecological properties and its conversational properties.

Ecological Properties

Ecological conceptions of the person and the intellect have been offered by experience-based and phenomenological philosophers for a number of years. Writers like Husserl (1965), Heidegger (1962, 1971), Merleau-Ponty (1962, 1964) and Buber (1958) have challenged Western definitions of humanness based upon human authority and dominance, independence, and rational agency. In contrast, they portray the world as a participant in consciousness, not just an object of consciousness. Mind and being extend beyond the person to include and enclose the world. One of Heidegger's interpreters, William Barrett, puts it concisely: 'Being is not something that takes place within [the] skin . . . ; Being, rather, is spread over a field or region which is the world of its care and concern' (1962: 217). Heidegger's term for 'field' or 'region' is *Dasein*, meaning literally in German 'Being-There' — the connecting of Being to World and Place. 'The Being of Dasein itself is to be made visible as care' (Heidegger, 1962: 83–4). Just as we might know a territory by the actions of its occupant, Dasein is known by the evidence of care.

The Being of Dasein asserts the primacy of interaction and relationship. By defining being human as 'hearing one's name in a field of care', Heidegger grounds the human condition as Being-in-the-World. Person is essentially linked to place; environment and context become essential to defining intelligence and humanity. Relationship, in effect, defines existence.

Likewise, Gregory Bateson (1972, 1979) has argued (from the point of view of biology, anthropology, and systems theory) that all mind or intelligence is ecological, that is, it is always relational to holistic systems of information and action. The human mind is immanent rather than transcendent and constitutes a 'system whose boundaries do not at all coincide with the boundaries either of the body or what is popularly called the "self" or "consciousness"' (Bateson, 1972: 319). Within the person these networks extend beyond conscious thought to include information and action embedded in the unconscious as well as in autonomic, neural and hormonal systems. Projected beyond the skin, these systems include all external pathways along which information can travel such as tool, object, light/sound, action. For Bateson, mind and intelligence are always a complex combination of organism plus environment.

The nature of these holistic and ecological systems has been proposed and described in a broad range of social science theories and research studies. Soviet activity theory (Vygostsky, 1962, 1978; Leontev, 1972) and its American derivative, sociohistorical analysis (Scribner, 1984, 1985; Wertsch, 1979) hold that neither mind as such nor behaviour as such can be taken as the principal category of analysis and understanding in the social and psychological sciences. Instead, this theory proposes that culturally organised human activities such as work, play, schooling, or artistic activities should be the starting point and basic unit of analysis and interpretation. Activities are defined as enduring, intellectually planned sequences of behaviour, directed toward particular objects and goals (Scribner,

1985). Rather than assert that thought and action are adaptive to a particular context or environment, activity theory portrays the interaction as 'constitutive'. Information and action flow in both directions, from environment to actor and from actor to environment, in a mutual and dialectical manner. The result is constitutive or constructed interaction, the creation of new systems of meaning, relationship and action that change both the actors and environment.

This work, as well as other research and theoretical work to be described below, supports the assertion that intelligence must be regarded ecologically. Human thought and action are produced conjointly with other actors and the context and operate as integrated and holistic systems. The nature of interaction in these systems is transactional and conversational.

Conversational Properties

Ecological intelligence is comprised of multi-person and multi-object systems of purpose, meaning and action. It is produced and composed in relation to such systems. The character of this production and composition is interactional and conversational. Studies of language learning and competence, social and cultural interaction, and learning and practice commonly portray meaning and action as jointly constructed, negotiated, and collectively defined and acted (Garfinkel, 1967; Mehan, 1979; Erickson, 1982; Cazden, 1986; Florio-Ruane, 1989; Dreyfus and Dreyfus, 1986). These interchanges are conversational in nature in that they are situated, responsive, reciprocal, and often improvisational. Like spoken conversations these interchanges both convey information and establish relationship. Ecological intelligence differs from notions of technical intelligence in that control and decision-making are negotiated and relational. Bateson (1972: 316) asserts that 'in no system which shows mental characteristics can any part have unilateral control over the whole.' The intelligence is in the whole system, not just in some parts. By acting conversationally, information flows, relationship is established and maintained, and action is constituted in human interaction.

Ecological Intelligence and Working Knowledge

With the shift of metaphor from technical intelligence to ecological intelligence and the consequent decentralisation of knowledge as the property of an individual, how to characterise and capture knowledge becomes a pertinent issue. Taking the lead from this conceptual shift, one can frame the issue like this: If knowledge is not solely in the mind of the individual, then where is it? We propose that knowledge is inherent in systems: in cultural systems, in physical and material systems, in social systems, historical systems, and in personal systems. The knowledge inherent in each of these systems can be best understood when it is in action. When a person engages in activity, the knowledge inherent in different systems helps to determine structure and meaning in the activity.

Following is an overview of the literature examining the way knowledge is expressed and used in various frameworks or systems. Although these studies focus on different aspects of how knowledge is used, we view these distinctions as being artificial, largely due to the application of different disciplinary orientations.

For example, in any particular situation, it is difficult to distinguish social knowledge from cultural knowledge or from historical knowledge. Trying to attribute any particular knowledge to only one system is somewhat arbitrary. Many times these disciplines study the same phenomenon, so the systems we have identified cannot be regarded as discrete, mutually exclusive categories. For purposes of explanation and illustration, we will often identify the systems separately, mainly as a reminder of the range of systems contributing to a given activity.

Systems of Knowledge

Cultural Systems

That cultural systems help to determine working knowledge was made evident during the 1960s and 1970s. The move to school the people of traditional, often nonliterate, societies and the apparent lack of success of these efforts as well as the academic problems experienced by America's own ethnic minority children provided the impetus and opportunity for studying cultural knowledge in a variety of situations. Early research testing the performance of traditional peoples often included completing logical syllogisms. Low scores on such tests were explained by deficiencies in the knowledge of traditional people. Interpretations of these 'failures' included the absence of logic, failure to integrate and retain information, and the absence of theoretical thought (Scribner, 1977). However, observing the practical activities of these people (Kpelle, Mayan-speaking and Spanish-speaking villagers in the Yucatan, Mexico, Vai, [as in Cole, 1988; Scribner, 1977]) and allowing the indigenous culture to provide the context for working knowledge, the 'failures' vanished. Scribner found that although 'populations designated as "traditional" or "nonliterate" have just a somewhat better than a chance solution rate across all types of problem material' (p. 486), examining each answer individually, instead of regarding it as right or wrong, revealed logical thinking, use of empirical information, and theoretical explanations. The question for her became 'What are (how *we* can conceive the nature of) the pre-existing schemas into which verbal logic problems can be assimilated?' (emphasis ours, p. 497). In a later review of the literature Cole (1988) concluded that cultural differences in cognition reside more in the contexts within which cognitive processes manifest themselves than in the presence of a particular process (such as logical memory or theoretical responses to syllogisms) in one culture and absence in other.

> A society's culture consists of whatever it is one has to know or believe in order to operate in a manner acceptable to its member. . . . It is the form of things that people have in mind, their models for perceiving, relating, and otherwise interpreting them (Goodenough, in Yinger, 1987).

Goodenough's definition identifies culture as the determinant of working knowledge. Yet as cognitive anthropologists have attested, assigning the character of working knowledge to culture fully can lead to circular logic and cannot account for the observance of intracultural variations in uniformity:

> [Pelto and Pelto, (1975) concluded that] the monolithic view of behavioural causation that makes culture the cause of culture — with perpetuation of

cultural patterns neatly through generations by means of child training and other socialisation — must be discarded (in Lave, 1988, p. 9).

More specifically, Geertz advised 'cutting [the] culture concept down to size,' in order to reveal more and obscure less (1973: 4), a charge that has produced diverse theories. Keesing (1974) has grouped theories of culture around four focal areas, three of which provide perspectives useful for understanding the cultural systems of working knowledge: culture as cognitive systems, culture as adaptive systems, and culture as symbolic systems. Each of these perspectives of culture has contributed in different ways to theories of working knowledge. This is not to say that the citations used by researchers (many simply acknowledge a cultural context and focus on other components) can be traced back to these theoretical homes — remember, we are lumping — but features of each of these cultural systems are compatible with the contextual features described in theories of working knowledge.

Culture as cognitive systems.
Culture as cognitive systems has already been discussed in terms of Scribner's and Cole's work. In asking, 'What are the pre-existing schemas into which verbal logic can be assimilated?' (1977: 497), Scribner, in fact, was trying to discern which components of the cognitive system of one culture could be seen to correspond with the cognitive component Western culture identified as logic. It is not simply that the schemas of different cultures produce different answers to given problems, but that the cognitive system determines what information is critical, what information is disregarded, and how that information is used to draw new conclusions, conclusions that can only be judged within the framework of the culture's cognitive system (p. 488).

Cultures as adaptive systems.
Using an evolutionary perspective, the focus of this notion is that 'cultures are systems (of socially transmitted behaviour patterns) that serve to relate human communities to their ecological settings' (Keesing, 1974: 44). Although theories of working knowledge have decidedly not arisen from Marxism or Neo-Marxism, emphasis has been placed on the role of the physical system (including the natural and artificial environments) as structuring components of activity and thought. Although 'seen as adaptive systems, cultures [can be said to] change in the direction of equilibrium within ecosystems' (p. 46); disequilibrium caused by environmental, demographic, technological, and other systemic changes is also possible. Yinger (1990) argues that many elements within our Western culture are at such disequilibrium with the ecosystem that their very futures are threatened. Demographic and technological changes in farming, for example, have produced methods so at odds with the ecosystem that, unless we immediately strive to work in harmony with the physical environment, we might not be able to feed ourselves (p. 75). The crises in the professions of medicine, law, architecture and teaching have been attributed to technological changes which have had the effect of distancing current practitioners from the values and beliefs traditional to each practice (p. 74).

Cultures as symbolic systems.
Within the culture as symbolic systems perspective, the focus is on interaction, on shared meanings, understandings and symbols. This understanding of culture has

been used by theorists of working knowledge to illustrate how individuals acquire knowledge that can be put to use, that is, how individuals learn. Brown, Collins and Duguid (1989), Harper (1987), and other researchers employ this perspective to discuss the social integration and/or the communal nature of knowledge. Typically the cultural system is localised into a smaller community of practitioners, such as mathematicians (Brown *et al.*, 1989); tailors (Lave, 1977); blacksmiths (Harper, 1987); and teachers and students (Yinger, 1987, 1990). Novices become members of these communities by participation in a continually negotiated and evolving process (interaction) in which the novice acquires not only the system of understanding and values of the community, but also the ability to make use of the understanding and values. Prominent in the theories of working knowledge that use the symbolic systems perspective is the metaphor of conceptual knowledge as tools (Wertsch, 1987; Cole, 1988; Brown *et al.*, 1989), perhaps best characterised by Brown and his colleagues:

> People who use tools actively rather than just acquire them, by contrast, build an increasingly rich implicit understanding of the world in which they use the tools and of the tools themselves. The understanding, both of the world and of the tool, continually changes as a result of their interaction. Learning and acting are interestingly indistinct, learning being a continuous, life-long process resulting from acting in situations. (1989: 33)

Physical Systems

The role of physical systems in the notion of ecological intelligence stands in sharp contrast to the decontextualised assumptions of technological intelligence. Place is considered as much as a participant in interaction as the practitioner and the collaborators (students, clients, audience) in Yinger's conceptualisation of knowledge at work as 'the conversation of practice':

> This interaction always takes place in a particular place — an identifiable world made up of specific patterns, structures, substances and meanings. This practical world is physical, cultural and communal and possesses a tradition grounded in history, knowledge and belief. To practise a particular occupation, craft, or art one must enter into a relationship with participants and place. Neither of these partners can be safely ignored. (Yinger, 1990: 82)

Both the natural and artificial environment comprise the physical system.

Natural environment.
As suggested in the culture as adaptive systems discussion, the participation of the physical system becomes apparent when, for whatever reason, the information it contains is ignored. Disregard for (or simply the inability to combat change in) traditional forms of work, family, neighbourhood and community has led to corporate owned farms interested more in short-term gains at the expense of the erosion of 4 billion tons of top soil a year and the loss of safe drinking water, interests which ultimately threaten our ability to produce food in the future.

Contrast the current situation with the cooperative work of people in rural and farming communities before World War II, a communal endeavour which, in hindsight, has proven to be highly efficient and ecologically sophisticated (Yinger, 1990).

Artificial environment.
One of the most detailed descriptions of the information contained in the artificial environment helping to structure activity is set forth by Lave (1988). She identifies two components: arena and setting. An arena is a 'public and durable entity [that] is physically, economically, politically and socially organised space-in-time' (p. 150), in this particular study, a supermarket. The interaction between the person engaged in shopping and the supermarket (the arena) constitutes the setting. In this perspective, 'neither the setting nor the activity exists in realised form, except in relation with the other' (p. 151).

Now that the decontextualised assumption of technological intelligence that posits all knowledge in the individual has been questioned, the artificial environment is, perhaps, the easiest of all systems in which to see (literally) some examples of the information contained in the physical system as an integral part of the knowledge at work. The basic understanding is that a problem is situated in the 'task environment.' The task environment contributes to the structuring of the problem and of the resolution of the problem. Furthermore the task environment can reveal the adequacy of the solution in that successful resolution allows the activity to continue (Lave, 1988). Rather than computing three-quarters of two-thirds, for example, the dieter measures two-thirds of a cup of cottage cheese, dumps the cottage cheese on a cutting board, pats the mound into a circle, marks a cross on the mound, and spoons away one-quarter. Thus, the artificial environment was an essential part of the calculating process, and the statement of the problem (three-quarters of two-thirds) was, in fact, the solution (p. 165). Dairy loaders, in Scribner's study (1984), transformed literal problem statements written on order forms into representations corresponding to the cases and partial cases with which they were working to provide a 'least-physical-effort solution'. For example, 10 quarts of chocolate milk can be reconfigured to removing 6 from a case of 16 quarts or to adding 2 quarts to a partial case of 8, a solution arrived at because of the existence of the partial case of 8 in the task environment.

As the previous examples suggest, recognising the representation of the problem as, in part, a contribution of information from the physical system and, thus, as a part of the solution is often easier to do in non-school settings. Consider Levi-Strauss's description of the process of the *bricolage*:

> His (sic) first practical step is retrospective. He has to turn back to an already existent set made up of tools and materials, to consider or reconsider what it contains, and above all, to engage in a sort of dialogue with it, and before choosing between them, to index the possible answers which the whole set can offer his problem. . . . [His options are] the contingent result of all the occasions there have been to renew or enrich the stock or to maintain it with the remains of previous constructions or destructions. (1966: 21)

A more modern example (although increasingly rare to find) is in the contrast between the knowledge and skill of a 'parts changer' and an experienced mechanic.

The experienced mechanic, in repairing a machine, does not simply see a defective part, but because of his knowledge of materials and the characteristics of a given machine at work, comes to understand why a part deteriorated in the first place and, in effect, remedies an engineering flaw in repairing a machine (Harper, 1987: 73).

Although mechanical examples are more specific in showing how the physical system contributes information to the problem-solving process, more abstracted illustrations exist. Physicists, when thinking about a particular formula, will mentally construct a physical environment, 'which then provides support for inferences and approximations' (Brown *et al.*, 1989). Polynesian navigators, who work without any instrumentation, rely on mental representations (distinctly non-Western representations) arising from and correlated with the observable physical features of their environment to navigate in a method deemed superior to any. The navigators observe the physical features of the seascape rotating toward them, while they, in the boat, remain fixed (Oatley, 1977).

Social Systems

The seemingly solitary activity of an individual going about the everyday business of life can be understood as structured by social relationships (Lave, 1988: 124) Quite often computing a best-buy in the supermarket is not simply a matter of converting the amounts and prices to ratios; such issues as family customary meals and storage capacity in the kitchen make an impact on what is considered to be the best-buy (p. 162). Nor is the mathematics involved in managing the family finances an application of basic operations and processes. Money as a standard and uniform medium of exchange would seem particularly conducive to a technological intelligence, but a quick review of one's own personal finances reveals the multitude of social relations structuring on its management.

An increasing number of studies suggest that learning activities embedded in social interaction engender more comprehensive understandings. Brown *et al.* (1989) contend that one of the benefits of collaborative learning is not simply the accumulation of the knowledge of individual members. Social interactions 'give rise synergistically to insights and solutions that would not come about without them', that is, structures and meaning that do not exist in isolated or disconnected activity emerge via the social system.

Brown *et al.* further characterise academic disciplines or manual trades as cultures. The conceptual knowledge of a discipline or trade, like a set of tools, is not fully understood until used, in a way that a practitioner would, which includes the accumulated insights and belief system of the culture. Typically classroom learning takes place within the culture of school, an inauthentic culture devoid of the support of structures and information that enable members of the authentic culture to practise. The social systems of schools, Brown *et al.* argue, prevent students from gaining access to 'meanings and purposes [that] are socially constructed through negotiations among past and present members.' However, students need not become experts in order to become enculturated. To provide for students to become 'cognitive apprentices' in, for example, a maths class, Brown recommends beginning by embedding a task in familiar activity which will legitimise the students' implicit knowledge (available for scaffolding in unfamiliar tasks), by showing different decompositions which stress that heuristics should be assessed relative to the task and not as absolutes, and by encouraging students to seek their own solutions.

The social systems' contribution to working knowledge is also illustrated by examining situations in which the activity has lost its social connectedness. As discussed earlier, not only have farming practices disregarded the information of the physical system, but the communal relationships that supported small-scale farming have disintegrated. Similarly Yinger argues that 'once a central form of expression and understanding in everyday life, poetry is now rarely read by people other than students of literature and other poets' (1990: 78). A growing consensus attributes poetry's lack of audience to subject matter that no longer includes human relationships but, instead, focuses on the poet's inner world, presented in language that denies entry into the poem's world rather than facilitates it (Berry, 1983; Levertov, 1973; Snyder, 1980; Muir, 1962; Ransom, 1968). By disregarding the socially structured value of striving to speak to an audience, poetry has lost much of its audience.

Historical Systems

Although some of the structuring and meaning making that occurs because an activity is socially integrated is of the moment (e.g., the synergistic insight in a collaborative learning activity or the temporary re-prioritising of the family budget to meet an unexpected need), other structures and information have been contributed by the historical system, both in the sense of a smaller community and a more broadly-based culture. Relying on a Vygotskian socio-historical understanding, Wertsch (1987) proposes a 'collective memory' to account for the means and methods available to members of a group engaged in social interaction and cooperative labour. The two broad categories contained in 'means and methods' are tool-like (instrumental) structures and their inclusion in a system of inter-relations with other people. Although Wertsch is primarily concerned with psychological processes, this understanding can be applied to the literal tools available to a culture. For example, woodworkers from another culture might not readily recognise a chisel and its function. Within our own culture a community of carpenters uses a chisel in a different way to a community of cabinet makers (Brown *et al.* 1989). All understandings (and lack of understandings) have been created throughout the history of a particular social group.

In extending Vygotsky's metaphor of socio-historical tools as the mediational means of human activities to a tool kit, Wertsch (1987) avoids 'viewing mediational means as ironclad determiners of these processes [and provides] a set of options that at least in principle allows some choice and some possibility of emancipation from established patterns' (avoiding the 'culture causes culture' trap). The transmission of the means and methods is only possible through actions and words. While an individual member shapes a situation by the tool selected, the member's consequent act is shaped by the tool (and, of course, by the limited number of tools in the tool kit, which has been determined historically). By acknowledging that there are reasons for the selection of one tool over another, Wertsch expands the scope of analysis to include not only the historical and collective mediational means, but also contemporary interpsychological functioning of group members.

To illustrate, Wertsch draws on the work of Bellah *et al.* (1985) on language and genre (the forms provided by the use of a particular language or the variation of 'one' language):

> . . . because a community . . . is in an important sense constituted by the history it shares, it must constantly retell its story, 'its constitutive narrative', but as should be clear by now, the way in which this story is told is shaped by the language the members of the community speak. Furthermore, this story will be shaped on particular occasions by the speakers' selection from among the various languages available to them. For example, instead of recounting a community's history by using the language of individualism, a speaker may use a language of communal commitment to create a nostalgic version of better times. Again, the choice of mediation to a great extent shapes what can and cannot be thought and said, or, in this case, remembered (1987: 22).

Personal Systems

Since the limitations of technological intelligence have been acknowledged, research stances that posit knowledge solely within the individual have declined. Nevertheless, one research avenue has focused on the knowledge of individuals, individuals engaged in the practice of teaching, most often identified as personal practical knowledge. Personal practical knowledge has been distinguished by Johnson (1989) according to a number of its central tenets, an account that suggests the relationships of the personal system with social and historical systems. He indicates that personal practical knowledge is clearly much more than theoretical knowledge of teaching, although it includes the way in which this theoretical knowledge informs the teacher's experiential knowledge as this is gained by first-hand experience in the classroom and the school as well as its wider community. Importantly, a further dimension includes the teacher's personal past history and understandings which are brought to bear either directly or indirectly on classroom activities. Johnson then draws on his earlier work (Johnson, 1987) to highlight the embodied nature of personal practical knowledge. This is reflected through a consideration of 'the teacher's aesthetic, that is, his or her mode of perceiving and interacting with the environment and with other people', as well as the need to view 'a person's understanding as their mode of being in, or having, a world' (Johnson, 1989: 362).

> And this, of course, is not merely a matter of beliefs held and decisions made; instead, it is people's way of experiencing their world, and it involves sensory experiences, bodily interactions, moods, feelings, and spatio-temporal orientations. To sum up, teachers' personal practical knowledge would include the entire way in which they have a structured world that they can make some sense of, and in which they can function with varying degrees of success. (pp. 362–3)

As with the other systems described, personal practical knowledge is not static and is closely related to other systems:

> The conceptualization of teachers' knowledge that we have evolved is based on the notion that teachers, as persons, bring to teaching a particular set of dispositions and personal knowledge gained through their particular life's history. This set of predispositions and personal knowledge that teachers bring from their private lives to the public act of teaching is termed the architecture-of-self. This continually evolving architecture-of-self is seen as having been learned or acquired through a life history of personal experiences of the teacher as person interacting with a variety of contexts. This process is viewed as continuing into the professional life of the teacher, who as an adult learner, continues to interact with a series of personal and professional contexts, resulting in the evolution of a personal form of professional knowledge which guides the way they think and act as a teacher. Teachers' knowledge, then, is grounded in, and shaped by, the stream of experiences that arose out of person/context interactions and existential responses to those experiences. (Butt, Raymond and Yamagishi, 1988: 151)

Although those who advocate a biographical approach subscribe to studying a teacher's history in order to understand current practice, personal practical knowledge incorporates a more complex, dynamic relationship between past, present and future. Personal practical knowledge is 'a kind of knowledge carved out of, and shaped by, situations' (Clandinin, 1989: 122), but as well as growing out of personal experiences, it is 'the very means of transformation of that experience. As a system, it both emerges from and restructures our world, and it has meaning and value only within the context of that experiential process of growth and change' (Johnson, 1989: 364).

This research, as well as the theoretical orientations described earlier, compel us to offer the following propositions about knowledge and action:

- Knowledge is inherent and widely dispersed across complex systems of information and action: cultural, physical, social, historical, and personal.
- Knowledge within these systems becomes available as working knowledge in particular activities and events.
- Working knowledge is constructed jointly through responsive interaction (conversation) among all the participants (systems) in an activity.

Working Knowledge in Use

Ecological intelligence can be said to be in use when the structures and information of the cultural, physical, social, historical, and personal systems converge within an activity. The milieu created by these systems is the field of action, concern, and care. Within this constitution, information and action from multiple systems combine in a mutual and dialectical manner. We have referred to this interaction as a conversation involving not only words, but also thought and action. This interactional conversation, in effect, creates new meanings and relationships that change the action and the systems.

For the purpose of explaining how ecological intelligence relates to the role of the teacher, we propose the classroom as the unit of analysis. We are using the classroom because typically the classroom as a unit of analysis is considered as an isolated system. The classroom is a location in which activity takes place involving a relatively stable group or community. However, the life of this community is not simply contained within the classroom, but is made up of lives that exist outside the classroom. These lives are constituted by the cultural, physical, social, historical, and personal systems, which exist both inside and outside the classroom.

The special role or responsibility of the teacher in the classroom is to understand the conversations which are occurring within and among all the systems and to recognise which are appropriate for the classroom activity. The teacher acts as guide to and translator of the structure, action and information contained in each system. The degree to which each system is contributing to the activity determines the authenticity of the conversation. The systems may not be contributing equally in every situation. Not all of the systems necessarily have contributions to make to the activity (that is, 'the conversation-of-the-moment'); however, over time all systems have vital contributions to make.

The effective teacher finds the appropriate conversation for the moment, one that continues prior conversations in each of the systems and connects these to ongoing conversations and sets the stage for future conversations. It is this notion of connectedness between past, present and future as well as among the systems that defines appropriateness of the conversation.

Equilibrium exists when classroom activity is functional, healthy and productive. These qualities can be assessed both internally and externally. Internally, classroom activity is in a state of equilibrium when conversation enables all of the appropriate systems to contribute to the accomplishment of the task at hand (e.g., learning new things, establishing or maintaining relationships, cooperation). Externally, classroom activity is in a state of equilibrium when conversations enable teachers and students to participate more fully in conversations outside of the classroom (family, work, and community activities and relationships). This ability to connect to broader systems of information and action has been referred by others in terms of relevance or transfer.

Systemic Conversation at Work

Lampert's (1986) experimental lessons for fourth grade mathematics provides an abundance of material with which to illustrate systemic conversation in the classroom. We have chosen Lampert's examples for two reasons: (1) the lessons she describes are generally regarded as being models of effective teaching and learning; and (2) these lessons have been discussed by others who have also been interested in understanding the nature of working knowledge (cf., Brown *et al.*, 1989). Because of the complexity of systemic conversation — how the information and structuring provided by one system interacts with and affects the other systems in a mutual and dialectical manner to create new meanings, relationships, and actions — her research will be discussed on two levels, a micro-level which has the authentic activity of mathematics (Brown *et al.*, 1989) as the conversation-of-the-moment and on a macro-level which will take a more ecological, holistic perspective to attaining equilibrium among the systems occurring in and brought to the classroom.

Systemic Mathematics

On the micro-level, our analysis draws upon Brown *et al*'s discussion of authentic activity, which characterises a knowledge domain, such as mathematics, as a community or culture. This characterisation is useful because it de-emphasises task completion as the goal of mathematics and emphasises robust, useful knowledge of concepts and tools. Learning, then, becomes enculturation, a process that accounts for the social construction of meaning and implicit knowledge embedded in an activity.

In her 1986 article, Lampert begins by describing the debate concerning elementary mathematics curriculum, a framework that fits well with our distinction between technological intelligence and ecological intelligence. She presents the four kinds of mathematical knowledge identified in the literature: intuitive, computational, concrete and principled. Intuitive knowledge arises out of and is tied to a particular situation; Scribner's diary loaders, for example, use intuitive knowledge. Computational knowledge is procedural. Concrete knowledge involves manipulating objects. Principled knowledge comes closest to pure mathematics and focuses on conceptual understanding. Of the four types of mathematical knowledge, computational and principled are pitted against each other in the curriculum debate. Many people — parents, teachers and school board members — see the teaching of mathematics as a choice between, in the language of folk models, 'knowing how' and 'knowing that'.

The goal of computational knowledge is for the student to apply a set of procedural rules to numerical symbols. Computational performance is assessed on the appropriate type of operation, the order in which the steps of the operation are used, and the placement of the answer. The instructional approach is for teachers to lecture, to demonstrate, to provide practice, and to test. Computational performance is dependent upon memorising addition and multiplication tables. The major criticism against emphasising computational knowledge is that students can arrive at correct answers without understanding the meaning of what they are doing. Computational knowledge corresponds with technological intelligence perspective in that it assumes a linear sender-receiver relationship (teacher to student) and its goal is for cognitive, as opposed to social and tacit, development.

In contrast to computation is principled knowledge. To have principled knowledge is to have an understanding of the formal mathematical laws and conventions. Performance with principled knowledge requires students to invent ways to work out the problem. The emphasis is not on the correct answer, but on the reasonableness of the invented strategy. Instructional approaches focus on the structure and compositions of numbers in all base systems in language that is abstract and symbolic. Although less often criticised as technological intelligence, principled knowledge can be considered such if the theoretical aims (abstract understandings) are valued over one's ability to practise mathematics, a charge levelled at the 'new' maths of the 1960s.

Brown *et al*'s metaphor of a mathematic enculturation overcomes the limitations of having to choose one kind of knowledge over another; to become enculturated, one must be able to use and continually develop all the kinds of knowledge necessary to interact with other members and to engage in the activities of the culture. To simplify the complexity of discussing what it takes to achieve ecological intelligence in the classroom, we will, for the moment, consider the four types of mathematical knowledge identified in the literature as systems in and of themselves and together comprising the culture of mathematics. Each of the areas of mathematics can be considered a separate system in that the knowledge inherent in each system contributes information and helps to structure the activity in different ways. For example, the perceptions of numbers and the repertoire of appropriate mathematical procedures available to the student engaging only in the computational system would be vastly different from those of students connecting with the intuitive, concrete, or principled systems. Lampert herself presents support from the literature for such an analysis by stating that 'the acquisition of "meaningful" mathematical knowledge [is] making explicit connections among different ways of knowing' (Davis, 1984, in Lampert, 1986: 313).

Analyzing the errors that her students have made in doing multidigit multi-plication led Lampert to believe that her students 'had reached an impasse in their knowledge of what to do when they got to the carrying part of the procedure and they invented a way to cope with it' (p. 314). However, since their coping strat-egies were not informed by intuitive, concrete, or principled knowledge systems, their strategies did not work to complete the problem successfully. This realisation led to the development of her experimental lessons designed to connect to the various systems of mathematics.

Lampert's first series of lessons on multiplication involved coin problems. Using coins draws upon the children's intuitive knowledge, the knowledge they have gained in their everyday lives handling money. This knowledge of coins is a strong, implicit, shared understanding (Brown *et al.*, 1989); that is, the class members, having had similar experiences with money, have a common basis for communication and activity, and this shared experience is legitimised at school. Although real coins were not used, the children's familiarity with coins provided tangible referents, that is, ready access to concrete knowledge. Lampert developed a notation system (3d for three dimes, 2p for two pennies) that 'provided a bridge between the concrete familiarity of the coins and a more abstract symbolic frame-work for representing mathematical relationships' (1986: 318).

One of the tasks in the lesson was to discover how many ways a dollar could be made using dimes and/or nickels. Because of their intuitive knowledge about using coins, the children were very unlikely to make computational errors. Such computing requires multiplying the number of each type of coin by the values and then adding the two products together. In this case, intuitive knowledge of money informs and structures the computational knowledge — the conversation between the intuitive knowledge system and the computational knowledge system work together to successfully complete the problem. Because Lampert designed the lesson as finding as many combinations of nickels and dimes to make a dollar as possible, the students discovered relationships between the number of coins and the values of the coins, learning the structure and compositions of numbers or the principled knowledge system. Thus, all systems conversed within the context of the les-son, allowing the students more comprehensive practice and understanding of mathematics.

Brown *et al.*, in arguing for the conception of a culture of mathematics, discuss social interaction as crucial to student learning or enculturation. We agree and will address this and other issues in the macro-level analysis because of our belief that social interaction in a classroom needs to be discussed more broadly as ecological intelligence.

Conversations Among Larger Systems

Although ecological intelligence exists when all of the appropriate internal and external systems are engaged over time, Lampert's published data and discussion of her work are not extensive enough to illustrate fully the concept of all the connections among systems. Some of the systems and connections can be identified, while others can reasonably be inferred.

We conceive of the teacher's role in the classroom as facilitating the interactions among systems — conversations with the appropriate systems for the particular activity, which includes introducing students to new conversations and connecting the conversation-of-the-moment to the systems and conversations brought by the students. One element of the ecological intelligence has already been indirectly discussed, introducing the students and the systems they bring to new conversations. Lampert achieved this by constructing situations in which the students brought their tacit and explicit cultural understanding of coins and engaged these understandings in the mathematical activities, activities informed and structured by the identified systems within the realm of mathematics.

Lampert's instructional approach is clearly conversational. Although she leads the conversation and directs the students, she is not the dispenser of knowledge, but rather the constructor of situations that elicit student knowledge, as attested to in her own description of her pedagogical style:

> In my discussion with students, I almost always followed an unexplained answer [provided by the student] with a question to probe how the student 'figured it out'. This strategy has two purposes. One is to give me some sense of the procedures students are using to arrive at their answers and how they are warranted; the other is to develop a habit of discourse in the classroom in which work in mathematics is referred back to the knower to answer the questions of reasonability. (p. 317)

This description of her pedagogy, supported by data used throughout the article, is important for a number of reasons. As Brown *et al.* stresses that through discussion of their activities the students are participating as mathematicians and 'are acquiring some of the culture's tools — a shared vocabulary and means to discuss, reflect upon, evaluate, and validate community procedures in a collaborative process' (1989: 38). Ko, one of Lampert's students, provides evidence of the enculturation process by volunteering that she had 'another way to think about it' (p. 329), that is, another way to conceive of the problem.

Cultural Systems

Lampert's experimental lessons are drawn from her personal experience teaching a heterogeneous group of twenty-eight fourth graders. Although the data she presents is focused to support conclusions drawn about the knowing, doing and teaching of mathematics, the data also suggest that Lampert has successfully enabled classroom discussion. Each culture has an implicit set of communication patterns that govern such things as turn-taking (e.g., who gets to speak when and for how long), listening (e.g., should the listener be silent or vocal), and speaking (e.g., should one or more people speak at once, what are the conditions that determine how many people can speak at once?). Erickson (1982) characterises these patterns as 'participation structures'. For effective communication to take place in heterogeneous classrooms, 'culturally congruent styles of interaction' must occur (Erickson and Mohatt, 1982). Because of the quantity and quality of communication exhibited in the data provided by Lampert, we can infer the existence of culturally appropriate participation structures. Perhaps the most detailed account of a school connecting with its students' cultural system is in the literature concerning the Kamehameha Elementary Education Program (cf., Au, 1979; Au and Jordan, 1981; Au and Mason, 1981).

The contexts Lampert builds to provide situational supports (discussed in detail later) for the abstract work of mathematics are clearly part of the cultural system. One series of lessons uses coins problems. A monetary system is a cultural feature, assigning an arbitrary value to an arbitrary object. Coins are symbolic representations in a similar way that numbers are symbolic representations of a different kind of value system, a correspondence that Lampert points out. Another illustration Lampert uses is that of planets and exploring astronauts, a cultural indicator guaranteed to capture many students' imagination.

Physical System

Lampert brings the physical system into the classroom as much as is possible when the goal is the learning of multidigit mathematics. As she points out, it is possible to make fourteen groups of thirty-two objects and then count the total, but such a method is 'inefficient and technically problematic' (p. 307). Rather than using physical objects, Lampert evokes the physical system, the knowledge and structure it contributes to the activity, and the students' tacit and embodied knowledge of the physical (their personal systems). Lampert characterises these representations as visual cues with which the students can check the reasonableness of their answers. But as indicated in the following example, the physical system can contribute a knowledge of its own. To illustrate 28×65, the class constructed the context of 28 glasses, each containing 65 drops of water. Since Lampert did not want to draw 28 glasses, she suggested two jugs, each containing 10 glasses worth of water (650 drops) plus eight glasses (65 drops per glass). After the class solved the problem, one of the students suggested what evidently was to her, and would be to almost everybody who has had experience measuring liquids, an easier way to handle such quantities of water:

> I thought you could have three jugs. Two would have 650 drops in them, just like you said there. But if you put 650 drops in the third one, you'd have too much. You'd have to take out two glasses because there are not 30 glasses in the story, but 28 (p. 329).

Social Systems

Evidence of the social system engaged permeates the article. Lampert's story and illustration lessons require social construction of context in order to create meaning.

> *Teacher*: Can anyone give me a story that could go with this multiplication ... 12 × 4?
> *Jessica*: There was 12 jars, and each had 4 butterflies in it.
> *Teacher*: And if I did this multiplication and found the answer, what would I know about those jars?

According to the student's direction, Lampert draws the twelve jars of butterflies on the chalk board and continues by asking other students to participate in solving the problem. Because of the way the data are presented, it is difficult to 'prove' that one student's contribution to the conversation-of-the-moment helps to engage another student's participation, but it is also difficult to deny. Later on, in this same lesson, after ten of the jars have been circled to represent the principle of decomposition, a student who does not know his times table (and in a different sort of classroom could not participate in a multiplication problem) can discuss the remaining two jars, each with four butterflies. What other ways Lampert's effort to elicit and articulate one student's working knowledge helps to clarify and engage another student's working knowledge cannot be determined from the article. Nevertheless, it seems reasonable to conclude that a group of children engaged as a social system in the classroom ecology support each other's learning and discovery.

Personal Systems

By asking a child to volunteer to create a story or to imagine a drawing to represent a given mathematical abstraction, Lampert is asking the student to rely on his or her personal system to 'construct a way to give meaning to an operation' (p. 322). Research within the realm of personal systems identifies narrative unity as 'a continuum within a person's experience' which renders those experiences meaningful because of the sense of unity they give the person (Connelly and Clandinin, 1988: 74). Lampert provides the students with opportunities to connect their sense of the world with the culture of mathematics. Lampert further provides for each child's personal system by encouraging multiple problem-solving strategies. One student, when looking at a representation of six jars, each containing four butterflies, responded by multiplying 6 × 4. Another student, looking at the same configuration, responded with 3 × 8, evidently, according to Lampert, seeing three pairs of jars, each pair containing eight butterflies.

Classrooms as Ecosystems

Earlier we argued, along with Bateson, that all mind or intelligence is ecological, that is, always relational to holistic systems of information and action. A system, according to Bateson (1972: 315), is a self-corrective unit that processes information. This self-correction will be oriented either toward homeostasis (balance or equilibrium) or toward the maximisation of certain variables. Homeostasis is not a static state but an active process involving give and take, cycling among various states or conditions. Lampert's lessons provide illustrations of how these processes might be functioning in classrooms.

Self-Correction

Lampert cleverly allows for the self-corrective process in the system by praising the number of and the inventiveness of students' strategies to decompose and recompose the problems and by accepting 'errors' as a matter of course. To help her students discover as many combinations of nickels and dimes totalling one dollar as possible, Lampert has developed a chart. The first entry on one student's chart is 5 dimes and 10 nickels equals a dollar. The next entry 6 dimes and 9 nickels, which the student discovers equal $1.05, so he draws a line through the entry to show he realises the conditions have not been met, and he tries again with 6 dimes and 8 nickels equals a dollar. The fourth entry appears to have used the same strategy as the second entry, adding one coin to the dimes (7 dimes) and removing one coin from the nickels (7 nickels) for a total of $1.05. The fifth entry, 8 dimes and 4 nickels equals one dollar, and the sixth entry, 9 dimes and 2 nickels equals one dollar, indicate a change in the child's strategy. No longer is the child adding one coin to the dimes and removing one coin from the nickels, but appears to be adding one dime and removing two nickels. By focusing on inventiveness of strategy and not on 'getting the right answer', the child's personal system interacting with the complete mathematical culture has self-corrected. Presumably when children are involved in a group activity, the social system would offer alternatives, that is, the other children in the group would provide the correcting force.

Maximisation of Certain Variables

By the end of the series of lessons, an ecological equilibrium seems to have been reached by the class. The cultural system, the social system, the physical system and personal systems have interacted with the four systems of the mathematical culture, the intuitive, the concrete, the computational and the principled. However, there are periods of time during which Lampert has created a purposeful imbalance. Throughout most of the lessons, the primary goal has been to enable the students to connect with the principled mathematical knowledge, the computational knowledge seeming, at times, almost incidental. An extremely large amount of time is spent 'doing' 28×65 — constructing stories and representations, discussing and exploring different means of decomposition and recomposition — compared to the amount of time spent on 28×65 in more conventional classrooms. Nevertheless, because Lampert wants to enculturate the students into the complete culture of mathematics, the time and effort can be considered a self-correction toward the maximisation of certain variables. As Lampert explains:

> Alternative algorithms are usually less efficient as a procedure for getting an answer; once students have learned a 'quick and easy' method for calculating the answer and have come to believe that the answer is what really matters, they are understandably less tolerant of more cumbersome alternatives (p. 331).

Thus, in order to counterbalance the demands of technological intelligence — efficient, decontextualised, product-oriented as opposed to process oriented —

Lampert has constructed the lessons to maximise the students' opportunities to work with certain variables, the variables of intuitive knowledge, concrete knowledge, and principled knowledge.

Homeostasis

Equilibrium exists when classroom activity is functional, healthy and productive, qualities that can be assessed internally and externally. Our analysis thus far has concerned itself with describing internal classroom activity in the state of equilibrium, defined as all appropriate systems conversing in order to accomplish the task at hand. Homeostasis of the ecosystem is most easily assessed using a larger perspective. One of the most basic questions that can be used to address homeostasis is: have the classroom experiences enabled the teachers and students to converse with the more encompassing systems existing externally to the classroom? Can the students engage in and interact with the systems that contribute to the construction of family activities, work activities and community activities?

Conclusion

We have proposed in this chapter a view of working knowledge grounded in systemic and holistic notions of learning, knowledge, practice and relationships. Ecological intelligence is proposed as a model of knowledge and action having three characteristics: (1) knowledge is inherent and widely dispersed in systems; (2) knowledge becomes available as working knowledge in particular activities and events; (3) working knowledge is constructed jointly by participants (systems) in an activity. This view stands in contrast to widely held notions of knowledge being solely acquired and applied by an individual. It also questions theories of practice assuming unilateral design and control by the practitioner, cultural neutrality, and objectivity of perception, language and thought.

Effective practice is a matter of ecological intelligence. We use 'ecological' because the term conveys the idea of complex systems interacting and affecting each other. Furthermore, it allows us to look at systems individually without disregarding the connectedness of the ecological unit. The systems contributing to effective practice are cultural, physical, social, historical and personal systems.

Ecological intelligence is when the thought and action in all of these systems interact in a mutual and dialectical manner to create new meanings, relationships and actions. The process is bounded by the structure and process of existing systems and, at the same time, is responsive to the moment and gradually structured and unfolding, that is, improvised. These are the features that make the interaction conversational.

In educational settings, teachers and learners find themselves a part of complex classroom ecologies. These are special kinds of ecologies because the information and action directed toward learning, development and relationship is found in highly artificial conditions (decontextualised, abstract, symbolically dominated, and institutionalised). To be effective, classroom practice (meaning both teaching and learning) must overcome these constraints. By developing links (conversations) with the relevant systems within and surrounding the classroom, activity can become appropriately contextualised, tangible, meaning-full, and communal. The teacher's task in an alive classroom is to facilitate conversations with the appropriate systems for the particular activity. This includes both introducing students to new conversations and connecting the 'conversation-of-the-moment' to the systems and conversations brought by students. Instructional conversations are corrected toward (have as purpose) the achievement of both particular relationships among participant systems and particular conversational abilities and repertoire (patterned knowledge).

The job of the student is connecting, a job made much easier if they are allowed to take part as full participants. This means students enter a classroom already engaged in systemic conversations. The classroom activity can either build upon these or ignore them. By building upon and incorporating the students' conversations, they directly connect with the knowledge contained in the cultural, physical, social, historical and other personal systems of which they are, in fact, a part. Ecological intelligence (homeostasis) is achieved when these interactions are adaptive, i.e., serve to maintain constancy of appropriate relationship between an individual and the environment. We call this learning.

References

ACKOFF, R. (1979) 'The future of operations research is past', *Journal of Operational Research Society*, **30**, pp. 93–104.

ALEXANDER, C. (1964) *Notes on the synthesis of form*, Cambridge: Harvard University Press.

AU, K.H. (1979) 'Using the experience-text relationship with minority children', *The Reading Teacher*, **326**, pp. 677–9.

AU, K.H. and JORDAN, C. (1981) 'Teaching reading to Hawaiian children: Finding a culturally appropriate solution', in TRUEBA, H.H., GUTHERIE, G.P., AU, K.H. (Eds) *Culture in the bilingual classroom*, pp. 139–52.

AU, K.H. and MASON, J. (1981) 'Social organizational factors in learning to read: The balance of rights hypothesis', *Reading Research Quarterly*, **171**, pp. 115–52.

BARRETT, W. (1962) *Irrational man*, New York: Anchor.

BATESON, G. (1972) *Steps to an ecology of mind*, New York: Ballantine.

BATESON, G. (1979) *Mind and nature: A necessary unity*, New York: Bantam.

BELLAH, R.N., MADSEN, R., SULLIVAN, W.M., SWIDLER, A. and TIPTON, S.M. (1985) *Habits of the heart: Individualism and commitment in American life*, New York: Harper and Row.

BERGER, P., BERGER, B. and KELLNER, J. (1974) *The homeless mind: Modernization and consciousness*, New York: Vintage.

BERRY, W. (1983) *Standing by words*, San Francisco: North Point Press.

BOWERS, C.A. and FLINDERS, D.J. (1990) *Responsive Teaching: An ecological approach to classroom patterns of language, culture, and thought*, New York: Teachers College Press.

BROWN, J., COLLINS, A. and DUGUID, P. (1989) 'Situated cognition and the culture of learning', *Educational Researcher*, **18**, 1, pp. 32–42.

BUBER, M. (1965) *Knowledge of man*, New York: Harper and Row.

BUTT, R., RAYMOND, D. and YAMAGISHI, L. (1988) 'Autobiographic praxis: studying the formation of teachers' knowledge', *Journal of Curriculum Theorizing*, **7**(4), pp. 87–164.

CAMPBELL, D. (1978) 'Qualitative Knowing in Action Research', in MARSH, P. and BRENNER, M. (Eds) *The Social Context of Method*, New York: St. Martin's Press.

CAZDEN, C. (1986) 'Classroom discourse', in WITTROCK, M.C. (Ed.) *Handbook of Research on Teaching*, Third Edition. New York: Macmillan.

CLANDININ, D.J. (1989) 'Developing rhythm in teaching: the narrative study of a beginning teacher's personal practical knolwedge of classrooms', *Curriculum Inquiry*, **19**(2), pp. 121–41.

COLE, M. (1988) 'Cross-cultural research in the sociohistorical tradition', *Human Development*, **31**, pp. 137–52.

CONNELLY, F.M. and CLANDININ, D.J. (1988) *Teachers as Curriculum Planners*, New York: Teachers College Press.

CRONBACH, L. (1975) 'Beyond the two disciplines of scientific psychology', American Psychologist, **30**, pp. 116–27.

DOYLE, W. (1986) 'Classroom organization and management', in WITTROCK, M.C. (Ed.) *Handbook of Research on Teaching*, Third Edition, New York: Macmillan.

DREYFUS, H. and DREYFUS, S. (1986) *Mind over machine: The power of human intuition and expertise in the era of the computer*, New York: Free Press.

ERICKSON, F. (1982) 'Classroom discourse as improvisation: Relationships between academic task structure and social participation structure in lessons', in WILKINSON, C.C. (Ed.) *Communicating in the classroom*, New York: Academic Press.

ERICKSON, F. and MOHATT, G. (1982) 'Cultural organization of participation structures in two classrooms of Indian students', in SPINDLER, G. (Ed.) *Doing the ethnography of schooling*, New York: Holt, Rinehart and Winston.

ERICKSON, F. and SHULTZ, J. (1982) *The Counsellor as Gatekeeper: Social Interaction in Interviews*, New York: Academic Press.

FENSTERMACHER, G. (1978) 'A philosophical consideration of recent research on teacher effectiveness', in SHULMAN, L. (Ed.) *Review of Research in Education — 6*, Itasca, IL: F.E. Peacock.

FLORIO-RUANE, S. (1989) 'Social organization of classes and schools', in REYNOLDS, M.C. (Ed.) *Knowledge base for the beginning teacher*, New York: Pergamon.

GARFINKEL, H. (1967) *Studies in Ethnomethodology*, New York: Prentice Hall.

GEERTZ, C. (1973) *Interpretation of cultures*, New York: Basic Books.

GRICE, H. (1975) 'Logic and conversation', in COBE, P. and MORGAN, J. (Eds) *Syntax and Semantics, Volume 3, Speech Acts*, New York: Academic Press.

HARPER, D. (1987) *Working knowledge*, Chicago: University of Chicago Press.

HEIDDEGER, M. (1962) *Being and time*, New York: Harper and Row (Original work published 1927).

HEIDDEGER, M. (1971) *Poetry, language and thought*, New York: Harper and Row.

HUSSERL, E. (1965) *Phenomenology and the crises of philosophy*, New York.

JACKSON, W. (1980) *New roots for agriculture*, Lincoln, Nebraska: University of Nebraska Press.

JOHNSON, M. (1987) *The body in the mind: The bodily basis of meaning, imagination, and reason*, Chicago: University of Chicago Press.

JOHNSON, M. (1989) 'Embodied knowledge', *Curriculum Inquiry*, **19**(4), pp. 361–77.

KEESING, R.M. (1974) 'Theories of culture', *Annual Review of Anthropology*, **3**, pp. 73–97.

KERR, D. (1981) 'The structure of quality in teaching', in SOLTIS, J. (Ed.) *Philosophy and Education*, Eightieth Yearbook of the National Society for the Study of Education, Part I, Chicago: University of Chicago Press.

LAKOFF, G. (1987) *Women, fire, and dangerous things: What categories reveal about the mind*, Chicago: University of Chicago Press.

LAKOFF, G. and JOHNSON, M. (1980) *Metaphors we live by*, Chicago: University of Chicago Press.

LAMPERT, M. (1986) 'Knowing, doing, and teaching multiplication', *Cognition and Instruction*, **3**(4), pp. 305–42.

LAVE, J. (1977) 'Cognitive consequences of traditional apprenticeship training in West Africa', *Anthropology and Education Quarterly*, **8**(3), pp. 177–80.
— (1988) *Cognition in practice: Mind, mathematics and culture in everyday life*, New York: Cambridge University Press.
LEONT'EV, A. (1972) *Activity, consciousness, and personality*, Englewood Cliffs, NJ: Prentice-Hall.
LEVERTOV, D. (1973) *The poet in the world*, New York: New Directions Books.
LEVI-STRAUSS, C. (1966) *The savage mind*, Chicago: University of Chicago Press (originally published in 1962).
MEHAN, H. (1979) *Learning lessons: Social organization in the classroom*, Cambridge, MA: Harvard University Press.
MERLEAU-PONTY, M. (1962) *Phenomenology of perception*, New York.
— (1964) *Sense and nonsense*, Evanston, IL.
MUIR, E. (1962) *The estate of poetry*, Cambridge, MA: Harvard University Press.
OATLEY, K.G. (1977) 'Inference, navigation, and cognitive maps', in JOHNSON-LAIRD, P.N. and WASON, P.C. (Eds) *Thinking: readings in cognitive science*, Cambridge, MA: Cambridge University Press, pp. 537–50.
PELTO, P. and PELTO, G. (1975) 'Intraculture variation', *American Ethnologist*, **2**(1).
RANSOM, J.C. (1968) *The world's body*, Baton Rouge: Louisiana State University Press.
REID, W. (1979) 'Practical reasoning and curriculum theory: In search of a new paradigm', *Curriculum Inquiry*, **9**, pp. 187–207.
SCHON, D. (1983) *The reflective practitioner: How professionals think in action*, New York: Basic Books.
SCRIBNER, S. (1977) 'Modes of thinking and ways of speaking: Culture and logic reconsidered', in JOHNSON-LAIRD, P.N. and WASON, P.C. (Eds) *Thinking: readings in cognitive science*, Cambridge, MA: Cambridge University Press, pp. 483–500.
— (1984) 'Studying working intelligence', in ROGOFF, B. and LAVE, J. (Eds) *Everyday cognition: Its development in social context*, Cambridge, MA: Harvard University Press.
— (1985) 'Knowledge at work', *Anthropology and Education Quarterly*, **16**, pp. 199–206.
SNYDER, G. (1980) *The real work: Interviews and talks 1964–1979*, New York: New Directions Books.
VYGOTSKY, L. (1962) *Thought and language*, Cambridge, MA: MIT Press.
— (1978) *Mind in Society*, COLE, M., JOHN-STEINER, V., SCRIBNER, S. and SOUBERMAN, E. (Eds) Cambridge, MA: Harvard University Press.
WERTSCH, J. (1987) 'Collective Memory: Issues from a sociohistorical perspective', *Quarterly Newsletter of the Laboratory of Comparative Human Cognition*, **9**(1), pp. 19–22.
WERTSCH, J. (Ed.) (1979) *The concept of soviet psychology*, Armonk, NY: M.E. Sharpe.
YINGER, R.J. (1980) 'A Study of Teacher Planning', *The Elementary School Journal*, **80**(3), pp. 107–27.
— (1986) 'Examining thought in action: A theoretical and methodological critique of research on interactive teaching', *Teaching and Teacher Education*, **2**(3), pp. 263–82.
— (1987) 'Learning the language of practice', *Curriculum Inquiry*, **17**(3), pp. 293–318.
— (1988) *Community and place in the conversation of teaching*, paper prepared for the Florida Reflective Inquiry Conference, Orlando, Florida.
— (1989) *The conversation of teaching II: Teaching worth math checking homework*, paper presented at the annual meeting of the American Educational Research Association, San Francisco.
— (1990) 'The conversation of practice', in CLIFT, R., HOUSTON, R. and PUGACH M. (Eds) *Encouraging reflective practice in education*, New York: Teachers College Press.
YINGER, R.J., HENDRICKS-LEE, M.S. and JOHNSON, S. (1991) 'The character of working knowledge', paper presented at the annual meeting of the American Educational Research Association, Chicago.

Chapter 8

Teachers Generating Knowledge: Constructing Practical and Theoretical Understanding from Multi-site Case Studies

Bridget Somekh

This chapter is based on work undertaken by teachers in the Pupil Autonomy in Learning with Microcomputers Project (PALM). This was an action research project involving around 100 teachers investigating ways in which the use of computers can enable greater autonomy in learning. The combined research outcomes of the project represent a substantial body of theory, capable of generalisation, subject only to tests of validity. By re-examining the ways in which teachers validate their knowledge this chapter opens the door to generalisation of the project's outcomes, while at the same time re-examining the purposes and importance of generalisation from research findings per se.

In a review of two books of case studies, mainly written by teachers, Bristow (1991) confesses that although he 'should have been in his element' reviewing books of this kind, he was not. He goes on, 'Despite the quality of the individual contributors' chapters . . . despite the undoubted conviction and hard work that went into the carrying out of each project, these books are misguided in their expectations and aspirations when it comes to communication with teachers.' Why? Bristow, in referring to 'jargon', suggests that the origin of the case studies in their authors' work for higher degrees is to blame, but he implies that the case studies are no more rewarding for him to read than for the teachers. I have noticed a similar response in myself, for example, when two sets of case studies from funded projects (one set written by teachers, the other by researchers from higher education) lay unread in my in-tray at different times for several months. I think there may be a different reason, related to the genre of case study itself and the *genre expectations* of both writers and readers. Kress (1985) explains how genres circumscribe their writers:

> To some, in fact a significant, extent . . . the genre and the discourses construct the meaning of a text, irrespective of the writer. The author/ writer is to that extent a scribe obeying the demands of discourse and of

genre. Readers are not passive on the other hand and contribute in various ways to the meaning of a text, in the act of reconstruction of the text, which is what reading is (p. 42).

What I believe is the source of Bristow's (and my) problem, is that genres construct the readers' responses in the same way as they construct the writer's intentions. Case studies make different kinds of demands from other genres, for example that the reader will immerse themself in the text and engage in vicarious experience and interpretation, by means of empathy with the writer. A reader comes to a case study with the expectation that this case will be read singly and intensively. The case study genre does not invite us to read case studies in banks of six, ten . . . forty. Therefore, when collaborative projects produce multiple case studies they pose problems for readers. They cannot access the knowledge generated by the project without unreasonable effort, which in turn dulls the reconstructive creativity necessary for the task.

The teachers in the PALM Project,[1] writing mostly individually but in some cases in small groups, produced forty texts in the *Teachers' Voices* series. These were deliberately called *Teachers' Voices* rather than case studies, in an attempt to prevent readers from approaching them with the expectation that they would fit into an established genre. The teachers wrote with an audience of other teachers in mind. There was an emphasis on readability both in the authors' written style and in the design of the publications. In one sense, these precautions were unlikely to be more than superficially effective in reformulating the genre, since, according to Kress (*op.cit.*: 19), it is the occasion of writing rather than the name which is significant: 'The conventionalised forms of the occasions lead to conventionalised forms of texts, to specific *genres*.' However, a further complication is that the teacher-writers and their readers are unlikely to share exactly the same constructs about the occasion of writing which may create a mismatch of intentions between writer and reader. It is not only teacher-writers who face this problem. Related complexities are touched upon by Geertz (1988: 137) who describes the problems for anthropologists writing in the context of the shifting sands of post-modernist textual analysis: 'The pervasive questioning of standard modes of text deconstruction — and standard modes of reading — not only leaves easy realism less easy; it leaves it less persuasive.' Coming to many texts rather than one, and coming with a genre expectation which may not match the genre intention of the writer, readers of the PALM *Teachers' Voices* series may be ill-prepared to read constructively (in both senses of the word).

During the second year of the PALM Project, well before we knew the extent of the written product likely to emerge, the project team grappled with the problem of how we would make this knowledge accessible to and usable by others. We assumed that we would publish all the studies individually — and this has since been done — but we were directly challenged by a staff inspector from HMI who said, 'How will I know what you have found out. You can't expect me to read all the individual reports.' Despite my instinctive response that yes indeed he should read all the teachers' reports, his point had force. It has greater force now that I have come to believe that *no* reader could read *forty case studies* and engage in 'the act of reconstruction' which, as Kress says, is the only way in which knowledge can be generated from a written text, and which has to be of a different order and intensity for this genre.

The problem has many ramifications. It is, of course, tied up with complex issues about the nature of knowledge, how it is produced, and whether or not knowledge from a single case can be generalised to other cases. The local focus and personal voice of action research reports — or of case studies more generally — may make the knowledge they generate of greater rather than lesser importance. At a time when knowledge is increasingly being seen as a product of particular social settings and the individual biographies of knowers, accounts of locally generated knowledge can be seen as carrying more force than generalised theories tacitly predicated upon a view of knowledge as rule-dependent.

In particular, the problem of how to make the PALM knowledge widely available poses a dilemma for me in my role as former PALM coordinator. On the one hand, I believe that the teachers' writing, as it stands, affords the best way for a reader to engage with their research, provided it is given the kind of reading the genre demands. On the other hand, I do not believe that publication of the individual texts alone will make the project's knowledge available to a wide audience — of either teachers, policymakers or academics. For some time this dilemma was complicated by my own feeling of insipient guilt in approaching the teachers' writing and 'doing things' to it. What right did I, an academic (albeit a sometime teacher), have to interfere with their writing, or presume that there was any need for me to mediate between their writing and readers. Would that not be a patronising stance to take? I have understood this feeling better since I read Geertz's account (1988: 130 and 134) of the 'pervasive nervousness' of anthropologists and what he calls their 'desire to distance themselves from the power asymmetries' which are the context for their ethnographic studies. Perhaps as a result, I have been able to stand back from the problem and got a better perspective. Many of the titles in the PALM *Teachers' Voices* series have now been on sale for nearly a year (PALM, 1990/91). Where are they? Who is reading them?

I have come to believe that anything I can do to make the knowledge generated by PALM more widely available is not only permissable, it is essential if the work of the teachers is to be valued. By merely publishing teachers' writing and doing nothing further to interpret it, proselytise about it, draw theory from it, or generally give it prominence, people in my position are reinforcing an insidious academic and bureaucratic hegemony. McTaggart (1989) has shown how 'teacher privatism' isolates teachers in their classrooms, preventing them from sharing their research or their knowledge with other teachers, and from 'competing with the knowledge claims' of the administrators of the school district. According to him, this is adhered to so closely by teachers that it 'appears to be an ethic of teaching.' My experience is that this applies as much if not more to teachers' attitude to publicising the knowledge contained in their writing. To become prominent, the outcomes of research need to be presented in different forms and genres depending on the audience and purpose of writing; and academics who do not use their own power in the system to do this for teacher collaborators are, unintentionally or not, maintaining the established hegemony of academic knowledge.

To date, two approaches have been tried to making the knowledge generated by the PALM teachers accessible to a wider audience:

- The first was by quoting substantial extracts from teachers' case studies as a means of drawing out a selection of what seemed to be important points.

This has been used in two short articles in the *Times Educational Supplement* and *Educational Computing* (Somekh, 1990a and 1990b), and in a paper for the *Cambridge Journal of Education* (Somekh, 1991) which aims at a mixed audience of academics and teachers. This method had the advantages of presenting knowledge within a theoretical frame while retaining a flavour of its original context, but the disadvantage of being highly selective and idiosyncratic.

• The second was by presenting a model of a pedagogy for information technology based on a detailed content analysis of all of the case studies undertaken by Richard Davies (1990). This had the advantage of being systematic but the disadvantage of disembedding the knowledge from its context in classroom practice (Somekh and Davies, 1991).

The purpose of this chapter is to outline and comment upon a third approach to presenting the knowledge generated by PALM teachers.

Dialectical Interpretation: A Method for Constructing Practical and Theoretical Understanding from Multi-site Case Studies

(a) Rationale.
Dialectical interpretation is a flexible procedure for constructing practical and theoretical understanding from multiple case studies, such as the texts in the *Teachers' Voices* series. It is designed to enable readers to interact intensively with one study while collaborating in the process of constructing a knowledge base from a larger number of the studies. It places a premium on the quality of the dialogue with, and about, individual texts rather than on complete coverage of all the texts in the series. Its philosophical base lies in the theories of *dialectics* and *scientific realism*.

Winter (1989: 46–51) develops a theory of *dialectics* by which understanding of reality is only possible through:

(i) 'Identifying objects within the set of relationships which define them (like the point of overlap in the middle of a Venn diagram) rather than trying to define them in isolation as single entities.'

(ii) Searching 'for the combination of the overall unity of a phenomenon and the diversity of its elements.'

(iii) Considering 'how and why what we carefully observed yesterday will certainly be different tomorrow.'

The complexity of reality as construed by *dialectics* leads to a particular definition of the cause-effect explanations of social action (p. 65). It is not possible to identify a single cause for any particular effect. Indeed, the relationship between phenonema is not uni-directional but interdependent. According to Winter the debate about the relationship between theory and practice misses the essential fact, that they too are interdependent. Thus reflection or 'dialectical critique' is a process of: 'questioning the reflective base on which practical actions have been carried out. This is the theoretical phase, in which theory questions practice. But it is followed by a contrary movement, in which practice questions theory . . . (asking) which of these newly recalled possibilities is practically feasible; which of these insights is usable?' (pp. 66–67).

House (1991: 2–9) applies the theory of *scientific realism* to educational research and evaluation. Like *dialectics*, *scientific realism* reconstrues the cause-effect relationship. It rejects the logical positivist identification of reality with 'our sense impressions of it' and construes it instead as 'complex and stratified so that one is always discovering more complex layers of reality to explain other levels.' Causation is, therefore, seen 'in terms of tendencies and probabilities, since events are the outcomes of complex causal configurations, which sometimes cancel each other out.' From the viewpoint of *scientific realism* 'explaining events' is more important than 'documenting their sequence,' and 'explanation requires knowledge of the causal structure of the entity and a notion of the history of other interacting mechanisms.' According to House, *scientific realism* leads to the conclusion that since cause and effect are far too complex to be determined in social settings, social science should focus on explanation and on discerning, through meta-analysis, 'tendencies which may or may not be present on given occasions.' In relation to the theory-practice debate, teachers become important in this process of meta-analysis, because, 'the teacher possesses specific causal knowledge built on inferences made over a period of time from different sources and focused on particular students and the concrete conditions of the classroom.'

(b) Procedure.
Dialectical interpretation involves the following steps:

1 A reader selects one text for close attention.
2 The text is given a preliminary reading.
3 The reader decides upon a procedure for reading the text more closely and analysing it, in order to:
   (i) identify/reconstruct knowledge presented by the author which might have implications for the reader's own field of practice (whether as teacher, teacher-researcher, policymaker, academic or academic-researcher);
   (ii) construct knowledge in response to the text (although not explicitly presented by the author) which might have implications for the reader's own field of practice.
4 The reader undertakes a close reading of the text and makes some notes of knowledge which is either interesting or useful and might, in some form, have implications for practice. This may be made available to other readers, if appropriate, to start the process of building a shared knowledge base.
5 If at all possible, the reader comes together with other readers and each in turn presents and discusses the knowledge constructions from the text he or she has analyzed, drawing upon the text as evidence to support conclusions.
6 The group collaborates in drawing up a summary of emerging themes or tendencies (House's meta-analysis, 1991, *op.cit.*) which are recorded as a contribution to a shared knowledge base.
7 The group confronts any notes of knowledge constructions from other individuals or groups, or any overview summary which has already been

extrapolated from the case studies (e.g., the PALM pedagogic model, see Somekh and Davies, 1991, *op.cit.*) with their own findings on the basis of 1–6 above and through a process of dialogue incorporates or rejects each element.

8   Each individual decides whether, and if so how, she or he will apply any of the knowledge acquired in this way to his or her field of practice (application to practice, in this sense, could include storing up ideas to inform future thinking).

(c) Dialectical interpretation: an example.
In order to demonstrate the procedure, in so far as it is possible within the limits of this chapter, I have undertaken steps 1 to 4 above. My status in carrying out the analysis is no greater by virtue of my prior knowledge as coordinator of the PALM project, than that of any other reader. However, like all other readers, my purpose must be to engage with the text from my own unique perspective and, perforce, my privileged knowledge makes my analysis untypical — not more valuable or less valuable, but different.

(d) Choice of the text.
In principle, this method presupposes that any one of the forty case studies in the PALM *Teachers' Voices* series could have been chosen as the first piece to be analyzed. In practice, Jean Edwards' case study (1991) was chosen for the following reasons and the reader must judge whether the spirit of this random selection has been maintained.

(i)   I had not quoted substantial extracts from it in making points in any previous papers. Therefore I would be able to come to its analysis freshly.

(ii)   It is a substantial but not extremely extended piece of work, twenty pages in length, from which a good core should emerge as a foundation for constructing a PALM knowledge base.

(iii)   It is one of the studies with which I was least familiar, partly as a result of it being one of the later PALM publications. Again, this would enable me to come to its analysis freshly.

The same criteria were later used to select Geoff Osborne's study, *'Don't Touch the Dongle!' pupils' autonomy in using the Atari 1040STFM microprocessor and the C-Lab Notator music software* (1991) as a second text for analysis.

(e) Deciding upon a method of analysis.
The purpose of the analysis is to enable me, as a reader, to immerse myself in the narrative and engage with it in sufficient depth to undertake the complex processes of interpretation and inference. In addition, the possible misunderstandings between the writer and myself-as-reader, brought about by the different discourse groups we belong to, need to be addressed by the analysis. Put another way, I am bound to engage with the text on the basis of my own values as a member of the research community and previously a secondary school teacher over fourteen years, so the method of analysis needs to help me bridge the gap between my assumptions and expectations and those of the authors. *It should be clear that the method I use is tailored to my own needs and is not suggested as a model for other readers.*

I began by using the criteria suggested by Lincoln and Guba (1990: 53) to make an assessment, on the basis of my knowledge of the texts and my own values, of the likely strengths and weaknesses of the PALM case studies.

(i) Resonance criteria
According to Lincoln and Guba these are criteria which 'reflect the multiple realities constructed by the respondents in the inquiry . . . reject generalisability . . . display and take account of the value influences' . . . and demonstrate 'conscious reflexivity.' PALM teacher-researchers are unfamiliar with the distinction between propositional knowledge and knowledge seen as 'multiple realities constructed by the respondents in the inquiry.' They are, therefore, likely to engage in generalisations in a way not acceptable to professional researchers, and are unlikely to 'display and take acount of the value influences that impinge on the inquiry.'

(ii) Rhetoric criteria
According to Lincoln and Guba these are criteria which are 'relevant to assessing the form, structure, and presentational characteristics of the case study,' such as narrative power, creativity and persuasive force. These include 'structural characteristics such as coherence and corroboration' and craftsmanship which is apparent, for example, when the study has 'power and elegance', 'displays courage', 'displays egalitarianism' and is 'open and problematic.' PALM teacher-researchers are likely to have a number of rhetorical skills, for example, in telling a story or describing people and events. However, they are unlikely to meet all the expectations of professional researchers, for example in corroborating all assertions, displaying the 'open and problematic' nature of the study, or going 'a step beyond present constructions and understanding, proposing novel ideas and/or new grounds for negotiation of reconstructions.'

(iii) Empowerment criteria
According to Lincoln and Guba these are criteria which assess 'the ability of the case study to evoke and facilitate action on the part of readers,' including, 'fairness, educativeness, and actionability.' Case studies should avoid ending their narratives only with 'suggestions for further research.' They should make clear 'what action steps are indicated by the inquiry — not just what we have, but what our findings say about where we should be going.' PALM teacher-researchers are likely to meet the empowerment criteria in 'making clear what action steps are indicated by the inquiry', since this is a central focus for action research.

(iv) Applicability criteria
According to Lincoln and Guba these are criteria which 'assess the extent to which the case study facilitates the drawing of inferences by the reader that may have applicability in his or her own context or situation.' Inferences in this sense are different from generalisations. They draw a distinction between inferences made between similar contexts, and those made between dissimilar contexts.

They mention the importance of 'thick description . . . in the sense that Geertz (1973) uses the term, as making clear levels of meaning', particularly when inferences are made between similar contexts. PALM teacher-researchers are likely to meet the applicability criteria for readers whose situation is similar, only occasionally. They are not likely to have the rhetorical skills to reveal 'levels of meaning' by using 'thick description'. For those whose situations are dissimilar, they are likely to meet applicability criteria frequently by providing 'a sense of vicarious, *déjà vu* experience'; a basis for making comparisons and drawing out similarities and differences; and 'a basis for re-examining and reconstructing one's own construction of a given phenomenon.'

On the basis of this assessment I decided to focus my analysis of Jean Edwards' study upon:

(i) clarifying values and value inferences by means of construct analysis;
(ii) clarifying the problematic nature of the study;
(iii) exploring the extent to which assertions are related to research findings or to the author's values and beliefs;
(iv) developing any inferences and novel ideas arising from the reading of the case;
(v) highlighting any suggested action steps.

(f) An extract from the analysis of Jean Edwards' case study in the Teachers' Voices *series.* There is not space here to include the whole of my analysis of Jean Edwards' writing, so I have selected extracts from the narrative account which sets the scene, and part of my analysis of her second research focus. No extracts are given here of my analysis of Geoff Osborne's study.

Narrative to set the scene
Jean writes:

> Gladstone Primary School is an inner-city multicultural primary school of four hundred and twenty pupils. Ninety per cent of our pupils are Urdu/Punjabi-speaking Muslims. . . . The school is divided into four teams. Each team comprises four classes of children plus a team teacher who divides his or her time equally among the four classes, working with either a group of children or taking the majority of the class whilst the class teacher works with a small group. Each team plans a termly or a yearly topic so that full exchange of ideas can take place and we can call upon each other's strengths in various areas of the curriculum. I am working in the middle school team, year 4, 8 to 9-year-old boys and girls, approximately 28 in the class. . . .

As an initial research focus, Jean decided to evaluate the change to a new system of teaching reading, agreed upon by the staff as a whole. Under the old system there was 'a limited supply of story books based within the classroom and a further supply of colour coded graded reading books based in the corridor, available to all the school.' Under the new system there would be 'a free choice of reading material within the classroom' and during half-hour reading sessions, when children gathered in the carpeted book corner, they would have two aims: 'reading "secretly" in our heads' and reading aloud quietly in pairs. The aim was to overcome recognised problems: '(i) hearing every child read at least once a week; (ii) monitoring children's behaviour while out of the classroom; (iii) the limited amount of reading materials; (iv) the outdated and unappealing stock.' Emphasis would be placed on books 'with good illustrations, non-racist, non-sexist, . . . those which embraced repetition, rhyme, humour, books with a good plot, those with large format and pop up books. . . . Emphasis was placed on a good plot/story so that children would read with sense and within a context, rather than reading sentences in isolation.'

The second research focus

(a) Narrative account

Jean's second research focus was on 'using the microcomputer as an aid to reading'. Her aims were:

    (i)   to enable the children to work in pairs or in threes, where each child was able to contribute and feel its contribution was valued;

    (ii)   children should help each other with their reading and understanding aided by discussion and the sharing of ideas;

    (iii) 'after initial instruction in keyboard organisation, leave myself free to give individual or group help to the other children';

    (iv) that computer activities should 'stimulate language and at the same time be self-explanatory, yet open to investigative work';

For hardware, the class had access to one Acorn BBC computer for two and a half days per week ('as it was being shared with the parallel class in our double-bayed classroom').

For software, Jean chose two programs, *Nature Park* and *Animal Rescue*, for the following reasons:

    (i)   'The children were able to identify with the subject matter';

    (ii)   'They were both adventure games written in three parts, where children could work at one part at a time, and then come back to the next part at a later date yet not lose the continuity of the story';

    (iii) Both had good quality, appealing text and graphics;

    (iv) 'The programs both involved reading, logical thinking, some number work but mostly reading and understanding';

    (v)   'All the children, even those with very limited English, would enjoy and learn from the programs'.

(b) The problematic nature of the study

Jean built upon the data collection methods she had already used:

- She divided the class into groups of three of varying composition: mixed ability and sexes; same sexes and mixed ability; same ability — 'The permutation seemed endless'.
- She undertook general observation of groups using the computer.
- She took still photographs.
- Another member of the team, Mrs Baker, interviewed one group of children using the photographs as a stimulus. This was tape-recorded and transcribed.

Interpretation

Jean's confidence in herself as a researcher means that she is now using a narrower range of data collection methods. She has decided to abandon testing and the use of a control group — partly perhaps because these are not methods PALM is actively suggesting, but partly, it seems likely, because of the ethical problem raised by differential treatment of one group of children. To me, both as a reader, and as the PALM coordinator, this seems to be a good idea. I judge that the comparison of test scores between the control group and the PALM group was useful as alternative data which confirmed the analysis of observation and interviews, but a similar approach in having one group using a computer and one not would raise even more ethical problems and might make the research very complicated.

(c) Values and value inferences
Analysis
Once again, as a reader, I carry out a construct analysis to help me identify with the values Jean is expressing implicitly rather than explicitly. A second construct analysis enables me to identify with the values of a small group of children. As a reader, I am looking for evidence of change at a deeper level rather than merely at the surface level (see Bussis, Chittenden and Amarel, 1976), and this is likely to be expressed in terms of a change in Jean's values. Changes in values are also, of course, a necessary part of curriculum development because of the value-laden nature of curriculum.

Jean's values: constructs for judging the children's computer work on the basis of her own observation.

Much discussion in both English and Punjabi.	————————	
Supportive of each other.	————————	Dominate control of keyboard.
Reading together.	————————	Rush to press spacebar before other read.
Enjoyment. Confidence. Participant.	————————	Passive onlooker.
Worked well together.	————————	Did not gel.
'Much language including pointing at the screen, arm waiving.'	————————	Dominant child, taking crucial decision disregarding opinions of others.
'Arguments, especially if a mistake was made.'	————————	
'Very intent upon what was happening on the screen, to the exclusion of all else.'	————————	

The values of one group of children: constructs for judging their computer work revealed in their discussion with Mrs Baker.

(The children in this group are described by Jean as, 'Sajid, a Muslim boy, Jangeer, a Muslim boy of mixed English/Pakistani parentage who had many behavioural difficulties, and Rukhsana, a shy retiring girl of Pakistani parentage.')

Doing the space bar.	————————	Couldn't do nothing.
Looking.		Didn't know how to do that.

Making something.	——————————— Trying to do something (but by implication not succeeding).
Hand on the button.	——————————— Letting (others) have a go.
Turning the computer off and on ('put my finger on break and shift and it came back on').	———————————

Interpretation

Two things are noticeable from the construct analysis. First that some of Jean's constructs for judging the children are more detailed and multi-faceted than the ones she used in her earlier research. These give the impression that she is seeing more in her observation of the children. In reading the earlier section I felt that Jean was categorising the children rather easily, for example as 'participants' or 'fiddling about', now she seems to categorise them in a more complex way — she is either much more interested in the research or she is beginning to see the children more as individuals. Second, that the children's constructs for judging their own work are different from Jean's. (She notes this: 'Immediately apparent was the fact that there was a conflict between my perception of the children's involvement with the computer and how they themselves perceive their own involvement.') Jean's constructs concentrate on language and reading, theirs on controlling the technology and 'doing something.' I find myself disagreeing a little with Jean's interpretation. She thinks the children are mainly interested in operating the computer and interested scarcely at all in the task they are engaged in on the computer. I find myself wondering what they mean by 'making something' and 'couldn't do nothing', — what constitutes 'making' and 'doing'? But I certainly agree with the main thrust of Jean's point, that they do not value the same aspects of the task that she values — there has been a shift of task between the setting and the doing. The implications of this interest me in relation to a lot of other computer-related tasks.

(d) Knowledge constructions

From Jean's analysis it is possible to identify three areas of knowledge she feels she has gained from this second research focus.

(i) 'The children did not rate ideas and program content as highly' as 'mechanical control';

(ii) Rukhsana's contribution to the discussion was 'quiet and reflective' and as her contribution increased 'the boys began to value her contribution and suggestions . . . they saw her in a new light.'

(iii) Both she and the children had gained 'knowledge and self-confidence' in using the computer.

Of these, the one which appears to be of most interest to Jean is the change in the boys' appreciation of Rukhsana's capabilities. She comments on this at some length:

As an onlooker I found this blossoming of Rukhsana's confidence very illuminating and it made me wonder what other hidden depths could be revealed by not only Rukhsana but by other pupils also. Analysis of tape transcripts together with close observation does tell you a lot about a child and his/her potential.

Towards the end of the story the boys were valuing Rukhsana's contribution, letting her suggest strategies. I too, have learnt something of value here . . . to build Rukhsana's confidence in the future by giving her tasks in all areas of the curriculum in which she can show leadership. Above all, she must feel that her contributions are valued.

During 1988–9, in particular, I had been able to gain insight into children's capabilities and learnt never to prejudge what they were capable of.

Interpretation

Once again, not surprisingly, the knowledge Jean gains is consonant with her prior values. It is derived from small group work in which emphasis is placed on children working collaboratively. However, within this frame of values the knowledge is very specific. For example, Jean does not formulate her new understanding in terms of:

anti-sexism —————————— sexism

but instead in terms of the broader construct of:

valuing an individual's contribution —————————— prejudging

As a reader I was surprised that Jean did not comment on what appeared to me from her description to be sexism in the attitudes of the boys to Rukhsana. This surprise was reinforced when I came to a comment later in the text about 'one pupil, a boy, who was not motivated during the first months of writing stories, the reasons being "boredom" and being paired with a girl!' I shall return to this point in commenting on the hypotheses in which Jean frames her understandings of the knowledge she has gained from her research, because one refers explicitly to this point. Reflection on the text provided me with some clues, however. Jean describes the context of the school with its high proportion (over 90 per cent) of Muslim pupils. I am aware of at least some of the differences between non-Muslim and Muslim culture in England, enough to know that in promoting *both* anti-sexism and anti-racism Jean is likely to be faced with some dilemmas. If she respects all aspects of the culture of the children she must respect their assumptions about the different roles appropriate for men and women, a stance which appears to be incompatible with anti-sexism. In the light of this interpretation I see Jean's focus on valuing every individual's contribution, as opposed to valuing every girl's contribution, as a way around the dilemma. I cannot feel it is a satisfactory resolution of the problem, but I feel I have learnt a great deal from reflecting upon this point, rather than allowing my initial surprise, with its easy assumption of superior insight, to stand unchallenged.

At the beginning of the case study there is not the same sense that Jean is focusing her attention on individuals, instead the focus appears to be the group. At the beginning of the second research focus on the computer an expressed aim is that, 'each child was able to contribute and feel its contribution was valued', but the force of the narrative suggests to me as I read that this is only fully realised by Jean, it only becomes a meaningful concept, after her analysis of the interactions of Rukhsana, Sajid and Jangeer.

In addition, my impression is that Jean now has a much more accurate idea of the children's approach to their work, their self-expectations and attitudes to each other. She has been surprised by the difference between their constructs and her own. The interpretation of his knowledge is again particular. What is specially interesting for me is that it is not in terms of the social construct:

engagement with task ——————— non-engagement with task

(that is she does not assume that the children were not really engaging with the task she had set), but instead in terms of the cognitive construct:

focus of task on active ——————— lack of focus of task on
comprehension   active comprehension

In other words, the action she feels she needs to take is not based on the assumption that the children did not engage in the task *as a result of some failure on their part*, but on the assumption that *it was not the right kind of task* to engage their attention.

(f) Suggested action steps
This time it is, if anything, even clearer that the knowledge Jean has gained is action-orientated, immediately suggesting actions she could take to improve the reading curriculum for these children and the others in her class:

(i)   'to build Rukhsana's confidence . . . by giving her tasks in all areas of the curriculum, in which she can show leadership.'
(ii)   'I felt that pairings would be better in the future and that more intensive exchange of ideas would take place.'
(iii) 'I decided to partner children who were on the same level academically or friendship pairings. I hoped a boy/girl mix might work well.'
(iv)   'I hoped to concentrate on programs which gave children a chance to construct stories of their own.'
(v)   'I thought that the focus in the future had to be on comprehension.'

Interpretation
In all of these plans for action it seems to me that there is a noticeable shift towards greater emphasis on cognitive development. I was struck that the majority of the constructs Jean used in her original observations, and a good proportion of the constructs she used in her observations of the computer work, seemed to be social constructs — framed in terms of children's behaviour. At this point I find myself wondering whether some shift of focus away from organisation of the group towards setting tasks for individuals is enabling Jean to turn her attention more towards concern for the children's cognitive development, for the nature of their thinking and learning. On the other hand, it may be as a result of PALM's focus on developing autonomy in learning. When the project began that was my assumption, but I now realise that it does not follow automatically. Jackson (1968) found that teachers concentrated mainly on organising activities and maintaining discipline rather than on children's learning *as a short term aim*. The PALM teachers' research taught me that autonomy in learning cannot take place without

careful structuring of the framing context, in terms of the organisation of activities. I have come to understand that *both* social and cognitive issues are important in enabling autonomy in learning, but that, for many teachers, the balance of their interest needs to shift more towards cognitive issues to enable effective curriculum development to take place.

(g) Summary

Dialectical interpretation is designed as a means of enabling readers to learn from case study reports of action research. It presupposes that learning from reading entails an interactive process of reconstructing and questioning the author's meaning and constructing new meanings in response (Winter, 1989: *op.cit.*). It is consonant with a view of cause-effect relationships as complex and inter-dependent, understandable only through the continuous questioning of dialectics, or the meta-analysis of many-layered realities suggested in House's application of scientific realism to social settings (1991: *op.cit.*). It enables a Gadamerian conversation with the text.

Reflections on Teachers' Knowledge Construction through Action Research

Although I was working alone rather than with a group, and was therefore only able to engage in the first four steps, the process of dialectical interpretation led me to reflect on the way in which these teachers constructed and reported the knowledge resulting from their research. I learnt things of practical relevance to my role coordinating and facilitating action research. Close reading of one of the texts also enabled me to construct new understandings in relation to the series as a whole. This final part of the chapter is in two sections. The first is a meta-analysis of how teachers construct texts and represents part of my learning. The second is more speculative, setting out what I see as the role of dialectical interpretation in teachers' learning.

Creating the Text of a Teacher's Voice

What the PALM teachers engaged in through the process of action research can be construed as a semiotic interpretation of the culture of their own classrooms. According to this theory, as described by Geertz (1973: 448), the actions and interactions of each child and the teacher, their daily routines, and important events such as the introduction of a computer into the classroom for the first time have symbolic meanings which can be interpreted in the same way as a written text. Drawing on Max Weber, Geertz (*op.cit.*: 5), sees mankind as 'an animal suspended in webs of significance he himself has spun' and the purpose of the anthropologist or social researcher as one of 'interpretation in search of meaning'. Elsewhere in the same book he refers to the texts produced by researchers as 'fictions, in the sense that they are "something made" "something fashioned" — the original meaning of *fictio* — not that they are false, unfactual, or merely "as if thought experiments"' (*op.cit.*: 15).

Construed in this way, in one sense the validation of the *Teachers' Voices* texts becomes irrelevant. They represent the interpretations of the author at a particular time and place. However, in another sense they lack validity until their meanings are reconstructed by another reader who can interpret the whole 'fiction' *including* the author's own role as participant, interpreter and reporter. Teachers can be seen as making *both* first order interpretations by, so to speak, reading the texts of their own classrooms, *and* second order interpretations of the perceptions of children and colleagues (e.g. interview data) and the records of classroom events (e.g. observation notes, photographs and tape transcripts); whereas readers of the texts make only second order interpretations, engaging in conversations with the text itself. The validity of the text is established through the dialectical interaction of reader and author. The reader validates the text by measuring both its congruence and its revelationary power against his or her own experience (for further discussion of this approach to validation see Adelman, Jenkins and Kemmis, 1975: 3; Elliott, 1990: 59; Altrichter, 1986: 133–34, 141 and Lincoln and Guba, 1990: 53); whereas the teachers validate their texts by recording their 'knowledge of concrete causal entities' (House, 1991, *op.cit.*: 9) and their own developing 'artistry' as teachers and 'cultivation of educational *connoisseurship*' (Eisner, 1985: 91/92).

Accumulating Knowledge Incrementally from the PALM Teachers' Voices

The PALM *Teachers' Voices* were not written in isolation from one another. Although there was not as much interaction between all the project teachers as would have been desirable, particularly between teachers working for different Local Education Authorities, there were a number of points of contact. First, almost all the teachers had other PALM teacher researchers in their own school. They were all supported by a project officer who was part of the central team and whose role included providing a rationale for action research and practical help with methods of data collection and analysis. The project also had a newsletter, *PALMLEAVES* which published articles by teachers and central team members, providing examples of research in progress and suggestions (for example of software to use, available reading and ways of getting started with writing). Just under half of the teachers attended a weekend conference at the end of the first year which resulted in the identification of several key questions to serve as a focus for research in the second year (PALM, 1989). As many again attended a second conference half way through the second year and took part in joint reading and analysis of all the writing which existed at the time (whether in finished or draft form). This led to the development of a set of hypotheses of what as a whole project group we felt we had found out. Therefore, to some extent all the writing was produced with a consciousness or *background echo* of the common understanding being generated by the project as a whole. Attendance at the conferences in particular appears to have been a formative experience in many cases (Crawford, 1990) which may be compared with Smith's (1989) observation about the power of such an event: 'How will it play at St Hilda's became the summary way of speaking. . . . In our view, having an image of such an audience is a very powerful factor in shaping and finishing a piece of inquiry.' As my colleague, Richard Davies, puts it in his detailed analysis of the *Teachers' Voices* series, from which we developed the PALM pedagogic model:

A kind of working validity is found in the subjective recognition of one's own experiences in the experiences of others in broadly similar contexts (the context in this case of teachers, schools, micros, PALM, the shared historical epoch, etc). The subjective character of this 'validity' is reduced in proportion to the size of the consensus or the number of people who recognise their own experience in the accounts of others. What one has is a kind of vernacular triangulation conferring shared significance (or common meaning) which becomes itself a form of valid generalisation, or knowledge of sufficient confidence to support change. (Davies, *op.cit.*, 1990: 3)

In this way, the authors' confidence in what they had come to know from their research, increased through cross-referencing it to the research of other PALM teachers. For example, it is very clear at the end of Jean Edwards' study that she is using the PALM questions and the set of hypotheses generated at the second conference from the teachers' analysis of the PALM writing (PALM, 1990) as a check list for writing her conclusion. In that sense her research can be seen as informing her selection of some hypotheses from the conference (and not others), while in their turn the hypotheses provided her with increased confidence in her findings. This process can be compared to some extent with the peer validation sessions in the 'dialogic research community' advocated by Whitehead (1987), but it differs in being open and consultative rather than taking place in a particular session and in the form of answering questions in defence of knowledge claims. It is a process which invites the reader to take up the conversation where it was left off and continue the process of cross-reference and inter-textual dialogue. It also makes it important that individual case studies should be read, where possible, in the context of knowledge generated by the project as a whole.

The Role of Assertions and Generalisations in Knowledge Construction

The *Teachers' Voices* case studies were not written only on the basis of data formally collected, recorded and analyzed. Michael Eraut, in a seminar at the Centre for Applied Research in Education in 1989, referred to the large body of informal, contextual data — for example, memories of things said in chance conversations — which cannot but be taken into account by any researcher. In the case of the PALM teacher researchers there was a vast quantity of this informal data in their past and current experience of teaching these children, in this school, in this LEA. Perforce this influenced the confidence with which they felt able to accept or reject the findings of their research — it either rang true to their experience or it did not. This can be seen as a process of informal validation on the basis of which they felt able, or not, to generalise their research knowledge to other settings and events in the course of their practice.

In terms of their written reports there were differences in language registers used by different teachers. Some may have been more familiar than others with the genre of research reports, or influenced to different degrees by some knowledge of the procedures of traditional scientific research in terms of validity, reliability and replicability. Geoff Osborne, for example, uses tentative language in putting forward what he has learnt from his research, and distances himself from his statements by adopting a slightly ironic, comic tone (Osborne, 1991); whereas Jean Edwards makes more definite assertions and appears to be generalising her findings at least to other situations within her own projected experience. However, it might be inaccurate to conclude that Geoff has a better understanding of the hypothetical nature of his findings. He might simply be more familiar with the genre. Another construction might be that as Jean has attended the second conference, read the other PALM writing, and taken part in the joint development of hypotheses, she has developed greater confidence in the validity of her work than Geoff, who was unable to attend the conference. Richard Davies clarifies the status he accords to the series as a whole:

> These materials are indeed about teachers talking to themselves and each other in their endeavour to develop suitable pedagogies for what may be a transforming addition to the classroom. From these statements we can make inferences not confident conclusions (Davies, 1990, *op.cit.*).

One way of thinking about assertions and generalisations is to see them as expressions of their author's underlying beliefs and values. The construct analyses I carried out on Jean Edwards' and Geoff Osborne's studies reveal that both have strong beliefs which underpin their actions. If anything, the tone of Geoff's allusions to 'musical intelligence' and having 'a good ear' appear more assertive because the constructs he uses for the computer are couched in comic irony (e.g. 'jungle of computer languages'). If assertions are seen in this light, it is worth considering what happens when new knowledge is acquired which may lead to the realignment of those beliefs and values. It may become necessary to think through the exact implications of the new knowledge for all the ramifications of the existing value system. Max Weber's metaphor of nets is useful here in graphically representing the myriad of pulls, twists and realignments which may be necessary. And the more the knowledge grows, the more the process of reflection may weave in upon itself and tangle the webs of the nets. Seen in this way, assertions on the basis of research become essential as statements of re-ordered beliefs and values. In the last two pages of Jean Edwards' study she constructs what amounts to a manifesto for her practice. It is irrelevant to me as a reader whether every statement can be validated on the basis of the data she has presented in the text, what matters to me is the passionate intensity with which her text comes to its conclusion.

Postscript

> Despite all this has autonomy taken place? Are there signs of autonomy developing? What has happened to these children during this period?

> They have entered a tunnel — warily at the narrow end, traversing the pitfalls and treasures and emerged into the daylight, larger, stronger, wider and far more confident, ready to enter a new tunnel with eagerness and anticipation.

> From all this research, it is apparent that children are supporting each other and relying on each other's knowledge and respecting the other's

innate ability, cooperation and self-reliance as their joint learned skills. They have helped each other to a common goal despite the massive hurdle of speaking and operating in a different language.

The computer becomes a third person in a relationship with a life of its own: with foibles and problems like anyone else, which the children accept. Like any other child, it often feels off form!

The autonomy lies in the developing relationship between the children using the computer as a catalyst. The activities created an atmosphere in an insular, escapist world where divisions have to be made, creating a sub-culture where different rules apply and control is available over the ultimate goal and the paths to it (Edwards, 1991: 20).

Assertions, seen in this way, are expressions of the passionately held meanings and enthusiasms whose spark enlivens and enriches the routine of practice. It is at least reasonable to suppose that when an individual's values and beliefs are changed as the result of research it is only through asserting the implications for practice that change comes to seem worthwhile or even sensible. In fact, making the assertions — whether or not they are expressed in writing — may be seen as a prerequisite for changing values and beliefs in the first place.

In case it may seem that I am putting forward special pleading on behalf of the PALM teachers (and indeed I make no pretence to be neutral), it is worth stating that assertions and generalisations are a feature of all the great texts which make an impact on human ideas. Whether it is Amiens' song in *As You Like It*:

'Blow, blow, thou winter winde,
Thou art not so unkind
    As man's ingratitude:' (Shakespeare, 1926, 2.7.174)

or T S Eliot's:

    'Human kind
Cannot bear very much reality.' (Eliot, 1963)

We relate to the power of a statement to evoke a reciprocal passion in our own understandings of human experience. Moving from art to research, much of our thinking is shaped by generalisations made by key thinkers on the basis of powerful but relatively thin data. To demonstrate what may be lost by rejection of generalisations ungrounded in rigorous research practice, Jackson (1990) asks us to 'imagine what a well-trained and hard-nosed ethnographer would make of Piaget's casual observations of his own children.' Similarly the enormous influence of Freud on twentieth century thought is based on interpretation of case studies from which he generalises extensive theories of human psychology. Geertz describes the textual brilliance of Ruth Benedict's *The Chrysanthemum and The Sword* (1967) in the following way:

The Us/Not-us motif is pursued through an enormous range of wildly assorted materials derived from wildly assorted sources . . . with the sort of single-mindedness that compels either general belief or an equally general skepticism (Geertz, 1988: 120).

And concludes that it is Benedict's control over language rather than the power of ideas or the rigour of methodology which persuades the reader. Since assertions appear in this way in respected and influential texts it is unreasonable to criticise less experienced researchers for making use of them in their writing.

Another way of looking at the role of assertions is to view the readers of case studies as learners. In order to persuade and inform, i.e. to enable their learning to take place, we need to solicit our readers with the power of ideas. If we wish other teachers, politicians or policymakers to engage with our knowledge constructions the tentative language of research is likely to be ineffective. We need the more passionate language of assertion, linked to judiciously selected evidence and carefully tuned to the expected reader. In this way we can argue that just as Evans-Pritchard's 'gunboat linguistics' is persuasive for upper middle-class readers from the home counties of England (Geertz, 1973), so Joan Edwards' metaphor of children 'traversing the pitfalls and treasures of a series of tunnels and emerging into the daylight stronger and more confident' is persuasive for teachers in English primary schools.

The Role of Dialectical Interpretation in Teachers' Learning

(a) Teachers' learning about teaching.
If then we think of the PALM *Teachers' Voices* writing as a means of communicating the project's knowledge to other teachers, assertions can play an important role in adding to the persuasive power of the texts. What the method of dialectical interpretation endeavours to do is to focus on the response of individual readers to that persuasive power rather than categorising knowledge across texts. The problem of the latter approach can be seen in Tripp's (1985) proposals for setting up an archive of case studies, in which suggested indexing categories, such as 'changed self image' or 'less sex stereotyping', are neither intellectually compelling nor likely to be adequate to the job of categorising knowledge bound into rich and varied contexts.

The dialectical interpretation can be construed, therefore, as a means of enabling readers to learn. More specifically, dialectical interpretation of the *Teachers' Voices* texts engages reader-learners in actively constructing knowledge. A peculiarity of current research into teachers' thinking seems to be its concentration on teachers' thinking about teaching, rather than on the way in which teachers' learn. The emphasis is on philosophy and social theory rather than cognitive psychology. Certainly, this is true of those writers who draw their inspiration from the traditions of action research or teacher-as-researcher. The work of Elliott is philosophical, moral and intuitive in origin, that of Stenhouse philosophical and historico-ethnographic (e.g. Elliott, 1988, 1991; Stenhouse, 1975). Both derive their theories of the central role of teachers in curriculum development (in which they are strongly influenced by each other) empirically from their experience of working with teachers on curriculum projects.

What light would a more explicit focus on teachers' cognitive experience shed upon the method of dialectical interpretation? Desforges (1989: 18) makes the assertion that 'teachers need a vision for learning, some notion of high quality intellectual life which they seek for their pupils.' It is a small step to conclude that in addition teachers need a 'high quality intellectual life' of their own. Intellectual life, however, is not to be found in the abstract — although it will be enhanced by the contemplative thought advocated by Buchmann (1990) — but through interaction with situations. The theory of 'situated cognition' is described by Brown, Collins and Duguid (1989: 32–42). Its first emphasis is on the supportive context for learning, in which part of the cognitive task is 'off-loaded onto the environment', in contrast to de-contextualised learning in which an extra (and irrelevant) layer of conceptual difficulty is added 'because explication often lifts implicit and possibly even nonconceptual constraints (Cussins, 1988) out of the embedding world and tries to make them explicit or conceptual.' This pre-supposes that practice should at least precede rather than follow conceptualisation, to which they are 'epistemologically prior — at a nonceptual level.'

Several writers emphasise the role of discussion in cognitive learning. Desforges, in writing about children's learning, stresses the importance of 'engaging in critical, socratic conversation.' Prawat (1991: 3–10), in developing the theory of learning through *immersion* (see below), stresses that it 'places a high premium on dialogue or discourse during learning.' Brown, Collins and Duguid (*op.cit.*) see collaboration as a necessary part of situated cognition, partly because of the importance of shared narratives:

> If as we propose, learning is a process of enculturating that is supported
> in part through social interaction and the circulation of narrative, groups
> of practitioners are particularly important, for it is only within groups
> that social interaction and conversation can take place (p. 40).

Bereiter (1991: 10–16) describes how until very recently the predominant theory of cognitive learning has been one of *information processing*. The developments in artificial intelligence in modelling the human brain have in themselves become a controlling metaphor for thinking about human intelligence. However, this view is beginning to lose favour, perhaps because the information processing model proved to be inadequate as a basis for artificial intelligence. Prawat sees two strands in the theories of cognitive learning which are on the ascendance. One, embedded learning (or situated cognition) has already been put forward, the other, immersion learning, stresses thinking itself rather than its context. According to this theory learning takes place as a result of engagement with 'powerful ideas' which 'serve as "lenses",' for our perceptions. The engagement with ideas is so intense that learners experience periods of time when they lose all sense of themselves as learners or the context which surrounds them. Prawat compares this with Csikszentmihalyi's (1982) concept of 'flow' as the 'peak-performance frame of mind enjoyed by those who are totally absorbed in a particular task.' (Prawat, *op.cit.*: 5). The immersion theory of learning stresses the key role of perception. Prawat quotes Neisser (1976: 9): 'Perception is where cognition and reality meet.' According to immersion theory learning is creative and heuristic rather than being predominantly a process of sorting, categorising and hypothesising; it is founded in a view of knowledge as constructions of the human mind rather than know-ledge as the uncovering of rules and laws about the natural world. For Prawat (*op.cit.*) the next step in the process is the laying down of what has been learnt in mental structures known as schemata which 'function both as formats for incoming information and as plans for finding out more about the environment.' These schemata may be more or less fixed, but Prawat asserts, 'The environment has its own set of demands, and we must be prepared to transform and adapt our schemata accordingly.' Learning is, therefore, a process whereby human thought is solicited by and focused upon powerful ideas, through the act of perception, and recorded in patterns of more or less fully constructed mental schemata which, in their turn, lead to refocusing upon other powerful ideas. It is a circular process which is partly self-generating and partly results from what Desforges (*op.cit.*: 23) calls 'challenges' from the learning context. In referring to the teacher's role in student learning he talks of 'challenging pupils' schemas (by) setting problems and investigations, posing questions and engaging in critical, socratic conversation.' It is clear that this should be applied equally to teachers' own learning.

One feature of this recent trend in cognitive learning theory is that it is inclusive and pleuralistic rather than exclusive and tied to one set of values. The theory, in this way, models its own view of knowledge. Bereiter, for example, points out that 'rules and rulelike statements — definitions, principles, explicit premises, and conclusions' are central to the intellectual discourse of Western culture, (Bereiter, *op.cit.*: 15), and there remains an important place for them in knowledge construction. The difference is in the status we accord to rules:

> Once we recognise rules as part of public discourse rather than as lines of mental program code, we can afford to be entirely pragmatic about their use in education.

Nevertheless, the thrust of both immersion theory and the theory of situated cognition is that learning results from interaction with particular events/ideas arising from the learner's immediate environment or his or her own intensive thought processes. Thus, according to Bereiter (citing Elliott, 1988, *op.cit.*) the learning context needs to be flexible and learner-sensitive. It follows that generalisation or transfer of knowledge needs to take place in relation to particularities rather than overarching rules, so that learner's can enter into a dialogue between their own understanding and the meaning they construct from other situated examples. Thus, according to Prawat:

> The view of transfer that is beginning to emerge from this body of work is, in many ways, the mirror image of the traditional approach. This view, which stresses the importance of contextualisation instead of decontextualisation, has been strongly influenced by the work of Brown and colleagues (Brown, Collins and Duguid, 1989; Collins, Brown, and Newman, 1989). (Prawat, *op.cit.*: 9).

(b) Learning through dialectical interpretation of case studies.
At the heart of *dialectical interpretation* lies a creative tension. Dialectics is a process of rational inquiry through posing alternative views: interpretation is a process of systematic searching and hermeneutic reconstruction. The method of dialectical interpretation was designed, as my account should have made clear, as a means of resolving the problem of presenting the knowledge from the PALM *Teachers' Voices* series in a more succinct form. The intention is to make this knowledge accessible to other teachers, policymakers and members of the research community in order to enable it to influence educational policy and practice.

Dialectical interpretation involves individuals engaging in detailed reading of a single text and recording their constructions and interpretations in summary form. The dialectical or rational questioning lies in the reader's interrogation of the text, the hermeneutic interpretation results in the reader's reconstructed knowledge. This interaction of individual readers with single texts is then itself opened up to further dialectical interpretation through discussion with other individual readers. This enables the collaborative group to cross-reference their knowledge constructions and identify points of agreement and points of ambiguity between different texts. In the case of the PALM *Teachers' Voices* texts this approach continues the process of cross-referencing and cross-validation which the PALM teachers were engaging in with each other at the time of carrying out the research and drafting and completing their writing. In relation to the learning theories of situated cognition and immersion this has several advantages:

(i)   It provides the conditions for building Desforges' 'high quality intellectual life' by subjecting individual accounts to scrutiny in order to draw out powerful ideas.

(ii) It promotes the intensity of vicarious experience from reading case studies, and thereby makes possible the transferance of contextualised knowledge, through creative reconstruction rather than unthinking replication.

(iii) It promotes reflection and collaborative learning through dialogue.

The method of dialectical interpretation builds on Winter's (1989 *op.cit.*: 52–5) notion of dialectical critique, it also supports dissemination of the outcomes of action research studies to other teachers. It is a method which has obvious advantages for those able to work in groups, such as teachers on LEA in-service training courses or students registered for degree courses in higher education. Additionally, through accumulation of the summary outcomes of each individual dialectical interpretation a knowledge base can be established incrementally and made available to individual readers, such as researchers and policymakers. Such a knowledge base provides an access point to the individual *Teachers' Voices* texts rather than replacing a reading of the texts themselves.

Note

1   The Pupil Autonomy in Learning with Microcomputers Project, 1988–90, was funded by the National Council for Educational Technology in collaboration with Cambridgeshire, Essex and Norfolk LEAs, and based at the University of East Anglia. As coordinator I led a project team made up of Erica Brown (Essex), Bob Davison (Norfolk), Jon Pratt (Cambridgeshire), Laura Tickner and Richard Davies (UEA). PALM was directed by John Elliott.

References

ADELMAN, C., JENKINS, D. and KEMMIS, S. (1975) 'Rethinking Case Study: notes from the second Cambridge conference', unpublished paper available from CARE, University of East Anglia, UK.

ALTRICHTER, H. (1986) 'Visiting two worlds: an excursion into the methodological jungle including an optional evening's entertainment at the Rigour Club', *Cambridge Journal of Education*, **Vol.16**, No.2, pp. 131–142.

BENEDICT, R. (1967) *The Chrysanthemum and the Sword: Patterns of Japanese Culture*, London: Routledge.

BEREITER, C. (1991) 'Implications of Connectionism for Thinking about Rules', *Educational Researcher*, **Vol.20**, No.3, pp. 10–16.

BRISTOW, S. (1991) 'Review of Practitioner Research in the Primary School', WEBB, R. (Ed.) and Managing Staff Development in Schools, LOMAX, P. (Ed.), *Research Intelligence, BERA Newsletter*, Summer 1991, pp. 28–29.

BROWN, J.S., COLLINS, A. and DUGUID, P. (1989) 'Situated Cognition and the Culture of Learning', in *Educational Researcher*, **Vol.32**, Jan–Feb 1989, pp. 32–42.

BUCHMANN, M. (1990) 'How Practical is Contemplation in Teaching?' in DAY, C. *et al.*, *Insight into Teachers' Thinking and Practice*, London, New York and Philadelphia: Falmer.

BUSSIS, C. and A. (1976) *Beyond Surface Curriculum*, Boulder, Colerado: Westnow Press.

CRAWFORD, K. (1990) 'From the Outside Looking In: observations of teachers and their research', in SOMEKH, B. *et al.*, 'PALM: The Inside Story, Final Report of the Pupil Autonomy in Learning with Microcomputers Project.' Available from CARE, University of East Anglia, UK.

CSIKSZENTMIHALYI, M. (1982) 'Towards a Psychology of Optimal Experience', in WHEELER, L. (Ed.) *Review of personality and social psychology*, **Vol.2**, Beverly Hills, CA: Sage, pp. 13–36.

CUSSINS, A. (1988) *The Connectionist Construction of Concepts*, (SSL Research Report). Palo Alto, CA: Xerox Palo Alto Research Centre.

DAVIES, R. (1990) 'Shared Perspectives', PALM Project working paper, CARE, University of East Anglia, UK.

DESFORGES, C. (1989) 'Understanding Learning for Teaching', *Westminster Studies in Education*, **Vol.12**, pp. 17–29.

EDWARDS, J. (1991) '*I like to read*' — computers and children's reading, PALM Project, CARE, University of East Anglia, UK.

EISNER, E.W. (1985) *The Art of Educational Evaluation*, London and Philadelphia: Falmer Press.

ELIOT, T.S. (1963) 'B . . . Norton, The Four Quartets', in *Collected Poems 1909–1962*, London: Faber and Faber.

ELLIOTT, J. (1988) 'Teachers as researchers: Implications for supervision and teacher education', paper presented at annual meeting of American Education Research Association, New Orleans.

— (1990) 'Validating Case Studies', *Westminster Studies in Education*, **Vol.13**, pp. 47–60.

— (1991) *Action Research for Educational Change*, Milton Keynes: Open University Press.

GADAMER, H.-G. (1975) *Truth and Method*, London: Sheed and Ward.

GEERTZ, C. (1973) *The Interpretation of Cultures*, New York: Basic Books.

— (1988) *Works and Lives: the anthropoligist as author*, Cambridge, UK: Polity Press.

HOUSE, E.R. (1991) 'Realism in Research', *Educational Researcher*, **Vol.20**, No.6, pp. 2–25.

JACKSON, P.W. (1990) 'The Functions of Educational Research', *Educational Researcher*, **Vol.19**, No.7, pp. 3–9.

KRESS, G. (1985) *Linguistic Processes in Sociocultural Practice*, 1985, Victoria: Deakin University Press, and 1989, Milton Keynes: Open University Press.

LINCOLN, Y. and GUBA, E. (1990) 'Judging the Quality of Case Study Reports', *International Journal of Qualitative Studies in Education*, **Vol.3**, No.1.

McTAGGART, R. (1989) 'Bureaucratic rationality and the self-educating profession: the problem of teacher privatism'. *Journal of Curriculum Studies*, **Vol.21**, No.4, pp. 345 – 261.

NEISSER, U. (1976) *Cognition and Reality*, San Francisco: Freeman.

OSBORNE, G. (1991) *'Don't Touch the Dongle!'* — *Pupils autonomy in using the ATari 104OSTFM microprocessor and the C-Lab Notator music software*, PALM Project, University of East Anglia, UK: CARE.

PALM (1989) *PALMLEAVES*, No.3, September 1989, University of East Anglia, Norwich NR4 7TJ: PALM Publications, CARE.

PALM (1990) *PALMLEAVES*, No.6, June 1990, University of East Anglia, Norwich NR4 7TJ: PALM Publications, CARE.

PALM (1990/1991) *Teachers' Voices*, University of East Anglia, UK: PALM Project, CARE.

PRAWAT (1991) 'The Value of Ideas: The Immersion Approach to the Development of Thinking', *Educational Researcher*, **Vol.20**, No.2, pp. 3–10.

SHAKESPEARE, WILLIAM (1926) *As You Like It*, The New Shakespeare, Cambridge UK: Cambridge University Press.

SMITH, L.M. (1989) 'One Road to Historical Inquiry: extending one's repertory of qualitative methods', in EATON, W. (Ed.) *Shaping in Supremacy*, New York: Teacher's College Press.

SOMEKH, B. (1990a) 'Palmistry', *Times Educational Supplement*, 15.6.90, p. B18.

— (1990b) 'Learning Autonomy', *Educational Computing and Technology*, **Vol.11**, Issue 5, June 1990, pp. 19–22.

— (1991) 'Pupil Autonomy in Learning with Microcomputers: rhetoric or reality? An Action Research Study', *Cambridge Journal of Education*, **Vol.21**, No.1, pp. 47–64.

SOMEKH, B. and DAVIES, R. (1991) 'Towards a Pedagogy for Information Technology', *The Curriculum Journal*, **Vol.2**, No.2.

STENHOUSE, L. (1975) *An Introduction to Curriculum Research and Development*, London: Heinemann.

TRIPP, D.H. (1985) 'Case Study Generalisation: an agenda for action', *British Educational Research Journal*, **Vol.11**, No.1, pp. 33–43.

WHITEHEAD, J. (1987) 'How can we produce a living educational theory in the context of the politics of educational knowledge?', paper presented at the British Educational Research Association conference, 1987.

WINTER, R. (1989) *Learning from Experience*, London and Philadelphia: Falmer.

Part 3 Developing Knowledge and Practice

Chapter 9

Teachers' Stories: An Analysis of the Themes

Marguerite Hansen Nelson

The research reported here was designed to investigate what it means to be a teacher from the perspective of practising teachers. This issue has been a concern since the debates between Socrates and the Sophists (Johnson, 1986). Yet, it is only in the past ten years that research regarding teaching has taken teachers' thoughts and behaviour into consideration (Day, Pope and Denicolo, 1990; Floden and Klinzing, 1990; Warren, 1989).

Despite the increase in investigations of teacher thinking, it is still acknowledged that teachers' voices are muted and their perspective overlooked in the knowledge base about teaching (Cochran-Smith and Lytle, 1990; Schubert, 1990). Unless the experience of teaching is considered from teachers' perspectives, teaching becomes an abstraction (Coles, 1971; Hart, 1976).

In designing research to respond to this need, it seemed important to utilise a method that would evoke the reality of teaching and diminish the tendency for teachers to say what they thought we wanted to hear about their profession. The theory of narrative provided a method that helped to reduce the influence of investigator expectations. Rather than soliciting a direct response to a question about what it means to be a teacher, this study analyzed teachers' stories using the approach of narrative inquiry (Connelly and Clandinin, 1990).

Theoretical Rationale for the Research Design

Stories were an appropriate medium because the language of folklore represents what a culture values (Barthes, 1985; Campbell, 1972). Teacher lore has recently become a sanctioned subject of research and source of insight (Schubert, 1989, 1990, 1991).

The theory of narrative indicates that humans are natural storytellers and that the study of narrative reveals how humans experience and create their lives (Britton and Pellegrini, 1990; Bruner, 1986, 1987; Connelly and Clandinin, 1990). Narratives allow access to the community (Jackson, 1987) and to the cognition of the storyteller (Britton and Pellegrini, 1990). If narratives provide manifestations of the models constructed by the mind (Chafe, 1990), then stories about teaching should reveal the storytellers' models of teaching.

Procedures

Permission was granted to solicit stories from teachers in a suburban school district. Letters were sent to the entire teaching staff (N = 630) asking them to share a story or stories about memorable or meaningful moments in their teaching careers. The letter explained that the stories could be in the form of informal anecdotes. The teachers who agreed to participate taped their stories independently so the investigator was unobtrusive. The tapes were subsequently transcribed verbatim.

The themes by which the stories would be categorised were not anticipated so the important dimensions of teaching were derived without preconceptions (Patton, 1980). The themes were suggested after the initial reading of the stories and corroborated by the literature on teaching.

The stories were categorised into eight themes by three independent reader/ judges. Limiting the number of categories to eight was intended to assist the retention of the labels while reading (Miller, 1956). The theme that was assigned to each story was determined by consensus among multiple judges.

The controversial selections were referred to two additional judges until a majority opinion prevailed or the story was considered such an amalgam of categories or an aberration from the categories that it was unclassifiable. The low frequency of stories that could not be assigned to a category bolsters the credibility of the category system (Patton, 1980).

Since Lortie (1973) encouraged imagination and thoroughness in research about teaching, a discriminant function analysis was conducted to determine if the themes could be predicted by some combination of the demographic data provided by the participants. Informal inspection indicated that the same themes recurred regardless of the teachers' gender, level, longevity, subject or educational attainment. This impression provided the null hypothesis that would be tested by the discriminant function analysis.

Participants

The participants were teachers from a large suburban school district with a reputation for excellence that has been cited in *The New York Times*. The status of the district suggests that the participants could be considered 'the reasonably successful and experienced practitioner to model or identify critical elements significant to teaching' (Leinhardt, 1990: 19).

Sixty-four teachers or 10 per cent of those contacted agreed to participate and fifty-five (8.7%) people actually contributed stories. The participants provided demographic data along with their tapes. The sample consisted of a fairly even distribution of ages in ten-year intervals from the twenties (16%) to the fifties (24%). Their teaching experience was also well distributed across five-year intervals ranging from one (25.5%) to thirty years (25.5%). Most respondents were women (85%) and the majority were permanently certified (82%) and had earned a masters' degree or beyond (87%).

Most of the participants (75%) taught at the elementary level. Only 9 per cent taught at the junior high and 16 per cent at the secondary level. It follows that most of the participants were classroom teachers (47.2%) responsible for all subjects.

Special education had the next highest representation with 21.8 per cent. Other specialties included: library (7.3%), reading (5%), science (3.6%), language (5.5%), art (5.5%), and speech (1.8%). There were no respondents with specialisation in maths, music, social studies, technology, or home and careers.

Most of these teachers had intended to be teachers when they started college (71%). Some of the participants had more than two years of experience in another field (35%). The sample was split almost in half in regard to changing assignments within the teaching field.

Results

The fifty-five participating teachers contributed a total of 146 stories. Individual contributions ranged from one to ten stories and individual stories ranged from one to six pages when typed. Although the teachers were currently employed in a suburban school district, there were stories that recounted experiences in inner cities, rural areas, the Far East, and South America.

Teachers as storytellers.
The analogies between the teachers' stories and realistic fiction contribute to establishing the verisimilitude of the data. In the tradition of oral tale-telling (Manning, 1985), the stories are straightforward with the emphasis on actions and are told in simple, concrete, colloquial language that is powerful and colourful. They are recounted from the first person point of view that is typical of the oral medium (Gardner, 1983).

The teachers' stories contain concrete details from observation. There are picturesque descriptions of the setting that contribute to the impact of the story. Deliberate repetition is utilised as it is in folktales to alert and impress the reader (Yolen, 1986).

The sequence of causal events provides profluence as demonstrated in the frequency of the verb, 'proceeded'. There is evidence of foreshadowing and the tension of suspense and surprising dramatic climaxes. Following the climactic incident, there is often denouement during which the tension of anticipation relaxes but the outcome or significance of the story is explored.

Readers are touched by the characters and the drama, not the commentary of the storyteller. The reader participates vicariously in the characters' experiences which the teachers succeed in making vivid and intense. Those who read the stories reported being provoked to cry, laugh aloud, and shiver with sighs.

The content can be considered significant to teachers because the intensity of interest experienced by the readers can only be aroused if the storyteller has a vital interest in the subject matter and cares about the characters. A story only has 'real interest if the central character is . . . an agent struggling for his or her own goals . . . and the nobler the goal, the more interesting the story' (Gardner, 1983: 65).

Categorisation of the stories.
Sorting the stories into categories was necessary to determine the important and valid aspects of the experiences (Leinhardt, 1990). Even though the stories were self-selected in response to an open invitation, the similarities among them invited categorisation. The patterns revealed the consistency of perspectives, values and insights (Leinhardt, 1990).

The categories were suggested by the obvious themes of the stories. 'Theme, . . . is not imposed on the story but evoked from within it' (Gardner, 1983: 177). Since the surface truth of tone and topic provides access to more universal truths, values can be abstracted from the interpretation of the story as a whole (Gardner, 1983). So the themes of the stories suggest what is valued by teachers in their work. The degree of consensus in classifying the stories indicated that the categories that emerged were effective for organising and explaining the data.

Description and validation of the categories.

The first category was labelled, 'Above and Beyond' (ANB). Stories in this category describe a situation in which the teacher goes beyond his or her regular expected responsibilities or roles. Highet (1976) confirms that, 'teachers are selfless people, giving out of themselves far more than they ever expect to get back' (p. 56).

'Communication' (COM) was the second category. In these stories there is an attempt to share information or a point of view. In some instances this attempt is frustrated. Heck and Williams (1984) confirm that 'teaching is, in so many of its dimensions, a mode of encounter and of communication' (p. 4).

The third category was labelled 'Contribution/ Impact/ Appreciation' (CIA) and applies to stories that describe the satisfaction that a teacher gets from making a contribution to a student's well-being, having an impact on a student's life, or being appreciated or acknowledged by students or their parents. 'Above all, teaching is a way . . . of making an impact on the world' (Freud, 1980: 10).

A fourth category was 'Job Description' (JOB) which accounts for stories or statements that delineate or highlight the challenges, responsibilities, or rewards of teaching.

The fifth category was 'Reflection' (REF) which involves a thoughtful consideration of a situation in retrospect for the purpose of evaluating and/or learning from the experience and frequently from students. The National Board for Professional Teaching Standards [NBPTS] (1990) claims that reflection is an essential attribute of professionalism because it contributes to critical pedagogy (Ayers, 1986; Britzman, 1986; Greene, 1986).

'Relationship' (RLA) describes stories that reveal the bond, affection, or mutual appreciation between students and teachers. Highet (1976) confirms that 'rapport is essential' (p. 80). Teaching has been described as a social relationship (Britzman, 1986), a means for sharing oneself (Freud, 1980), and activating the value of care (Greene, 1986). Professionalism requires an ethic of service (NBPTS, 1990). Influential teachers tend to be empathic (Lightfoot, 1983), considerate (Ross and Houtz, 1979), and accessible (Csikszentmihalyi and McCormack, 1986).

The category of 'Student Perspective' (STP) might be considered a subcategory of 'Communication'. In this category, the power or punch line of the story is provided by the revelation of a student's unique and often unanticipated perceptions. The refinement of communication to take student perspective into account is described by Booth (1988) as 'moments of genuine exchange, not simply moments when I give and they receive' (p. 259).

The final category was entitled 'Surprisingly Successful Student' (SSS). Stories in this category relate the sequence of events that culminates in a breakthrough, achievement, or any obvious dramatic change in a student. NBPTS (1990) cites teaching as the most democratic profession because of teachers' tendency to empower their students to learn, achieve, and even surpass their visions for them. Teachers reap satisfaction (Ayers, 1986) from these 'gratifying graduates' (Lortie, 1975: 123).

These categories are consistent with the aspects of teaching revealed in the study by Roueche and Baker (1986). The components cited in their study included commitment, interpersonal skills, and cognitive skills. The categories of ANB, CIA, JOB and SSS reflect their component of commitment. This incorporates both dedication and appreciation of the teaching-learning process. The themes of COM, RLA and STP reiterate their component of interpersonal skills which incorporates the listening, rapport, and empathy reflected in the stories. The theme of REF is the vehicle for their component of cognitive skills which includes learning from experience and being lifelong learners.

Exemplars of the categories.
The stories classified as 'Above and Beyond' (3.4%) described situations in which the teachers' involvement with their students exceeded society's expectations for their role. For example, in one story a teacher made a compact to give up smoking if a sixth grader would try to quit. Another special education teacher took students from an impoverished background to her apartment on a weekend before the holidays to decorate the tree and make cookies which they shared with the other children in school on Monday. A speech therapist enlisted the help of children in the neighborhood so that one of her students wouldn't be teased for stuttering.

The most powerful story of exceeding regular responsibilities involved a teacher and student he coached in track. The student was disadvantaged and placed in a group home in a predominantly affluent community. The student succeeded in winning a scholarship to college because of his achievements as an athlete. The teacher and the student stayed in contact through college and beyond. After an enduring relationship, communication from the student became sporadic. There was one aspect of the young man's life that he had not discussed with his former coach.

> When I finally did hear about my friend, it was with the news that he was not feeling well . . . I did successfully call him and I found out that the illness he had was in fact, a terminal illness known as AIDS. . . . It was in October during the school year when I understood finally that he was very ill and I asked my principal if I could go and visit and try and see him through this difficult period of time . . . I cared for him for a period of about three or four days until he could in fact get hospice care . . . I returned to school and called him on a daily basis . . . and then finally, there was the day that I had received the call that he had passed away.

It is clear in the teacher's voice on the tape and the sequence of the story that he is not sharing this story to praise his own behaviour. In fact, when the dying man's friends express amazement that he would come on such a mission, he is honest about his mixture of motives.

> It was as much for selfish, as well as for altruistic reasons. The selfishness being the completeness of the bridge that I had started years before (19B).

This story might be considered the quintessential teacher's story in this study since it is so comprehensive. It incorporates the other categories of communication, contribution, relationship, reflection, and, at the time of earning the scholarship, the successful student.

Stories (4%) in the category of communication (COM) reveal the challenge of communicating effectively. A humorous illustration is the story in which a first-year teacher thinks the principal is asking when he has band, only to find out that his principal was inquiring about the time he taught maths. This same teacher had mismatched mothers and children at Open House and added to the confusion while talking to one of their fathers the next day.

Another teacher recounts getting detoured into the principal's office on her way to return a set of antlers to a student. Feeling in the holiday spirit, she held the antlers on her head while the principal proceeded to discuss budget matters without even acknowledging her bizarre appearance. On another occasion, this same teacher was frustrated by her first graders' infatuation with a celebrity stuntman and told them that she was going to be marrying him. After gaining their attention in this way and having a successful lesson, the teacher confessed that the wedding was a joke. However, the children persisted in believing it and the news spread throughout the community with hilarious complications.

Other stories of communication describe children's insightful grasp of concepts. For instance, after reading and discussing *The Ugly Duckling*, a second-grade boy whose English was a second language told his teacher privately, 'You know that little girl who sits next to me? . . . She is beautiful inside and outside' (p. 23). Another student insisted upon referring to his English teacher at the junior high school as 'Mr'. The teacher tried repeatedly to clarify the correct use of titles only to learn that the student was not confused, but was using the title deliberately because of her authoritative style which he associated with masculinity.

Other stories (8%) emphasise the satisfaction that teachers glean from making a contribution, having an impact, or being appreciated (CIA). Since tangible indications of success are scarce, teachers have to rely on subjective reports from former students (Roueche and Baker, 1986). In many of these stories students return years later and teachers are amazed at what they remember and at their expressions of appreciation. These occasions evoke reflection on professional responsibilities and a rationale for persevering in the profession.

> It did make you realise that sometimes you do touch them in ways that you don't even realise. I felt so marvellous after seeing him . . . I guess one like that every seventeen years is enough to make you go on teaching (p. 17).

Another story involved a thirteen-year-old special education student who had been an elective mute since kindergarten. The teacher had initiated a home visit and the process of finding appropriate alternative placement for the near future. As the story progressed the teacher's voice became husky with emotion.

> I got a terrific letter from her mother the other day, very touching, telling me how she feels her daughter has changed so much within the last two months. . . . She's extremely pleased that I took the time. . . . Her mother is very very thankful and I was very touched by the letter

that she wrote. It truly feels great to know that you've made a difference in somebody's life (p. 45).

Another teacher encountered a former student while jogging and they ran together for a time. As a student, this young man had been a reluctant reader. Now at twenty-seven, his job involves a considerable amount of reading.

And he said, 'I really hated reading as a kid, but I remember that in fifth grade you always used to read to us.' And he started to name a few of the books that I read to the class which I myself had forgotten. And he said, 'You know, you really were the one that taught me that there could be joy in reading. And I have really come to love reading. . .' (p. 48).

In this story, we see the surprise again about what the students remember.

That really really pleased me so much to know not only that I had that effect on somebody but to see that we all really make an impact on our students, more than we can know and more than we can even remember (p. 48).

These opportunities to have an impact confirm the professional choice of many teachers. In a survey of 22,000 teachers by the Carnegie Foundation, 77 per cent reported satisfaction with their jobs. A stated source of this satisfaction was the chance to be a change agent (Tifft, 1990).

Some teachers delineated the responsibilities, pressures, or pleasures of their positions in the category of JOB (15.7%). One recounts the pressure of being observed and evaluated. Another teacher elaborates on her professional responsibility. Other teachers describe their philosophy for success and what represents success to a teacher.

My philosophy about kids is that generally they'll live up to your expectations. If you expect nothing, that's what you'll get and, on the other hand, if you believe in them and you have very high expectations, with some support and some help and guidance, they're going to get there (p. 49).

I've come to the conclusion that when we get a class if they're two years behind, I guess the best thing we can do is to help them to feel good about themselves and to grow as much as possible while they're in our care . . . Then we've done them a great deed even if they're not on grade level when they leave our class (p. 28).

On a day to day basis, I find that I am learning from the children all the time, as well as my being able to give them new ways of thinking about themselves and the world that they live in . . . I want to instill in them my love for learning and the fact that I feel I can always improve myself and there is always so much out there for me to learn (p. 39).

Another teacher relates her involvement with a dysfunctional family as if it provides an illustration of her philosophy which is stated at the conclusion.

Teaching is 'risky' business. I believe that teachers need to go with their gut feelings and confrontation is both a responsibility and an obligation. I can't help but feel that our intervention did make a difference. We may never know just how much! (p. 42)

Other stories (8.2%) both represent and engender reflection (REF) on teachers' work. In these instances, the teachers tend to evaluate themselves and consider what they have learned from the situation and their students.

A novice teacher evaluates and reiterates her philosophy as her first year approaches its conclusion. An experienced teacher recalls an incident from her early years of teaching in which she discovers after trying multiple approaches that a child did not understand the meaning of the word 'equals' in an equation. She reminisces about this momentary instructional impasse because of what she learned from it.

I realised then and there how important language was to the understanding of mathematics and, indeed, to a child's understanding of all subjects . . . I have never forgotten that early experience and to this day, take great care in introducing the definitions of words I am going to use (p. 22).

A physical education teacher tells of doubting the student report that his partner had done sixty-two sit-ups in a minute.

With recent results of fitness testing being rather low, I was a little sceptical of this score, and . . . I asked the student to return at another time and do the test over again with me. Well, to my surprise when I did retest this third grade student who was a female, the student proceeded to do sixty-four sit-ups. I was a little amazed. . . . It was probably the last time I ever really doubted a student's score (p. 30).

In another case, a teacher had a student who was a new entry. When she left in the spring the teacher learned that this little girl had been sleeping on the floor since September.

And I guess the point of the whole story is that sometimes children sit in front of us and look perfectly normal and behave normally and sometimes there's so much going on at home that we don't know about. . . . It's something that I've tried to keep in mind in the years since. . . . We never really have a right to make the assumption that if everything looks great, it must be great. And that was the feeling or lesson that I learned from this little girl many years ago (p. 28).

A dramatic example of learning from students through reflection was contributed by a high school chemistry teacher. He prefaced the story by referring to the tendency toward a 'know-it-all attitude' in the early phase of his career. He recalled giving a struggling student 'a circled sixty-five' at the end of the course only because of the effort he had made.

The student earned an athletic scholarship to college and had to take a science course. He avoided chemistry because of his prior experience, but became so enthralled with biology that he switched to a pre-med major. Eventually, through determination, he earned his medical degree. The teacher has been telling this story to his classes and reminding himself of its message for twenty-five years.

> That boy taught me the most powerful lesson in all my years of teaching — that motivation is far more important than innate ability. I will never in my life say to any kid, 'You can't make it'. Given sufficient motivation and a moderate amount of ability to match it, anyone can achieve anything he or she sets his heart on (p. 34).

The relationship (RLA) between teachers and students was an underlying theme in most stories, but there were some in which it was the primary focus (12%). One teacher's voice swelled with emotion as she obviously restrained herself from crying over the recollection of this incident.

> I remember one incident over ten years ago when my own Dad passed away . . . and when I returned back, there was just so much concern . . . as to how I felt about having lost someone close to me. We often are concerned about the children and their problems and making them feel good and here was a case where even very young ones were concerned about me and how I felt (p. 39C).

This story suggests the mutuality of the empathy, sympathy, love, respect and kindness that the teachers in Koerner's (1990) study viewed as the bonding ingredients in the student-teacher relationship.

A mature teacher recounts a story from her early field experience in which she had introduced a program dealing with self-esteem that was called, '*I am special*'.

> On my last day the class honored me with a party and a beautiful grapevine wreath. One little shy Haitian girl came to me with a small package wrapped in toilet tissue. She quietly told me that I was special, too. Her gift to me was a slightly used spool of pink thread. This gift from the heart is among my most treasured possessions (p. 47).

Another teacher notices a child's unspoken sadness and inquires compassionately if anything is wrong. When the student stammers, 'My, my cat died!' the teacher reassures her, 'It's O.K. to cry'. and then, overwhelmed with empathy joins the child in crying over the death of her cat. Another time when a special education student unexpectedly declares, 'I need you', she responds warmly with the eloquence of sincerity, 'Well, I need you, too' (p. 38). In another setting, a teacher finds herself crying with most of the class as she reads a student's favourite story about the love between a mother and a child (p. 53A). These teachers did not distance themselves from students by hiding their emotions (McPherson, 1972 in Lightfoot, 1983).

This theme is best summarised by the reflections of a teacher about how his accumulation of several years' experience has affected him.

> I'm noticing . . . you care more about the students in so many ways. You really care about them academically, more than you ever thought you

could and about them socially, and about their physical welfare . . . and you start to really worry. . . . And you hear stories about a student . . . about how well they're doing or if you hear a bad story about them, it hurts (p. 32D).

Like the teachers in Millie's (1990) research, these teachers value their students as human beings and develop the concern that is inherent in a personal relationship. The ultimate description of this relationship was dramatic and ironic since it was appended to a story that ended with the student's death.

It is a significant bond that teachers develop with their children and in fact, it's a bond that transcends time and place. It's as if we cut and paste time and reinsert it in a different location. And for that reason I view teachers as being immortal, living forever in the minds and the hearts of the children that they've had in their classes (p. 19B).

The most frequently occurring category (35%) was the subset of communication that involved the student's perspective (STP). This corroborates Koerner's (1990) research in which the characteristic being sensitive to the students' point of view was seen as the pre-eminent qualification for teachers, especially for elementary school teachers. In our sample, this theme occurred at all grade levels, although predominantly at the primary grades. In many of these stories the teachers are surprised and amused at their students' perceptions.

Any professional comedian would envy the effective punch lines that emerge from the children's unique perceptions. After a lesson on discriminating fiction from non-fiction books a student says, 'Hey, give me one of those *fake* books you were talking about' (p. 4). During a lesson in sixth grade, a teacher describes pubic hair as 'hair down below' and the student who asked for clarification exclaims, 'You mean I'm going to grow hair on my feet?' (p. 9A). During a lesson on fractions, the students were encouraged to cut their cookies and when asked what fractional parts they had now, one exuberant youngster responded seriously, 'Crumbs!' (p. 23A).

Other instances provoke thought rather than laughter. In one episode an underprivileged child in a matted fuzzy coat responds to her teacher's suggestion to button up her coat at recess with the retort, 'Oh, Mrs B. a girl is never cold in fur!' (p. 12A).

The most beautiful example of student perspective was evoked when a teacher declined to answer the question, 'Why are we here and who made us?' because she felt it was a religious question. However, another student said, 'Don't worry, Mrs C., I'll take care of this one', and proceeded with his rendition of creation.

Well, it was like this. One day God was sitting around doing nothing so he decided that he wanted to colour. So he got the biggest paper he could find . . . and the biggest box of crayons he could find. . . . When he was all finished, he looked over the paper and really liked it. He decided that he would just make it real. You see, it's simple and that's why we are here (p. 36A).

At the junior high level, students' perspectives are still amusing and informative. One teacher, who was rather cautious around birds, had a bird fly into the classroom one day. While waiting uncomfortably for the custodian to come to the classroom, the students observed her distress and the principal stopping by to laugh at the situation. One student studying English as a second language said, 'Miss L., one bird come in, you call the principal. Two birds come in, you call 911' (p. 35B).

A high school student who was deficient in verbal concepts went jogging with her teacher after school. When she saw a beautiful swan on the track 'she became very excited, pointed a finger and said, "I love those Gloria Vanderbilt's!"' and then 'was very embarrassed when she heard herself identifying it based on an insignia she had seen on a pair of jeans' (p. 3B). So we see that student perspective is an issue from kindergarten through high school.

Witnessing the progress of individual students (SSS) as described in 5 per cent of the stories is a source of pleasure and pride for teachers (Lightfoot, 1983), but their surprise also reflects the uncertainty of their profession (Jackson, 1986; Lortie, 1975). One has the sense that they are sharing their amazement more than their accomplishment. In fact, the unexpectedness was probably the reason for the selection of the story for sharing (Chafe, 1990). Teachers may be surprised by obvious success because in their work the outcomes are often amorphous (Lightfoot, 1983).

One teacher of English at the junior high level described the sequence in teaching writing to learning disabled students. One challenging student insisted that she did not need to learn to write and had a repertoire of excuses with which to stymy her teacher's efforts.

As the year progressed, the student began to feel more comfortable with writing. She had become one of the most descriptive writers I had ever come across (p. 44).

An art teacher persisted for weeks to counter a student's discouragement with a papier mâché project. The student would dispose of it quietly and then just sit idly. Every time the student threw it out, the teacher retrieved it and calmly showed him how it could be salvaged. As the figure is thrown out and retrieved for four weeks in a row, the story builds to a climax of exasperation that never comes.

So he proceeded to work on it and then he kept calling me over when he was having some difficulty. And at that point in time I saw that he was asking more questions of how to complete this project and started to be happy with his work (p. 38I).

Other success stories described long-awaited breakthroughs and unexpected progress. One story involved a student selecting and attempting to read a book from the library for the first time. Another involved a second grader who was convinced that he could not and would not read and write. With much encouragement he finally produced a phonetically spelled story of a few lines.

When I had the opportunity to call him up to my desk to show him his story I read it back to him and his face was so *surprised* that I could

Table 9.1: Intercorrelations Among Variables

	1	2	3	4	5	6	7	8	9	10	11
1 THEME	1.00	0.14	0.02	0.13	−0.02	−0.07	0.25	−0.11	0.00	−0.04	−0.17
2 SEX			0.11	0.07	−0.04	−0.12	−0.17	0.19	−0.24	−0.41	0.18
3 ELEM				−0.46	−0.29	0.11	0.37	−0.02	0.03	−0.35	−0.28
4 JRHI					0.05	−0.14	−0.17	−0.01	−0.02	−0.03	0.20
5 ED						0.54	−0.33	0.34	0.05	0.31	−0.05
6 EXPER							−0.25	0.41	0.00	0.15	−0.15
7 CLAS								−0.48	−0.08	−0.13	−0.60
8 HUM									−0.04	−0.08	−0.35
9 GYM										−0.01	−0.05
10 SCI											−0.10
11 SPED											1.00

ELEM : Elementary
HUM   : Humanities
SPED : Special Education
JRHI : Junior High
ED   : Educational attainment
EXPER : Professional Experience
CLAS : Classroom Teacher
GYM   : Gymnastics
SCI   : Science

actually *read* his story and the light went on in his eyes. He had made the leap. He understood finally, that he could do work in a way that could be transferred to another person. He understood what it meant to be a writer and a reader (p. 26).

These victorious moments are memorable and motivating to teachers. Their belief in the possibility of these breakthroughs is an incentive that sustains them (Tifft, 1988).

Statistical Analysis

A discriminant function analysis was conducted using SPSSX to determine if the themes of the stories could be predicted by any combination of the demographic data provided by the participants.

The information about the respondents that was utilised as predictor variables included: gender, level at which they taught, the subject that was their specialty, educational attainment and professional experience. Some specialties were combined. Language and art were subsumed under the label of the humanities, while speech therapy, remedial reading, and teaching the gifted were grouped with special education. Since the information about specialty was nominal, it was dummy coded. This resulted in a total of ten predictor variables. It was confirmed that the predictors are independent since many of them have low correlations. The moderate correlations (0.31–0.54) are compatible with a multivariate analysis (Stevens, 1986). The intercorrelations among the variables are listed in Table 9.1.

Table 9.2: Accuracy of Predicted Groups

Group (Theme)	No.of Cases in Group	No. Correctly Predicted	% Correctly Predicted
0	14	4	28.6
1	5	1	20.0
2	6	2	33.3
3	11	3	27.3
4	23	4	17.4
5	12	1	8.3
6	17	5	29.4
7	51	25	49.0
8	7	1	14.3

Overall Accuracy = 31.51%

Table 9.3: Correlations of Variables With Functions

Variables	Function 1
SEX	0.387
CLAS	0.321
JRHI	0.235
SCI	0.107
GYM	0.099
ELEM	0.047
EXPER	0.033
ED	−0.086
SPED	−0.147
HUM	−0.267

Findings

The accuracy with which the categories or themes were predicted was 31.51 per cent overall. The per cent of the cases that were accurately predicted in each category is shown in Table 9.2.

Since there were nine categories, there were eight possible discriminant functions. The first function was significant at 0.01. The correlations in Table 9.3 reveal the relationship between the predictor variables and the significant discriminant function. The variable that was most closely aligned (0.387) with the first function was gender. Being a classroom teacher has the next highest correlation (0.32).

Examination of the standardised canonical coefficients revealed that the variable that is not redundant is gender (1.09). When the information from the standardised canonical coefficients and the variable-function correlations are considered together, gender is the only consistency. This may be an artifact of the predominance of female classroom teachers at the elementary level in the sample.

Interpretation

Despite the fact that there was a significant function, the accuracy of prediction was low. In addition, the low correlations of the variables with the function discourage the meaningful association of some attributes of teachers with the themes of the stories (Stevens, 1986). Therefore, with this sample, the null hypothesis was confirmed. The low accuracy of prediction suggests that in this case the themes cannot be adequately predicted by the gender, level, specialty, experience, or educational attainment of the teacher. The inference could be made that the themes represent issues that are generic to teaching. Further research will need to be conducted to substantiate these suggestions with other samples and other variables.

Discussion

This analysis of teachers' stories has revealed recurrent themes. The themes were induced from their multiple manifestations in the narratives which contributes credibility to the findings. The themes were reiterated in other sources suggesting that the themes may represent a viable model of teaching.

These themes are also associated with excellence in teaching (Johnson, 1990; Roueche and Baker, 1986). Therefore, the themes not only represent features of the concept of teaching, but also what is valued in teaching. This is important because the concept of teaching cannot be dissociated from what is worthwhile in teaching (Hart, 1976). Since the themes could not be predicted with a high degree of accuracy from the characteristics of the teachers, they may represent the critical dimensions of teaching or its essence.

These stories have a pragmatic value since 'the powerful moment, the moving insight . . . is sometimes enough to create dynamic improvement in those who have access to it' (Schubert, 1990: 100). The function of the oral tradition is to transmute and transmit the culture that is its context (Olson, 1990).

The implication of the themes is that teachers are attuned to their students (RLA, STP, COM), want to make a difference in their students' lives (CIA, ANB), are eager for feedback (SSS, CIA), and are willing to think about their work for the purpose of self-development (REF, JOB). The challenge to educational institutions is to arrange for the organisation and administration of schools to supply and rely on what teachers value.

These stories offer potential stimulus material for thoughtfully considering the challenges and rewards of the profession (Coles, 1989). Exploring the profession in this way might be utilised for recruitment and retention of capable and committed teachers. Such stories might contribute to the burgeoning narrative tradition among teachers and the analytic apprenticeship that is recommended for achieving mastery of a practical craft (Tom, 1984). As one of the reader/judges said, 'I realised how much value this would have for anyone interested in teaching. . . . These stories are wonderful. . . . They really had something important to say.'

References

AYERS, W. (1986) 'Thinking about teachers and the curriculum', *Harvard Educational Review*, **56**(1), pp. 49–51.

BARTHES, R. (1985) *Mythologies*, New York: Hill and Wang.

BOOTH, W.C. (1988) 'A teacher's journal, 1972–1988', in BOOTH, W.C. *The vocation of a teacher*, Chicago: The University of Chicago Press, pp. 219–276.

BRITTON, B.K. and PELLEGRINI, A.D. (Eds) (1990) *Narrative thought and narrative language*, Hillsdale, New Jersey: Lawrence Erlbaum Associates, Inc.

BRITZMAN, D.P. (1986) 'Cultural myths in the making of a teacher: Biography and social interaction in teacher education', *Harvard Educational Review*, **56**(4), pp. 442–72.

BRUNER, J. (1986) *Actual minds, possible worlds*, Cambridge, Massachusetts: Harvard University Press.

BRUNER, J. (1987) 'Life as narrative', *Social Research*, **54**(1), pp. 11–32.

CAMPBELL, J. (1972) *Myths to live by*, New York: Viking Press.

CHAFE, W. (1990) 'Some things that narratives tell us about the mind', in BRITTON, B.K. and PELLEGRINI, A.D. (Eds) *Narrative thought and narrative language*, Hillsdale, New Jersey: Lawrence Erlbaum Associates, Publishers, pp. 79–98.

COCHRAN-SMITH, M. and LYTLE, S.L. (1990) 'Research on teaching and teacher research: the issues that divide', *Educational Researcher*, **19**(2), pp. 2–11.

COLES, R. (1971, Oct.) 'On the meaning of work', *Atlantic Monthly*, pp. 104–5.

— (1989) *The call of stories: Teaching and the moral imagination*, Boston: Houghton Mifflin Company.

CONNELLY, F.M. and CLANDININ, D.J. (1990) 'Stories of experience and narrative inquiry', *Educational Researcher*, **19**(5), pp. 2–14.

CSIKSZENTMIHALYI, M. and McCORMACK, J. (1986) 'The influence of teachers', *Phi Delta Kappan*, **67**(6), pp. 415–19.

DAY, C., POPE, M. and DENICOLO, P. (Eds) (1990) *Insights into teachers' thinking and practice*, London: The Falmer Press.

FLODEN, R.E. and KLINZING, H.G. (1990) 'What can research on teacher thinking contribute to teacher preparation? A second opinion', *Educational Researcher*, **19**(4), pp. 15–20.

FREUD, S. (1980) 'The passion and challenge of teaching', *Harvard Educational Review*, **50**(1), pp. 1–12.

GARDNER, J. (1983) 'The art of fiction', *Notes on craft for young writers*, New York: Alfred A. Knopf.

GREENE, M. (1986) 'In search of critical pedagogy', *Harvard Educational Review*, **56**(4), pp. 427–41.

HART, W.A. (1976) 'Is teaching what the philosopher understands by it?' *British Journal of Educational Studies*, **24**(2), pp. 155–70.

HECK, S.F. and WILLIAMS, C.R. (1984) *The complex roles of the teacher: An ecological perspective*, New York: Teachers College Press.

HIGHET, G. (1976) *The immortal profession: The joys of teaching and learning*, New York: Weybright and Talley.

JACKSON, P.W. (1986) *The practice of teaching*, New York: Teachers College Press.

JOHNSON, S.M. (1986) 'Incentives for teachers: what motivates, what matters', *Educational Administration Quarterly*, **22**(3), pp. 54–79.

JOHNSON, S.M. (1990) *Teachers at work: Achieving success in our schools*, New York: Basic Books, Inc.

KOERNER, M. (1990) 'Teachers' images: Their work and themselves', *Kappa Delta Pi Record*, **26**(4), pp. 111–15.

LEINHARDT, G. (1990) 'Capturing craft knowledge in teaching', *Educational Researcher*, **19**(2), pp. 18–25.

LIGHTFOOT, S.L. (1983) 'The lives of teachers', in SHULMAN, L.S. and SYKES, G. (Eds) *Handbook of teaching and policy*, New York: Longman, pp. 241–60.

LORTIE, D.C. (1973) 'Observations of teaching as work', in TRAVERS, R.M.W. (Ed.) *Second Handbook of Research on Teaching*, Chicago: Rand McNally and Company, pp. 474–97.

— (1975) *Schoolteacher: a sociological study*, Chicago: The University of Chicago Press.

MILLER, G.A. (1956) 'The magical number seven, plus or minus two: Some limits on our capacity for processing information', *Psychological Review*, **63**, pp. 81–97.

MILLIES, P.S. (1990) 'Aspects of the mental lives of teachers', *Kappa Delta Pi Record*, **26**(4), pp. 111–15.

NATIONAL BOARD FOR PROFESSIONAL TEACHING STANDARDS (1990) *Towards high and rigorous standards for the teaching profession*, Detroit, Michigan: Author.

PATTON, M.Q. (1980) *Qualitative evaluation methods*, Beverly Hills: Sage Publications.

ROSS, P.C. and HOUTZ, J.C. (1979) 'Students' ratings of satisfaction with industrial training predicted from instructors' leadership style and trainees' personality characteristics', *Psychological Reports*, **45**, pp. 63–73.

ROUECHE, J.E. and BAKER, G.A. (1986) *Profiling excellence in American's schools*, Arlington, Virginia: American Association of School Administrators.

SCHUBERT, W.H. (1989) 'Teacher lore: A neglected basis for understanding curriculum and supervision', *Journal of Curriculum and Supervision*, **4**(3), pp. 282–5.

— (1990) 'Acknowledging teachers' experiential knowledge: Reports from the teacher lore project', *Kappa Delta Pi Record*, **26**(4), pp. 99–100.

— (1991) 'Teacher lore: a basis for understanding praxis', in WITHERALL, C. and NODDINGS, N. (Eds) *The stories lives tell: Narrative and dialogue in educational research and practice*, New York: Teachers College Press.

STEVENS, J. (1986) *Applied multivariate statistics for the social sciences*, Hillsdale, New Jersey: Lawrence Erlbaum Associates, Publishers.

TIFFT, S. (1988, November) 'Who's teaching our children', *Time*, pp. 58–64.

— (1990, July) 'Crusaders in the classroom', *Time*, p. 66.

TOM, A.R. (1984) *Teaching as a moral craft*, New York: Longman.

WARREN, D. (Ed.) (1989) *American teachers: Histories of a Profession at Work*, Washington, D.C.: American Education Research Association.

YOLEN, J. (Ed.) (1986) *Favorite folktales from around the world*, New York: Pantheon Books.

Chapter 10

Construing Teachers' Personal Development: Reflections on Landmark Events Through Career Mapping

Michael Kompf

Views of development depend on domains of interest and epistemological orientation. Paradigm shifts evident in the central structures of science and society indicate renewed permeability in research applications. Studies of development are particularly in want of novel approaches when considered from a constructivist perspective. Kelly's (1955) assumptions of individuals' abilities to represent reality are used to adopt a bottom-up view of personal development. A technique of career mapping was devised to assist examination of long-term teacher reflection and anticipation. Thirty teachers recalled past events and projected future events (positive or negative) deemed to be 'landmark events' which were labelled, briefly described and considered for impact. A self-characterisation sketch was produced through synthesis of event narratives. Nearly all participants expressed surprise, new perspective and feelings of resolution and clarification of relations between self, important others and practice. Providing context for events brought out submerged constructs and patterns found by participants produced insights into constructs. Mapping produced visual representations of life and career and used Kelly's (1955) view of events over the span of life as opposed to the flicker of passing moments. Narrative enquiry and constructivist methods and assumptions are useful for nomothetic and idiographic approaches and may lead to productive research on the long-term effects of development on teachers actions.

Developing Knowledge

Developmental issues are evident in most disciplines and are dependent on the assumptions made about topics under study. Epistemological orientation (e.g., logical positivism, hermeneutics, critical theory[1]) determines the boundaries of inquiry and the structural, functional and valuational styles by which scientific thought and communication are characterised. While epistemological choice and investment provide clear paths to follow, any orientation, if mutually exclusive

from another, carries the disadvantage of narrowing ranges of conceptual conven-
ience and lessening permeability in personal, social and theoretical constructions
of knowledge (and produces what Kelly might have intended to convey as 'hardening of the categories').

Theories accounting for personal development are mainly grounded in psychology which, in its formative years, gained respectability as a science through
the adoption of rigorous procedural standards from the 'harder' sciences. As mainstream scientific paradigms began to shift and re-form,[2] resistance gave way to
permeability and the worlds of Galileo, Newton and Descartes surrendered to
those of Einstein, quantum mechanics and an emergent community of new age
scientists. Paradigmatic shifts in disciplines practising science are evident following the Industrial Revolution and during the late-nineteenth century. The
emerging field of psychology responded with its own paradigm shift through the
advance of Freud and the acknowledgement of the unconscious. Education was
led by John Dewey[3] and others who, through progressivism, challenged the
dominant traditionalist views of education. While the *zeitgeist* may have been right
for change, entrenchment of epistemological positions was often the response to
attempted change in practice or refutation of theory. Fragmentation, it appears,
was the corollary and legacy of the emergent twentieth century scientist.[4] Out of
such turmoil the basis for developmental considerations in many areas of scientific
investigation can be seen as, at least a research variable, at most a subsystem
within a larger framework. However, the central assumptions regarding the nature
of human interaction with perceived reality have remained largely unchanged over
time.

Developmental perspectives may be considered in three gross categories:
physical, cognitive and affective. Physical development is inexorable and measurable as any actuarial table demonstrates. Cognitive development is well accounted
for up to pubescence. Of main interest in this study were the more affective
modes of development, historically characterised by an eclectic series of movements
with various polarised epistemological leanings. Combined approaches mainly in
use since the mid-1970s have lessened some of the tension between quantitative
and qualitative methodologists and allowed more holistic views of persons to
surface with new potential for theoretical integration.

It is likely that emergent twenty-first century scientists are in the midst of a
new round of paradigmatic transition. Montgomery (1991) described an epistemological panic occurring throughout various theoretical and theological domains
as regards: the accuracy of attributing the four gospels to Jesus Christ; allegations
of concocted foundations in Freudian psychoanalysis; and the refutation of Einstein's central propositions. While excommunication and litigation are no longer
likely results of theological or theoretical deviation, vacuums have been created in
the central concepts of meaning and may serve to loosen the anchors by which
personal and professional scientists anticipate their lives. In other examples, de-
mocratisation has (in)validated countless politically and socially constructed belief
systems during recent years. Technological advances in communications and
information services illustrate both a symptom and a cause of paradigmatic and
epistemological transition. Epistemological permeability is increasingly evident in
environmental and natural sciences, psychology, education, medicine and many
other venues as a renewal of holistic perspectives of persons has accelerated the
growth and scope of lifespan and developmental theories.

Constructivism and Developmental Theories

From a constructivist perspective, personal state-trait and cognitive developmental theories can be considered as objective-diagnostic[5] theories. Such theories project and infer individual attributes largely by virtue of demographic or other generalisable characteristics. As objective-diagnostic types of tests (e.g., Intelligence Quotient (IQ)) elicit data from subjects within a predetermined response set to establish generalisable sets of parameters, much in the affective and cognitive domains is left untouched. Such approaches, while useful for making general assumptions and inferences about the statistical majority of persons tend to be approaches wherein process is inferred from content.

While the stance of person-as-scientist as advocated by Kelly (1955) endows individuals with representational and meaning-making abilities, such allowances outside of the constructivist domain are tempered by deference to positions held in the formal sciences. In practice, models are proposed to assist understanding for individuals or groups and become templets through which confirmation, extension or refutation of the model is sought. While such an approach may be 'good science' or even 'good theory', underlying assumptions about whether or not persons are knowable exposes several drawbacks accountable to paradigmatic and epistemological roots. An example of such a drawback is the Procrustean tendency inherent in generalisation which is convenient and useful for researchers and theorists and may be misleading and self-fulfilling for consumers of theory and research. Considered with the dated nature of much theory when overlaid with social progress, the professions in concert with the general public are left searching for stable anchors from which to venture into poorly explored psychical regions.

From a constructivist perspective, an anchor metaphor may be applied in several useful ways: sets of core or central constructions remain relatively stable throughout life; continual testing and revision of constructs and resultant understandings enhance the organisation, adaptiveness and therefore success of anticipations; and reflective processes ground construing 'in the perspective of the centuries rather than in the flicker of passing moments' (Kelly, 1969: 3). Constructive developmentalism attends to integration of the processes of personal construing (in addition to professional and social) rather than attending to the products (i.e., construct labels) as these are evaluated by the construer. Kelly's (1955) central assumption of constructive alternativism represents the essence of articulated choice in that acknowledgement of alternatives necessitates meaningful integration of constructs. The task of the developmental personal scientist thus becomes that of examining events in an historical context; establishing relevant construct pathways; analyzing interactions for operational or symbolic systems; and choosing among alternatives for the greater opportunity of system extension.[6] As may be understood from Kelly's (1955) corollaries, individual constructions: unite (sociality, commonality) and differentiate (individuality); extend (choice, modulation, experience) and limit (dichotomy, range); clarify (construction, organisation) and confuse (fragmentation) attempts at making sense and meaning out of lives and experiences.[7]

Individuals' inner lives are based on available perceptual resources and can only be construed as events are experienced. While infants and young children develop through experiences of acculturation, shaping, superego development, social reproduction, cultural production, novice and older adults experience more varied and sophisticated versions of the aforementioned processes. The increased availability of perceptual resources through the concomitant expansion of individual construct repertoires indicates perceptual, if not cognitive, complexity as an artifact of ageing. In addition, continual attempts at redefinition of self through construct activity supports developmental processes. Forging of new, event-dependent, construct pathways thus enhances organisational and adaptive processes for individuals navigating life passage.

The task of navigating life passage may be metaphorically viewed as using a destination-specific map. The macro view of how construct system interaction may be illustrated is by considering the differences in perspective obtained by superimposing a street map of Guildford, Surrey, UK, over the top of a world map. The world map represents the finite number of constructs which are the totality of perceptual and constructive resources. The local map represents that which is summoned forth to construe or anticipate a single event. The ability to zoom in expediently to a micro-perspective for a given construction may be considered as a form of constructivist prowess which enhances opportunities for speedy testing and revision of constructs. The macro view of an individual's construct system may be achieved through a process of life review during and in which an audit for consistency and efficacy is carried out on useful and not-so-useful constructs and construct systems (Kelly never did discuss what happens to abandoned constructions).

Life review is normally associated with crises, latter age/phase/cycle[8] aspects of development, or as a function of some psychotherapeutic process. It appears that some sense of serenity, perspective and resolution may be established by undertaking such reviews. As the latter stages of life are times of establishing a favourable ratio between integrity and despair, social and professional withdrawal or redirection has created opportunities for review. Redefinition of the latter stages and the likelihood of life review experiences indicates that older persons tell stories to bring about closure and resolution and because their life reviews are rendered more meaningful when exposed through verbalisation for scrutiny by self and others (Kompf, 1991).

It is a purpose of this discussion and research to explore the process and effects of reviewing landmark life events as experienced by a group of teachers. Self theories which might arise through construct system review are used to examine efficacy of developmental perspectives which might be applied to accrued life histories and professional trajectories. While this study was carried out on a group of teachers, the implications are likely to extend beyond teachers' personal development to a consideration of the broader perceptions persons have of their own development.

The Study

As part of a graduate level course[9] titled 'Lifespan Development and the Educative Process' thirty teachers[10] agreed to devise life-event impact maps by identifying and rating the significance of events deemed by them to be landmark events (i.e., important and significant occurrences which had residual effects on experienced or projected life trajectory).

From preliminary studies several issues were chosen as most important:

(1) landmark events must be identified by name/label; (2) events must be considered against a temporal framework relative to the age and experience of the participant; (3) a level of event impact (positive or negative) must be assessed; and (4) explanation of events and how perceptions of them were formed was necessary. A format was devised to facilitate comparisons between and among participants (see Figure 10.1).

The following instructions were given to participants:

1   At the left hand bottom of the life/event impact map enter the year of secondary school completion and continue across the grid in five-year intervals continuing past the present year.
2   On separate sheets develop lists of landmark: a) personal events; and b) professional events which have occurred throughout your life.
3   Consider each event as you now view its contribution to your life development and assign an impact value (negative or positive on a scale of −10 through 0 to +10) to the event.
4   Mark personal events in the appropriate cell. 4.a. Repeat step (4) with professional events.
5   Using a solid line connect impact rating markers for personal events across the grid; using a broken line connect impact ratings for professional events.
6   Project beyond the present year and speculate as to events (and their likely impact) you anticipate happening in your personal and professional life as far ahead as you are able (up to and past retirement if possible).
7   Using narrative format characterise yourself by describing and synthesising the events of each year and explain the impact value assigned to those events.

The requirements and format of the tasks were understood and able to be completed by all participants during a four-week period provided to complete maps and event narratives. It was agreed that anonymity would be preserved by only discussing the most general issues about submissions and that maps would not be shared or offered for comments between and among fellow participants.

Findings

In addition to the constructivist support for this research approach, the spirit of an understanding methodology was also included. The notion of understanding is based on Weber's concept of *verstehen* which Giddens (1976) discussed as a documentary method presupposing patterns derived from individual evidence, which is in turn interpreted on the basis of what is known about the underlying pattern, allowing each to elaborate the other. In the case of stimulated life review, a simple framework is provided for focus, structure and direction. Landmark events were: those deemed to be important by the participant; comprised of the participant's memory traces; endowed with meaning which is developed through the accumulation of subsequent experiences; and, self-elicited representations as currently construed.

The first level of analysis consisted of an examination of the type of events which were designated as landmark events. Some examples of items included

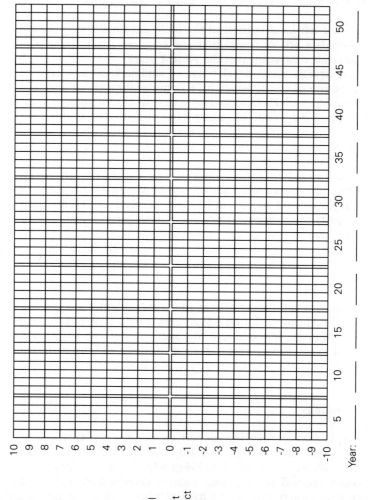

Figure 10.1:   Life/event impact map (actual map format is full page)

were: graduation from secondary school; first full-time job; acceptance into university; marriage; birth of children; promotion and/or change of employment or position; illness/death of a parent; purchase of home; separation and/or divorce; children attending school; second honeymoons; summer vacations; illness/death of child or spouse; major illnesses or accidents; turning 30, 40, or 50 years of age; beginning graduate education. Projected events included: purchasing newer/larger homes; investment opportunities; retirement; children leaving home; academic success; increased earnings.

The second level of analysis and of special interest were reaction comments regarding the juxtaposing of personal and professional events and the experience of bringing together meaningful events. Participants spoke metaphorically of the experience using such descriptions as 'an autobiography, a self-portrait, a "This is your life" experience' and the like. Most indicated that while certain events and/ or ages of their lives were subjected to periodic superficial review, such experiences were likely to be situation-specific and relate to an issue at hand. This is entirely consistent with several of Kelly's (1955) corollaries (e.g., construction, organisation, choice, experience) which govern the use of personal constructions. In this way an event may be treated as a larger construction which summarises and connects specific sets of constructs as may have been in use during the actual event. Moreover, developmental processes which occur naturally through ageing and the inevitable increase in construct repertoires provide advantages in retrospective, introspective analyses which diminish negative side-effects of memory dynamics. In other words, a process of meaning-making occurs by recapturing a series of events able to portray individual development as anchored by significant events.

The task was viewed in a number of ways and indicated a polarised reaction. Five of the thirty participants reported that during the period of time taken to complete mapping and interpretation, they had procrastinated, experienced nostalgia-induced mood swings and fought the concretising (i.e., writing down) of reflections. Among the remaining participants one expressed a process of 'near reverential awe while travelling down the halls of memory', others described amused embarrassment, mixtures of joy and sorrow and what appeared to be kinder, more gentle attributions to the self and others of past experiences. Major themes throughout submissions included summary catharsis and professional renewal. The highly personal and idiosyncratic character of each submission was evident in the passion with which the narratives were written. The benefits of the personal narrative which have been determined, while situation or event specific, are meaningful, important and centrally representative of an individual's perceived reality. In a summary sense, those events which are used to account for who the teachers were, why they had become that way and what the implications of responses to such questions had for anticipation of future events created the interest in participation.

Discussion

Articulation and analysis of personal theories of self-development were novel experiences for all participants. Reflections which clearly corresponded to examination of personal and professional paradigms included evidence of belief and epistemological systems. Changes and/or transitions were noted over periods of time which had been obscured at the occurrence of the event and new meanings were interpreted. Some found that the creation of distance between self and experienced events allowed multiple perspectives upon which the self could be reflected. At the end of the course of study one respondent commented:

> I have held a view of theory that is best explained by imagining myself in a house with many windows. Through each window a psychologist from a different orientation peers in; each has a different view of who and what I am and what I am up to. What their understandings of me amount to is only visible by how they assess problems or dysfunctions I might have; I might never know their opinion, just their categories. When I account for my history and what it has meant to me and meant in my life, the windows turn into mirrors and I am able to stand in front of each and see how I am understood from that perspective. While I do not agree with how I am portrayed by some of these views, the scope provided for projecting who I might be out of who and what I have become and how I got here is enriching and fulfilling.

Another teacher commented that she had resisted the whole experience vehemently and procrastinated at every turn. When she was eventually able to 'confine' her life to paper, she did so amidst feelings of anxiety and relieving old pains. After completion and return of her paper she said that she had burned it page by page. Upon completion of this 'ritual' she stated that a great sense of relief came over her and she felt like a 'Phoenix rising from the ashes'. Future research will deal with processes of debriefing which will address ethical issues and the therapy-like aspects of this type of research. Examples of post-mapping reflections conveyed a mixture of drama and passion sufficient to assume that the experience had a profound impact on most, if not all, participants. The gaining of additional self and life perspective assisted construction of a perceptual 'You are here!' sign according to one teacher.

Life experiences were viewed from three perspectives. First, a structural perspective of events (How is the event represented?) was assisted through the mapping exercise producing a visual representation of the event and its impact in the participants life. Second, a functional perspective of the event (What happened?) was facilitated by assigning a retrospective impact rating to the event so its contribution to present constructions of self might be assessed. Third, a valuational interpretation of the event (What impact and why?) was assisted through narrative interpretation.

Juxtaposing perspectives with the intent of making sense of an event is essentially a symbolic interactionist approach which questions the event for meaning (What meanings can be made?). Extraction of meaning involves choosing how new perspective might be incorporated into advantageous extension of individual construing. Asking 'What next?' is a way of operationalising constructive alternativism (see Figure 10.2). Constructive alternativism can thus be seen as a logical ending and/or beginning to an examination of events and or personal constructions.

Establishing new perspectives of the larger issues which had been thought to control individual lives (e.g., epistemologies, paradigms, theories, etc.) brought

Figure 10.2: *Pathways of personal theorising*

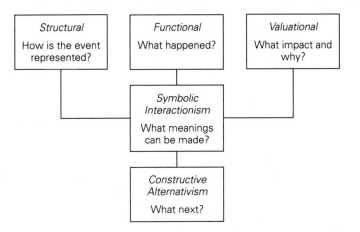

about a sense of personal empowerment. A reversal effect was achieved as the traditional view of persons (i.e., top-down as theory and philosophy dictate) gave way to a bottom-up view wherein individual perceptions and accounts of life passage were used as a window on the internal and external worlds of the present. Kelly's metaphor of person-as-scientist might well be extended to include the view of person-as-navigator in that, while scientist-like behaviour assists persons to gather and assess information for representation of personal constructions, choices among alternatives must be based on more than the 'flicker of passing moments' (Kelly, 1969: 3). The person-as-navigator constructs contextual, interactive maps which assist him or her to find his or her own way among constructed points of reference. Landmark events considered as representations of meaningful past experiences may also provide a way of, not changing personal history, but rather changing the way personal history is construed by focusing on the context its recollection provides which might contribute to successful anticipations of future events. Notions of paradigmatic shift and epistemological permeability as discussed in the beginning of this paper are precursors to scientific, social and personal transition. While such changes occur over generations, they are inexorable. The hallmark of change may not be the posing of new questions in new ways, but rather exploring more fully and rearranging the answers to past questions.[11]

Notes

1 See BREDO, E. and FEINBERG, W. (1982) *Knowledge and values in social and educational research*, Philadelphia: Temple University Press.
2 See KUHN, T.S. (1970) *The structure of scientific revolutions*, Chicago: The University of Chicago Press.
3 See BERNSTEIN, R.J. (1966) *John Dewey*, Atasacadero, California: Ridgeview Publishing Co.

4 'Fragmentation corollary: A person may successively employ a variety of construction subsystems which are inferentially incompatible with each other' (Kelly, 1969: 83).
5 See Kelly (1964) for an explanation of what he called 'the treatment-depends-on-objective-diagnosis stupidity' (p. 361).
6 Choice corollary: 'A person chooses for himself that alternative in a dichotomized construct through which he anticipates the greater possibility for extension and definition of his system' (Kelly, 1969: 64).
7 See KELLY, G.A. (1969) *A theory of personality: the psychology of personal constructs*, Chicago: W.W. Norton and Co., pp. 46–104.
8 See EVANS, R.J. (1967) *Dialogue with Erik Erikson*, New York: Harper and Row.
9 Offered in the Master of Education Program, Faculty of Education, Graduate Department, Brock University, Canada.
10 In spite of Leinhardt's (1990) comment that ISATT, representing teacher belief literature, had experienced an 'unfortunate turn of events . . . and . . . has accepted, somewhat anti-intellectually and mystically, self-realisation and all beliefs as equally wonderful manifestations of the deep inner knowledge of teachers' (p. 25), ordinary teachers were chosen for this study because of their deep inner knowledge which is wondrously manifested through self-realisation and examination of beliefs and for other anti-intellectual and mystical reasons.
11 Interesting approaches to these issues are presented by: WILBER, K. (Ed.) (1982) *The holographic paradigm and other paradoxes*, Boulder, Colorado: Shambhala Publications Inc. and SCHWARTZ, P. and OGILVY, J. (1980, June) *The emergent paradigm: towards an aesthetics of life*, paper presented at ESOMAR, Barcelona, Spain (available through SRI International, Menlo Park, California, 94825).

References

GIDDENS, A. (1976) *New rules of the sociological method: a positive critique of interpretive sociologies*, New York: Basic Books.
KELLY, G.A. (1955) *The psychology of personal constructs*, **Vols. 1 and 2**, Chicago: W.W. Norton and Co.
— (1964) 'Man's construction of his alternatives', in SOUTHWELL, E.A. and MERBAUM, M. (Eds) *Personality readings in theory and research*, Third Edition, Monterey, California: Brooks/Cole Publishing Co.
— (1969) *A theory of personality: the psychology of personal constructs*, Chicago: W.W. Norton and Co.
KOMPF, M. (1991) 'Reflected educational thought and action: construing retired teachers', *Teaching and Teacher Education*, **7**(5/6), pp. 479–90.
LEINHARDT, G. (1990) 'Capturing craft knowledge in teaching', *Educational Researcher*, **19**(2), pp. 18–25.
MONTGOMERY, D. (1991, April 7) 'Tough times at the top', *The Buffalo News*, Buffalo, New York, pp. F1, F2.

Chapter 11

The Identification, Development and Sharing of Professional Craft Knowledge

Margaret Batten

Teachers have few opportunities to stand back from the hectic demands of the classroom and to reflect on their practice in a sustained and systematic manner. The potential value of such considered and critical reflection to both practitioners and researchers in education has been underrated, but some recent studies of the identification and utilisation of professional craft knowledge have sought to remedy this neglect (Schön, 1983; Boylan et al., 1988; Brown and McIntyre, 1989).

A study of teachers' professional craft knowledge was undertaken in Australia (Batten, 1990) using a model developed by Brown and McIntyre in Britain.

Brown and McIntyre (1989: 5) define 'craft knowledge' as:

that part of their professional knowledge which teachers acquire primarily through their practical experience in the classroom rather than their formal training, which guides their day-to-day actions in classrooms, which is for the most part not articulated in words and which is brought to bear spontaneously, routinely and sometimes unconsciously on their teaching.

The Australian study was undertaken with twelve teachers of Year 9 classes in two secondary schools; there were four teachers in each of the three curriculum areas: humanities, science/mathematics, and practical subjects. To select the teachers, a survey was undertaken of all pupils in Years 9 and 10 in the two schools; they were asked to identify their best teachers, and to list the qualities that made them good teachers. Pupils were used for this task rather than principals or the teaching staff, because teachers are rarely observed for a sustained period by other teachers whereas the students, who are their clients, receive constant exposure to their professional practice. How these teachers would compare with 'good teachers' in other schools was not an issue for this study — these twelve people were acknowledged as good teachers in their schools, and it was in their schools that their reflections on successful teaching were to be used in the final stage of the study, a school-based professional development exercise.

Each of the twelve teachers was to be observed for three lessons (the number was reduced to eleven when one teacher left the school); after each lesson, the teacher was asked to talk about the positive aspects of his or her teaching in those lessons. Each lesson and follow-up interview was recorded and later transcribed. The interviews were relatively unstructured; the teachers were encouraged to reflect on and talk about the positive aspects of the lessons (which was, in effect, the application of their craft knowledge in the classroom). It was seen as important for the study that the basis for the articulation of a teacher's craft knowledge should be established by the teacher, not imposed by the researcher.

Analysis of the Interview Data

The teachers' comments contained in the transcripts could be said to comprise an articulation of craft knowledge in practice — not, of course, the complete craft knowledge repertoire of the teacher, but a slice of it. From these 'slices' it was planned to construct a pedagogical profile for each teacher. While this 'pedagogical profile' would reflect only a part of the teacher's craft knowledge, and might not even represent fully all the things a teacher was thinking and doing in those particular lessons, it was felt that it would give some indication of how and why the teachers operated as they did in the classroom.

The Construction of Pedagogical Profiles

For each of the eleven teachers, all the positive aspects of the lessons mentioned by the teacher were extracted from the three relevant transcripts, using the teacher's own words. Nearly always these statements were accompanied by supporting comments from the teacher which gave reasons why the given instances of teaching were successful, or described the ways in which success was achieved. The positive aspects of the lesson were called the *criteria for successful teaching*. Alongside these criteria were put the teacher's elaborations of the ways in which these positive aspects were exemplified in the lesson — called *associated strategies or reasons*. This framework could be more simply described as '*what*' (the positive aspects of the lesson, the criteria for successful teaching) allied to '*how*' and '*why*' (the associated strategies and reasons).

In order to give some coherence to the array of comments from each teacher, the positive aspects which seemed to have a similar orientation were clustered together within each profile. The profiles were discussed with the teachers who made some minor alterations, provided a label for each cluster, and confirmed that these were frequently occurring elements in their teaching practice. Figure 11.1 is an extract of two of the seven clusters of comments built up from the three lessons and interviews with Teacher A. The comments in the left hand column of the first cluster indicate that one of the criteria for successful teaching established by Teacher A was the maintenance of quietness in the classroom. In the right hand column are listed her descriptions of relevant strategies she employed in achieving her aims, such as not talking over classroom noise, and giving extra work to a girl

Figure 11.1: Extract from pedagogical profile of Teacher A

Criteria for Successful Teaching	Associated Strategies or Reasons
1 Settle the kids down	
'I waited for everyone to be quiet'	'I think one of the things I was not willing to do was talk over anyone in class'
'starting from the beginning . . . I got quiet	'I waited . . . and by me mentioning that there was going to be a test coming up, they were even more wary about listening'
'they simmered down'	'I said I was going to give more work to people that were going to misbehave . . . I had to carry out what I said so I gave her an extra problem.'
'everything was quiet after that'	'I said to John "Stop looking round at David; that is why I separated you" . . . That worked quite well'
'they settled down and did their work'	'When I said "Everyone is working well except you three" . . . they got the message . . . they were aware of me being aware of them'
2 Getting the kids to participate in what you're saying or discussing	
'the kids co-operated, they were willing to discuss and answer questions'	I made the discussion short'
'they will listen in and be ready for the question'	'I gave them a lot of praise when they got the answer right . . . also when I said "Hands down, I will choose you", that does enliven kids, it wakes them up . . . they don't want to be made a fool of.'
'participation of the kids was quite good'	'kids were putting their hands up. I chose some kids that didn't have their hands up.'

who had been given a warning. Student participation is the theme of the second cluster of comments for Teacher A; she talks of obtaining cooperation by keeping the discussion short and by praising students.

Elements of Successful Teaching

The next stage of the analysis of interview and profile data was an examination of the pedagogical profiles of all the teachers to see if the statements they used to describe the elements of successful teaching in their lessons could be categorised in some way.

From the descriptors provided by the teachers for each cluster in their profiles, a classification of elements of successful teaching practice was developed. The three major groupings in the categorisation were concerned with 'teachers', 'students', and 'the classroom'. Figure 11.2 gives the details of this classification. All the elements described by the teachers could be accommodated in the subcategories under these three headings. The elements of successful teaching most

Figure 11.2: Elements of successful teaching

CLASSROOM	TEACHERS
Classroom management: planning, structure, organisation* setting and achievement of objectives	*Teacher characteristics:* helping/focusing on individual students* fostering student involvement/participation awareness of student needs
Classroom environment: relaxed, friendly, comfortable atmosphere* positive teacher-student relationship* social interactions, group dynamics	positive reinforcement, encouragement providing a variety of activities monitoring work making students think low-key approach, don't force the kids
Classroom control: discipline, order* settling students down	explanation to ensure understanding

STUDENTS
Student learning/affective outcomes:
sense of achievement, progress*
working well, trying hard*
interest, enjoyment, keenness*
independent learning, self-motivation
self-awareness, self-analysis
confidence
tolerance
sense of responsibility

*elements most frequently mentioned by teachers

frequently referred to by the teachers are indicated by an asterisk in Figure 11.2; each of these nine elements was mentioned by four or more teachers.

The elements of successful teaching identified by the eleven teachers were elements that were of continuing importance to them in their teaching at all year levels. Similar elements were found in the interview transcripts of the secondary teachers in the Scottish study (Batten, 1989), which gives some validity to the suggestion that these elements may have relevance to teaching practice in schools other than the two involved in the study.

Differences in Teacher Perspectives across Subject Areas

An examination of the individual pedagogical profiles of the eleven teachers showed a fairly even spread across the three groupings of the classification represented in Figure 11.2 (Classroom, Teachers, and Students), but when the teacher profiles from similar curriculum areas were considered separately, some variation was noted, particularly in relation to 'teaching strategies' and 'student outcomes'. More emphasis was placed by humanities and science/mathematics teachers on 'teaching strategies' than on any other category, while teachers of practical subjects placed the greatest weight on elements of their teaching connected with 'student outcomes'. The differences between teachers was most marked in this last category: student outcomes were mentioned on five occasions by humanities teachers as successful elements in their teaching, on four occasions by science/mathematics teachers, and on twenty-one occasions by teachers of practical subjects.

One possible explanation of this difference between teachers of practical subjects and other teachers might be found in the way that practical classes operate. The practical subjects taught by the four teachers in this study were broadly representative of that curriculum area: their subjects were ceramics, woodwork, electrical work practices and physical education. Teachers in these subjects, particularly the first three, probably devote less time than humanities and science/mathematics teachers to interactions concerning the teacher and the whole class; in practical subjects there is more one-to-one interaction between teacher and student. It is understandable, therefore, that teachers of practical subjects should focus more on student outcomes and less on teaching strategies.

Another explanation of this difference between teachers could lie in the views of teachers of practical subjects about themselves as teachers. During the interviews held after the observed lessons, two of the teachers made the following comments on their roles as teachers:

> I certainly don't class myself as a good teacher, mainly because I am in an area where the kids like to be . . . I think I do handle kids well, I have a very good rapport with kids, I win kids very easily, but it still doesn't make me a good teacher . . . I would class some of the teachers that make the kids work, homework and things like that and the kids hate them, I class some of them as really good teachers.

> I just feel that my lessons, they are so informal anyway. It is as if I am teaching. I don't feel like I am teaching.

Perhaps teachers of practical subjects see themselves as woodwork or ceramic experts more than as teachers, and therefore they focus on student outcomes rather than on teaching strategies when reflecting on their lessons; but most of the teaching strategies mentioned by other teachers were present also in the observed lessons of practical subject teachers. Such teacher activities as 'helping individual students', 'positive reinforcement', 'monitoring work', 'fostering student involvement' were all strategies that were noted by the researcher in lesson observations, and commented on by the students of these teachers when they were writing about examples of good teaching in their lessons.

Students' Views on Good Teaching

At the conclusion of the third observed lesson for each of the eleven teachers, the students in the class were asked to spend a few minutes writing down their impressions of the positive aspects of the lesson. The instruction at the top of the sheet of paper handed to each student said:

> Please write down one or two things which you think were best about [teacher's name]'s teaching in this lesson.

Comment classifications were constructed for individual teachers, in which similar comments were grouped together; the students' own words were then used to label the categories. The individual classifications were amalgamated to form an overall classification which covered all eleven teachers and their students. In all, there were 154 students who wrote sometimes one but mostly two or more positive comments about their teacher.

The following ten specimens summarise the most common matters commented on by students:

- explains so you understand, shows you how to do things;
- helps with our work;
- caring, relates to students, understands what we say;
- controls the class well, doesn't yell;
- makes the work interesting and enjoyable;
- can joke around, combines humour with learning;
- doesn't rush us or force us, can work in my own way;
- we learn a lot;
- knows what she or he is talking about;
- fair, straightforward.

It can be seen that these comment categories cover a broad range of aspects of the interaction that takes place between teacher and student in the classroom. Some of the comments are to do with classroom management (control) and teacher attitude (care, humour, fairness). The other comments are related to teaching approaches (explanation, individual help, flexibility), subject expertise, and student outcomes (interest and learning acquisition).

Students' Views on Good Teaching in Different Curriculum Areas

The eleven teachers in the Australian study were chosen to represent three curriculum areas: humanities, science/mathematics and practical subjects. When the students' comments on good teaching in the last of the three observed lessons were clustered according to curriculum area, slightly different patterns emerged for the three areas (Figure 11.3). Taking the two most frequently mentioned comments for each area, it could be said that, according to these students, the typically successful mathematics or science teacher, above all else, explains well and maintains good control in the class, while the successful humanities teacher relates well to students and makes the classes interesting, and the successful teacher of practical subjects helps individual students and makes clear explanations. Other differences to be noted were that flexibility ('doesn't rush us', 'work in my own way') was seen by students to be more important in teachers of humanities than other subjects, while class control was less important; and the acquisition of learning was seen to be of particular importance in science and mathematics lessons.

Of course, these observations are not generalisable, because they are based on such a small number of teachers, but they do raise the possibility that teachers in different subject disciplines do approach teaching in different ways. Whether these differences are inherent in the subject or lie within the teachers themselves and their educational philosophies is a matter for further debate and research. Perhaps students look for and value different things in the teaching of certain

Figure 11.3: Students' comments on successful aspects of lessons: Most frequently mentioned comments in rank order

Mathematics/Science	Humanities	Practical Subjects
(3 teachers)	(4 teachers)	(4 teachers)
(39 students)	(51 students)	(64 students)
explains	cares	helps
control	interest	explains
humour	own way	control
helps	explains	fair
learn	helps	knows
interest	fair	interest
cares	control	own way
knows		cares
		humour

subjects. What the present study has shown is that the student perspective can make a valuable contribution to such debate.

Sharing Craft Knowledge: School-Based Professional Development

Most of the teachers who participated in the study said that they found it a valuable professional experience, as the following extract illustrates:

> I've enjoyed talking to you obviously, because it's interesting stuff and you don't always get the opportunity to have someone there that's listening and every now and then asking you questions. It forces you to focus on your lessons which you haven't done since you were doing teacher training, and then you always focused on the negative instead of the positive; so it's great. I think it would be good if everyone went through it, even though that would probably be impossible. You feel better about your teaching, by looking at positive things, and that somebody else sees them as being positive things, because sometimes you're not sure.

One of the strengths of the approach used in the study of teachers' craft knowledge was its emphasis on the positive aspects of a teachers' performance. The deficit model of teacher development has been the basis of too many in-service education courses; there is a place for programs which remedy deficiencies, but an overdose of this orientation in professional development can lead to an undermining of teacher morale and a consequent decline rather than improvement in teaching performance. Positive reinforcement is just as sound a principle for adult education as it is for child education. The teachers in the study all warmed to the task of reflecting on and articulating their craft knowledge as they came to realise that the environment in which they were operating (the input from researcher and students) did not threaten but provided support and acknowledgement of achievement.

The teachers in one of the schools in the study talked at length about the possibility of using the process in their school, starting with experienced teachers working with new teachers and extending to a whole staff involvement in pairs on a voluntary basis. What appealed to these teachers about the process was that it:

- stressed the positive and built on strengths;
- was directly related to day-by-day concerns in the classroom, while making it possible to set such concerns in the context of a cohesive and continually evolving personal repertoire;
- created the opportunity for a teacher to reflect on and put into words the constituents of this repertoire.
- had the potential to break down the isolation of the classroom by enabling teachers to observe and discuss each other's craft knowledge in action.

The process can be used by any school for the professional development of its teachers. The process could be used to advantage with newly recruited teachers, who could work with more experienced teachers to develop areas of potential and actual strength by observing lessons and being observed, and by learning to reflect on practice and by listening to experienced colleagues' reflections. Another way of using the process would be for all teachers in a school to teach, observe and reflect with a colleague and to construct some form of individual pedagogical profile. The profiles would form a common pool of information about the particular teaching strengths of staff members, so that teachers could choose to work with other teachers to develop particular areas of expertise. Another relevant area in which the reflective process and the development profiles could be used to advantage would be in teacher appraisal; it would be a way of actively and positively involving teachers in the appraisal process.

At a time when team work and cooperative endeavour are the hallmarks of many on-the-job training programs in business and industry, consideration should be given by school administrators and practitioners to the ways in which collaborative classroom-based professional development activities, such as those described above, can be incorporated into the operational fabric of the school.

References

BATTEN, M. (1989) 'Teacher and pupil perspectives on the positive aspects of classroom experience', *Scottish Educational Review*, **21**, pp. 48–57.
— (1990) 'The nature of teachers' professional craft knowledge', *VIER Bulletin*, **64**, pp. 1–15.
BOYLAN, C., WALLACE, A., BATTERSBY, D., RETALLICK, J., and EDWARDS, J. (1988) 'Towards an understanding of exemplary teaching', paper presented at the Annual Conference of the Australian Association for Research in Education, 30 November–4 December, Armidale, New South Wales.
BROWN, S. and McINTYRE, D. (1989) *Making Sense of Teaching*, Edinburgh: Scottish Council for Research in Education.
SCHÖN, D. (1983) *The Reflective Practitioner*, London: Temple-Smith.

Chapter 12

Transferring Knowledge to Classroom Teaching: Putting Knowledge into Action

Hannelore Börger and Harm Tillema

This chapter reports research on the transfer of pedagogical and didactical knowledge to classroom teaching. This problem of student teachers not using their didactical knowledge during their teaching is seen here as a lack of knowledge about how this learned didactical knowledge can be brought into action. Answers to the question of how these transfer problems can be studied and improved through training are sought in the domain of thinking skills. Two approaches are discussed within this domain that offer guidelines for the study of transfer: the embedding and the immersion approach. Both approaches combine in their own way cognitive and metacognitive aspects of thinking. Finally, a research proposal is made to further examine dichotomies and important variables within these theories, like situatedness, knowledge organisation and the accessibility of knowledge.

Introduction

A frequently encountered finding these days in studies of teacher and in-service education is that students who do have the theoretical knowledge that is required during their training do not use this knowledge in practice. Research points out that this distinction between trained pedagogical and didactical knowledge and professional acting in classroom situations is not due to a lack of theoretical knowledge, because this knowledge is available to novice teachers when asked for explicitly, for example during examinations (Wahl, 1991). Therefore this problem is seen as a lack of knowledge about how these learned theories should be brought into action, which causes a transfer problem between theoretical knowledge and its application to relevant practice situations.

A teacher, however, needs to have knowledge and skills relevant for teaching, and to be able to bring this body of knowledge and skills into action in the classroom. Research in the domain of expert/novice teacher differences has revealed the fact that teaching skills are based on various knowledge domains. Some of these knowledge domains are more concerned about the content of the topic to be taught, and others are more directed to the question of how these topics should be taught. The latter domains include more strategic knowledge about when to use what strategy or approach, and knowledge about analogies and other explanatory techniques (Wilson, Shulman and Richert, 1987). Reports about teacher thinking also direct much attention to the role of knowledge; they consider teaching to be a way of constant decision-making in which teachers rely heavily on their knowledge base. Research on effectiveness of diverse training methods and components has especially focused upon the process of knowledge acquisition. These knowledge acquisition theories traditionally concentrated on aspects of content and organisation (knowledge-based theories). These theories are based on the notions of the Associationist tradition that considered the concept of 'identical elements' as the determining factor for transfer of learning. They assumed that the greater the number of identical elements (Anderson: identical productions; Singley and Anderson, 1989) between the original and the transfer task, the greater the amount of transfer there would be. Transfer is thus guided by a process of associating identical elements between the original and the transfer task. So for transfer to occur it is important to have a rich knowledge base with much domain specific knowledge with which to associate new information. This S-R view initially stressed a specificity view. In the early 1960s a shift emerged towards the influence of more general processes to the transfer of learning. These processes are believed to be knowledge independent, and in the form of (metacognitive) strategies. Because of the generality that makes them applicable to more than one domain, these strategies can facilitate transfer. In addition the metacognitive strategies (like e.g. cognitive monitoring) can be used directly in the process of transfer, by students learning them as guidelines for transfer. This strategic based position is based on the Gestalt approach, that considers the process of thinking as reorganising, or linking various elements of a problem situation. This process should lead to structural understanding. Therefore the concepts 'insight' and 'meaning' are central to this approach. Transfer questions studied in the field of knowledge acquisition are focused on knowledge transfer between various domains or tasks.

A teacher, however, not only has to acquire relevant knowledge and skills, but also has to bring knowledge and skills into *action* in classroom practice. This means that teachers are not mere decision-makers, they also have to be flexible in their decision-making because of the ever changing demands of the environment. Therefore it is supposed that teaching takes place under 'executive control'. Joyce and Showers (1983) define this as a process of understanding the purpose and rationale of a skill and knowing how to adapt it to students, apply it to subject matter, modify or create instructional materials attendant to its use, organise students to use it, and blend it with other instructional approaches to develop a smooth and powerful whole.

Lack of usability of learned theories can be regarded as a serious problem in teacher education. This kind of knowledge transfer to adequate classroom application has, however, been the subject of a surprisingly small amount of research within effectiveness of diverse teacher-training methods and components. We will first discuss the research done in the field of transfer between tasks and knowledge domains, and effectiveness of training methods with regard to this transfer. Later on we will suggest a way to study the transfer of theoretical knowledge to practical use in the classroom.

Instruction of Transfer

The distinction can be made between knowledge-based and strategic theories. Both will now be discussed with regard to their opinions about how transfer can be enhanced.

Knowledge-Based Theories

Nowadays the emphasis of these theories is not so much on the acquisition of knowledge, but on the accessibility of knowledge. To increase this knowledge accessibility the right knowledge has to be learned, and this knowledge has to be organised in an adequate way. It is supposed that this can be accomplished by learning large amounts of facts and establishing the similarities and relationships between them, so that domain specific strategies can be formed that can help solve problems. According to Shuell (1990) the individual relies heavily, if not exclusively, on domain-specific strategies. This is in accordance with Singley and Anderson (1989) who believe that general methods are relatively unimportant in transfer. This process of knowledge organisation, however, does not take place automatically. To stimulate this process the learning instruction should include relevant examples, relations between concepts and knowledge should be highlighted ('building bridges'), various problems should be solved and mapping and representational methods should be used (see, for example, Prawat, 1989; Shuell, 1990; Singley and Anderson, 1989). So the process of knowledge utilisation in knowledge acquisition has to be addressed (Voss, 1989).

Beside these techniques to enhance structure and connectedness in knowledge, attention also has to be paid to the already existing structures and beliefs of the students. These preconceptions of students are very resistant to change. A possible explanation for this is that these preconceptions are based on 'common sense' or own experiences, and have been present for a long time. The student has, therefore, already experienced the benefit of these preconceptions, which form a stable ground in further learning (Wahl, 1991). A second aspect is that preconceptions are often in the form of procedures that direct actions in an automatic way (Anderson, 1982). These procedures are therefore hard to change. Some suggested ways for change are: confrontation with new information or examples (Corporaal and Boei, 1990), learning through own experiences (Wahl, 1991) or instruction of right hemisphere strategies (metaphors, images, rhythm, etc.) instead of the left hemispheric strategies that are mostly used (Wubbels, 1991).

Strategic-Based Theories

The strategic-based theories emphasise the learning of general thinking skills, because these skills are easily transferable and can be used to establish transfer actively. The assumption is that if you want transfer to occur, you have to teach how transfer should be established. Therefore flexibility has to be taught (for example, through reflection), persistence has to be shown, and 'deep understanding' has to be the goal of learning (Joyce and Showers, 1988). Awareness seems to be highly important to this approach. Awareness is needed to gain access to knowledge (Prawat, 1989). In order to bring strategies under conscious control one should rely on techniques like verbalisation or writing down one's own thoughts. Communication among peers and between teacher and student are thus very important (see, for example, Prawat, 1989; Joyce and Showers, 1988). Research has shown that the provision of a rich input domain is also fruitful to establish dynamic knowledge (Lebowitz, 1986).

A problem with both theories above mentioned is that their programs only lead to transfer within one domain and not to transfer between domains or contexts. Another problem (or maybe a causal problem) is the strict division between them. As Garner (1990) puts it, 'structures of knowledge and cognitive processes interact'. Therefore integration of the strategic and knowledge-based positions has started to take place. In this line of thinking there has been much criticism on teaching strategies which are domain independent. Linking strategies to a domain specific knowledge base yields better results in terms of transfer between domains (Perkins and Salomon, 1989).

A shift has emerged recently towards utilisation of knowledge (application of knowledge instead of accessibility of knowledge). Recent studies focus on methods of teaching theories in a way that they will be used in practice. They see knowledge as tools to be used differently in different contexts. This metaphor makes clear how both approaches view learning; as an active process in which the knowledge is not internalised precisely in accordance with the instructional form, but in which the knowledge is being worked upon by prior knowledge and becomes connected to it. In this way new tools are formed. The toolmaker is seen as the central executive, the 'internal agent of self-regulation' (Iran-Nejad, 1990).

This links to another new line of thinking that has emerged recently among researchers with a cognitive or information processing approach to human learning. Learners are now conceptualised as active constructors of knowledge rather than passive recipients of information; they actively seek to make sense of the environment. They can do this by imposing structure and order on stimuli encountered through experience. Shuell (1990) calls this kind of learning 'meaningful cognitive learning', this is described as an active, constructive and cumulative process that occurs over a period of time.

How can the Transfer of Educational Theory to Classroom Teaching be Studied?

The question remains how student-teachers' transfer between pedagogical and didactical theories can be facilitated. Only the transfer between various knowledge domains has been studied thus far. The above mentioned shifts (towards utilisation of knowledge and towards active learning) may, however, lead to very promising ways for looking at transfer from theory to practice in the domain of teaching. The question of how to teach a subject so that it will be used by the students in practice is also applicable to the transfer problem of teacher students. The model of seeing learners as active constructors of knowledge trying to make sense of their environment also suits the theories of teacher thinking skills. As mentioned earlier these theories see teachers as decision-makers, constantly making decisions as the environmental demands change, who rely on their prior knowledge and knowledge base.

Table 12.1: Most Salient Differences Between the Immersion and the Embedding Approach

Immersion	Embedding
Content of teaching:	
Content of thoughts (what).	Process of thoughts (how to).
Order of teaching:	
Teaching content knowledge and concepts first.	First teaching application rules and then how to use them or waiting for problems to arise: only providing 'know-how'.
Product of teaching:	
Implicit conceptual understanding.	Teaching for discrete know-how (explicit knowledge)
How to teach:	
Contextualising	De-contextualising
Providing an authentic context, creating and re-creating settings and tools which sustain learners' perceptual work	Providing (teaching) application rules, demonstrating
Guidelines for learning:	
Ideas	Thinking frames (executive control/critical thinking)

An interesting analogy to the teacher transfer problem can be found in research on thinking skills. Within this domain two approaches can be distinguished that examine the question of why theoretical knowledge is not transferred to usable knowledge. Within these approaches the notions of active learning and usability of knowledge can also be found. These approaches are very attractive for the study of knowledge transfer to classroom practice because of their roots in the theories of knowledge acquisition that are more empirically based and more well known. Furthermore they can be used effectively in the more specific field of teacher education because of their emphasis on the *use* of learned theories and skills. One of these approaches is more in line with the former strategic-based theories (immersion approach), while the other links up with the knowledge-based theories (embedding approach). The most salient distinctions are summarised in Table 12.1.

The Embedding Approach

The embedding approach integrates the knowledge-based and the cognitive theory by conceiving strategies as handles of knowledge domains. Through these handles domain-specific knowledge can be retrieved and used (Perkins and Salomon, 1989). Much attention is therefore paid to the process of knowledge use at the point of knowledge acquisition; How is the knowledge being stored? Is new information adequately integrated with prior knowledge? If this is the case, is it done within just one structure or in more structures? Because of this emphasis on structural aspects of knowledge acquisition this skill-learning approach links up with modern knowledge-based theories in which good learners are characterised by an adequately structured knowledge base and good information processing mechanisms. This makes them capable of relating new information to their existing knowledge, and hopefully to more than one structure. The knowledge of such learners is thus better organised and therefore less inert. Their knowledge has to be cued less, which is what makes these learners more flexible in their application of knowledge (Voss, 1987).

This approach sees learning as a process of organised storage, retrieval and use of information under the guidance of executive control. The products of this learning process should be critically evaluated. These general strategies (of executive control and critical thinking) should be taught within a specific knowledge domain to enhance their practical usability. Beside this it is very important to make hidden knowledge and processes as explicit as possible. To enhance transfer, relations between the learning and the practice situation have to be stressed and the overarching framework has to be made explicit. In this way the teacher can be certain that the right inferences are made by the learners, and that their knowledge becomes structured adequately.

The Immersion Approach

The immersion approach, on the other hand, argues for knowledge and processes to remain implicit so that the learners can abstract relevant knowledge out of the information themselves. The ideas the learners have about which knowledge is relevant and which is not play a crucial role in this approach (Prawat, 1991). According to the immersion approach these ideas guide the thinking process. In return these ideas will be adjusted to experience. So here learning is also seen as a cumulative process, this time not guided by the information provided (as is the case with the embedding approach) but by the ideas that learners have. Learning is much more an active process here in which the learners themselves are given the opportunity to make their own inferences. Inferring and generalising is based on one's own experiences.

To enhance inferring and generalising, the new information has to be provided in the context of meaningful activities. Transfer can be achieved by providing rich information and stimulating students to work actively with this information. One possibility of achieving this is by providing 'multiple perspectives on the same anchor or set of events' (The Cognition and Technology group at Vanderbilt, 1990). This instruction method is generally called 'cognitive apprenticeship' (for example, Brown, Collins and Duguid, 1989). Important aspects of this method are the active attitude of the students and the provision of rich information and feedback within a social setting to enhance active communication between the students and to enhance the number of alternative perspectives. Through the provision of rich information and training examples in which students are motivated to generate the problems themselves, it is believed that students learn general rules to detect relevant information and cues from the environment and rules of how to abstract a problem schema (Catrambone and Holyoak, 1989, The Cognition and Technology Group at Vanderbilt, 1990). The strength of this approach lies in the practice the students get in perceiving invariants and discovering serial and generic concepts in their learning environment (Gough, 1989). This aspect is very important because teaching is an occupation with relative little surveillance and few standard operating procedures. According to Joyce and

Showers (1983) one of the most important things for the effective use of a new skill or theory is knowing when to use it appropriately and what will be the consequences. Learning to pick the situations in which problems can be expected, or theory can be implemented, will help to pick the right spots in real classroom teaching. Furthermore, the principle of students searching for problem situations will lead to more dynamic knowledge, a very important aspect in an ill-structured and complex problem space (like classroom teaching) (Lebowitz, 1986).

Because of the resulting dynamic knowledge (the applications are learned in the context of the theory) the immersion approach seems more suited for the complex teaching situation than the embedding approach. There has not been much research comparing the embedding to the immersion approach. Prawat (1991) reports one such study of Brown and Palinscar which supports the notion that the immersion approach has more potential for influencing student thinking than the embedding approach does. Both approaches, however, seem very useful to transfer from theory to practice, because they emphasise the usability and application of the learned theory and skills. These approaches seem to be very useful for providing some guidelines for the study of theory to practice transfer.

Both approaches emphasise the organisation and accessibility of knowledge. A dichotomy however exists, as mentioned earlier, about how this can be established. Should de-contextualised strategies be taught, or should contextualised knowledge be provided? This dichotomy seems to be a first crucial question to be addressed. The embedding and the immersion approach both offer different strategies to instruct theories: the embedding approach in a more de-contextualised way, and the immersion approach in a very situated way. These strategies will be used in a first study to question the situatedness of transferrable knowledge. Further, the connectedness of the knowledge base is believed to be very important by those who promote the embedding approach, and the 'richness' of the information given seems to be the determining factor for the immersion approach; while the embedding approach, in contrast, has discrete know-how provided directly to the students. These variables were chosen first because of the importance they have for the approaches, but also because they reveal some of the crucial factors guiding transfer, and they provide information about methods to enhance the chance of theory-practice transfer to occur at a more instructional level.

In the following section a proposal for a research program concerning knowledge transfer is given. This program consists of three studies.

1 First of all a study is proposed to examine the most revealing variable: situatedness. In this study examples of how to use the learned theory in relevant practice situations are provided in two different ways, in a very strictly structured manner that assures that the examples will be learned as knowledge *per se* (in this way forming a strategic knowledge domain, linking strictly with the theory learned), and in another, more contextualised way (in a more active way linking the knowledge to the theory learned, leaving the occurrence of transfer to practice more under control of metacognitive strategies). It is hypothesised that the condition leading to contextualised knowledge will be most successful for the transfer from theory to practice, because this condition promotes the access of theoretical knowledge through cues out of the classroom environment. In this study the roles of the teacher and instruction are studied.

2 In a second study the two other variables above mentioned, that illustrate differences between the immersion and the embedding approach (richness of the information given and connectedness of the knowledge base), are plotted against each other. This study tries to explore further the results found in the first study. In this study the role (knowledge) of the learner is studied, as well as the influence of the context.

3 The final goal of these studies is to come to concrete recommendations for the teacher and in-service education programs. These studies may lead to a third study in which, for example, a combination of the embedding and the immersion approach are tested. As is shown in the literature, the immersion approach appears to have a slight advantage over the embedding approach in teaching students. This advantage lies probably in the fact that the knowledge students acquire by the immersion approach is more active than the knowledge brought about by the embedding approach. The disadvantage of the immersion approach, however, is the chance that false strategies will arise as a result of wrong inferences made by the students. This cannot be controlled as much as in the embedding approach. What thus seems a good compromise between the two approaches is to combine the openness of the immersion approach with the more controlling embedding approach by the provision of direct feedback, and correction of wrong strategies. Depending on the results of the suggested studies research can further lead in this direction.

Research Proposal

Study 1: Situatedness of the Acquisition of Usable Educational Theory

The first step is to pose the question of how domain specific the acquisition of usable educational theory is. The most obvious way to teach a theory in a manner that promotes the use of it, is to give examples of application situations. The question is then, how these examples should be provided to enhance the usage of theories. Knowledge-based research studies of transfer have shown that the provision of multiple sources of information (multiple examples or analogies) alone does not lead to inter-domain transfer. For transfer between domains to occur it is necessary that these domains or situations have the same salient features and that these features are highlighted (Singley and Anderson, 1989, Catrambone and Holyoak, 1989). Transfer can be enhanced by comparing diverse analogies and stressing the underlying structure. Singley and Anderson (1989) call this procedure structural analogy, this leads to generalisation of the resulting procedural representation. Translating this to the transfer from theoretical knowledge to practice, salient features between the theoretical and application situation have to be highlighted, application examples have to become clear, restrictions of the application domains have to be shown or experienced, etc. Both the immersion and the embedding approach support this notion, but each has a different view of accomplishing this knowledge.

According to the embedding approach, educational theory has to be acquired in a rather de-contextualised way that assures that the strategical knowledge learned from application examples will be learned as knowledge *per se* (in this way forming a strategic knowledge domain). This means that strategic knowledge about how to use the theory should be provided, illustrated by examples that are given by the teacher or generated by the students.

The immersion approach, however, argues that this theoretical (strategic) knowledge should be linked to the situations in which they emerge, leaving the occurrence of transfer to practice more under control of metacognitive strategies. This points in the direction of teaching these strategies in a more contextual way. In this study this is operationalised by using the method of 'self explanation' (Chi and Bassok 1984). Here worked-out examples are provided for the students that give a step-by-step description (in this case of a classroom situation in which the learned theory is used). The students are than stimulated to give as much expla-nation as possible for the steps that are taken in the example. In this way the application strategies are directly learned in the context of the theory and of the classroom situation. It is hypothesised that this condition, leading to contextualised knowledge, will be most successful for the transfer from theory to practice, be-cause this condition promotes the access of theoretical knowledge through cues out of the classroom environment.

To gain insight into the question of how situated the acquisition of a theory must be to be used in practice, both methods of using application examples can be compared. Furthermore, the influence of providing application examples itself can be studied by adding a baseline condition in which no such examples are given. This baseline condition is probably the most common form of teaching educational theories to teacher students.

Design.

As learning theory the 'Advance Organiser' theory of Ausubel (see, for example, Joyce and Weil, 1980) is chosen. The study material will be the text Verloop (1989) used for his thesis. This text will be revised for the following three conditions:

- providing worked out examples → letting the students generate rules (for practical application) themselves (self-explanations) (immersion approach)
- providing rules and strategies for application → giving or generating examples to/from the students (embedding approach)
- not providing strategic rules or examples (the baseline condition, which is probably mostly used in training).

The lesson content has to be further explicated; for the use of examples an instruc-tion-video from Verloop can be used. The lessons in the three conditions have to be of equal duration.

Testing material will include first of all a questionnaire to control for the amount of prior knowledge and reasoning ability the students have, and to test their perceptions about teaching theories in general. A triangulation of knowledge testing material is used to map the knowledge the students possess after having read the text. The testing material varies along two axes (see Table 12.2). This material has been validated and tested for reliability in a pilot study.

After the students have completed the lesson program they have to give a lesson according to the theory of Ausubel. This lesson will be recorded by a video camera, so the student can watch the tape as soon as the lesson has finished. During this viewing session stimulated recall will be used to find out what the

Table 12.2: Triangulation of the Knowledge-Tests

		KNOWLEDGE	
		organisation (relatedness)	content (concepts)
INSTRUCTIONAL FORM:	cued	giving weight to important links between concepts	questionnaire (for factual and strategic knowledge) video recognition
	non-cued	concept mapping	

student was thinking while teaching. The amount of theory being used can be rated by counting the amount of theory elements used in these verbal reports. This, however, only gives an indication for the used cognitive amount of theory. The real amount of theory brought into action can be observed by using the taped recordings of the lessons (here also scoring the theory elements used). Theory to practice transfer can in this way be compared with the instructional form of the lesson program followed and the acquired (types and form of) knowledge.

This study can be extended with a third question: what are the limits of the established transfer? This question can be studied by again contacting the students who cooperated (preferably by contacting only their teacher so the students will not directly link participation to the first studies). Transfer testing could take place with the aid of 'protocol' questions, in which a classroom situation is described. The students are then asked to define their reaction to such situations. In this way first of all the retention is assessed: Is the theory still active? (The answers can be compared to the also protocol-like questions of the questionnaire).

The form of the questions (protocol-like) makes it possible not only to say something about the mastery of the subject-matter, but also about the application of the theory by the learners. Research has shown that the amount of theory application depends largely upon the instruction the student has received. When instructed to bring the theory into practice the amount of theory application increases (Wahl, 1991). This is one of the problems in exploring theory to practice transfer. In this kind of research the question is whether the student brings the learned theory into practice, while the instruction is to apply the theory in the classroom. To get some insight into the size of this problem the first questions will be asked without reference to the theory of Ausubel, and the later questions with the instruction to make use of the learned theory of Ausubel.

A further question, about the limits of the knowledge transfer, can be answered by varying the domain to which the knowledge has to be transferred. To establish this the students can be given protocol questions about other subject content lesson situations.

Study 2: Conditions for the Occurrence of Theory-Practice Transfer

To study the differences between the immersion and embedding approaches two variables can be used that will have different influences according to both

Table 12.3: *Expected Results with Rich/Poor Contextual Information Given and Poor/ Well-Organised Knowledge*

	well organised knowledge (expert student teacher)	poorly organised knowledge (novice student teacher)
'rich contextual' information	immersion: + embedding: +	immersion: + embedding: −
'non-situated', more abstract information	immersion: − embedding: +	immersion: − embedding: −

approaches. The most salient difference lies in the knowledge that has to be provided.

According to the embedding approach the connectedness of the knowledge base and the information given is of great significance. A well-organised knowledge base does not need to be compensated for by rules or strategies (Garner, 1990). The information of the embedding approach is provided in such a way that no false inferences can be made and resulting inefficient or wrong strategies can be learned. The immersion approach, on the other hand, emphasises the importance of the 'situatedness' of the given information. If the information is not provided in such a way that the student can actively seek his own information and solutions to problems, this knowledge will not become active. According to the embedding approach, however, rich contextual information that is given to stimulate the student enhances the chance that the student may make the wrong inferences and learn the wrong strategies.

The variable 'connectedness of the knowledge base' can be tested by using expert and novice subjects. It is assumed that experts have a more structured knowledge base than novices (Garner, 1990). Research has shown that these differences also already exist between student teachers who have experienced shorter and longer training (Boei, 1990). By using first-year and third-year student teachers, knowledge structure is varied. The expectations between this condition and 'contextual richness' of the information given will differ between the immersion and the embedding approach. Table 12.3 shows the expected results according to the immersion and the embedding approach.

Design.
Expert and novice teacher students can respectively be selected out of the last year and the first year of the teacher education centre. These students have to be given the same lesson program in which a teaching theory is learned. It is then assumed that the expert students organise their knowledge in a more adequate way as the novice students (this has to be studied).This can be examined with the same knowledge tests as used in the study mentioned above, in which two tests examining the knowledge organisation were used (see Table 12.2). To test the application of the theory and to vary the amount of situatedness questions can be asked that sketch a classroom situation in which a problem arises. In the 'rich' condition this can be done with the aid of a video of a real classroom situation and the

problem can remain implicit. In the other condition the situation can be made less situated by not describing the whole classroom situation but only the teachers' part in it. It does not have to be a 'real' situation. In both cases the question will be: 'What would you do in this situation, keeping in mind the theory you have just learned?'. The answers can be scored in terms of the amount of theory elements used. In this study the limits of the established transfer can also be studied as in the first study.

Study 3: Influencing Knowledge Accessibility and Utilisation

In the last step of the research a training-method can be tested (either in the regular training or as a workshop) that seems most promising for theory-practice transfer. The content of this training-method will depend on the results of the first two studies. It is expected that a contextual and immersed approach will enhance the transfer from theoretical knowledge to classroom practice more than a de-contextual and embedded approach. In this case one teacher training program can consist of an active practical training with much use of cases, and the other training can be more strictly structured and theory-driven. It may be that a combination of the two approaches would be most promising, for example the contextual rich instruction of the immersion approach combined with the provision of feedback (this should limit the acquisition of wrong strategies, a thing that has to be controlled according to the embedding approach). Another result that can be expected from the results of former studies is that the conditions measured will have different effects in different phases of learning. Brooks and Dansereau (1987), for example, conclude from their review of content-skills transfer studies that meaningful (situated) learning will only be useful if the student already possesses some degree of content knowledge. Students without such prior knowledge are better off under more rote learning conditions. The goal of this last study is to come to concrete recommendations for teacher and in-service education programs. The resulting training-method can be presented in the form of a package that can be used in teacher training.

References

ANDERSON, J.R. (1982) Acquisition of cognitive skill, *Psychological Review*, **89**, pp. 369–406.

BOEI, F. (1990) *Ontwikkelingen in declaratieve kennis (Development of Declarative Knowledge)*, Thesis Leiden, De Lier: Academisch Boeken Centrum.

BROOKS, L.W. and DANSEREAU, D.F. (1987) 'Transfer of information: an instructional perspective', in CORMIER, S.M. and HAGMAN, J.S. (Eds) *Transfer of Learning: Contemporary Research and Applications*, London: Academic Press.

BROWN, J.S., COLLINS, A. and DUGUID, P. (1989) 'Situated cognition and the culture of learning', *Educational Researcher*, **18**, pp. 32–43.

CATRAMBONE, R. and HOLYOAK, K.J. (1989) 'Overcoming contextual limitations on problem-solving transfer', *Journal of Experimental Psychology: Learning, Memory and Cognition*, **15**, pp. 1147–1156.

CHI, M.T.H. and BASSOK, M. (1984) 'Learning from examples via self-explanations', in RESNICK, L.B. (Ed.) *Knowing, Learning and Instruction*, New Jersey: Lawrence Erlbaum.

GARNER, R. (1990) 'When children and adults do not use learning strategies: Toward a theory of settings', *Review of Educational Research,* **60**, pp. 517–29.

GOUGH, N. (1989) 'From epistemology to ecopolitics: Renewing a paradigm for curriculum', *Journal of Curriculum Studies*, **21**, pp. 225–41.

IRAN-NEJAD, A. (1990) 'Active and dynamic self-regulation of learning processes', *Review of Educational Research*, **60**, pp. 573–602.

JELSMA, O. (1989) *Instructional Control of Transfer*, Thesis. Enschede: Bijlstra and Van Merrienboer.

JOYCE, B.R. and SHOWERS, B. (1983) *Power in Staff Development through Research on Training*, Alexandria: ASCD.

— (1988) *Student Achievement through Staff Development*, New York: Longman.

JOYCE, B. and WEIL, M. (1980) *Models of Teaching*, Englewood Cliffs: Prentice-Hall.

LEBOWITZ, M. (1986) 'Concept learning in a rich input domain: Generalization-Based Memory', in MICHALSKI, R.S., CARBONELL, J.G. and MITCHELL, T.M. (Eds) *Machine Learning: An Artificial Intelligence Approach*, **Vol.II.**, Los Altos, Morgan Kaufmann Publishers, Inc.

PERKINS, D.N. and SALOMON, G. (1989) 'Are cognitive skills context-bound?', *Educational Researcher*, **18**, pp. 16–26.

PRAWAT, R.S. (1989) 'Promoting Access to Knowledge, Strategy, and Disposition in Students: A Research Synthesis', *Review of Educational Research*, **59**, pp. 1–44.

— (1991) 'The value of ideas: The immersion approach to the development of thinking', *Educational Researcher*, **20**, pp. 3–11.

SHUELL, TH. J. (1990) 'Phases of meaningful learning', *Review of Educational Research*, **60**, pp. 531–47.

SINGLEY, M.K. and ANDERSON, J.R. (1989) *The Transfer of Cognitive Skill*, London: Harvard University Press.

THE COGNITION AND TECHNOLOGY GROUP AT VANDERBILT (1990) 'Anchored instruction and its relationship to situated cognition', *Educational Researcher*, **19**, pp. 2–11.

VOSS, J.F. (1987) 'Learning and transfer in subject-matter learning: A problem solving model', *Educational Research*, **11**, pp. 607–22.

WAHL, D. (1991) *Handeln unter Druck; Der weite Weg vom Wissen Zum Handeln bei Lehrern, Hochshullehrern und Erwachsenenbildnern*, Weinheim: Duetscher Studien Verlag.

WILSON, S.M., SHULMAN, L.S. and RICHERT, A.E. (1987) ' "150 different ways" of knowing: Representations of knowledge in teaching', in CALDERHEAD, J. (Ed.) *Exploring Teachers' Thinking*, London: Cassell Educational Limited.

WUBBELS, TH. (1991) *Alternative Approaches to Influence (Student) Teachers' Conceptions*, paper presented at the ISATT conference.

Chapter 13

Teachers and their Career Story: A Biographical Perspective on Professional Development

Geert Kelchtermans

And because the stories were held here in fluid form, they retained the ability to change, to become new versions of themselves, to join up with other stories and so become yet other stories; . . . Salman Rushdie, Haroun and the Sea of Stories

Teachers' professional behaviour develops during their career. Terminating the teacher education program and receiving a teacher certificate doesn't mean the end of the training process and the achievement of competence. The further development of professional behaviour during a career is called 'professional development'. This notion is used in a descriptive as well as in a prescriptive way. In the descriptive sense, professional development refers to the way the teachers' evolution takes place during a career. The prescriptive meaning refers to interventions and training to direct the evolution in the professional behaviour in a more desirable way. In a recent review of the topic one reads: 'Professional development, now viewed as a career-long process, is, (. . .), being viewed as a major factor in efforts to improve schools' (Holly and McLoughlin, 1989: IX). This viewpoint, which is at the same time conclusive and programmatic, includes both the descriptive and the prescriptive meaning of professional development.

Teachers' Professional Behaviour Changes over Time[1]

In our research we try to gain more insight into the content as well as the form of professional development. We try to find ways to describe this developmental process. We do this from the so called 'biographical perspective'. The central idea in this approach is: teachers' professional behaviour[2] and its development can only be understood properly when situated in the broader context of their career and personal life history. More specifically, our research question is: 'Can the study of the teachers' life cycle provide insight into the factors and mechanisms that determine qualitative changes in teachers' professional behaviour?'

The biographical perspective gives a central place to the subjective interpretation of the teacher. We therefore don't study the formal career, but we look for the development in the professional life as it is experienced by the teachers themselves. We assume that the professional experiences of teachers result in a sense of professional self and a subjective educational theory.

This hermeneutic stance has consequences for the conceptual framework of our study as well as for the research method. In this chapter we present an overview of a broader research project. We will first clarify our conceptual framework. Central to this framework is our view of the teachers' self and a view on 'development' as a process. It will also become clear that our focus on the teachers' view, doesn't make us blind to the institutional context, in which teachers work. In other words: from the biographical perspective we study teachers' professional behaviour (and their 'thinking') about it in both the spatial and temporal context.

Taking the teachers' subjective stance seriously implies a narrative research method. Further, we will describe our research-procedure, centred around semi-structured biographical interviews. Next we report on a first study, which tested the usefulness and consistency of the framework. In our study we were guided by the grounded-theory-approach. As a result of this study the content of the conceptual framework was more fully elaborated. We will comment on these results further. Finally we explore some methodological issues and we briefly sketch the contours of a second study.

The Biographical Perspective

In order to understand career changes over time, we decided to study the professional development of teachers from the 'biographical perspective'. This means that we assume that the professional behaviour of a teacher is not only determined by the organisational context, but also by life history and related experiences. In other words, experiences from the past and expectations about the future, influence the perception of the present situation. 'Since no two people have the same life experiences, we all learn to perceive the world and ourselves as part of it in different ways' (Nias, 1989b: 156). This perception influences our daily decisions and behaviour.

Since the end of the 1970s, this approach has been adopted by a growing number of educational researchers. An early example is Peterson's study (1964), in which the role of age in the career of secondary school teachers and its relatedness to teacher effectiveness is studied. More recent studies deal with questions of how teachers perceive their career, how they react to changes in their job situation (for example, as a result of cut backs by the school administration) (Ball and Goodson, 1985; Goodson, 1992; Sikes *et al.*, 1985). Other studies look for the patterns that can be distinguished in the way teachers experience their career (Day in this volume); how educational innovations affect careers (Hirsch *et al.*, 1990; Huberman *et al.*, 1989a; Smith *et al.*, 1986) and how teachers' self-concept develops over time (Hirsch, 1990; Nias, 1989a).

Also in teacher thinking research several authors acknowledge the importance of biographical experiences in the teachers' personal opinions and implicit theories about education (Butt, 1984; Butt *et al.*, 1986; Clark and Peterson, 1986; Connelly and Clandinin, 1988a and 1988b; Elbaz, 1983, 1990). The importance of life experiences and personal background as determinants of teachers' thinking and professional behaviour is further demonstrated by the research on teacher socialisation (Grant and Sleeter, 1985: 212; Zeichner, 1986: 264).[3]

Professional Self and Subjective Educational Theory:
Key Concepts

Several authors make clear that being a teacher is a job that strongly involves the teacher as a person. 'In understanding something so intensely personal as teaching it is critical we know about the person the teacher is' (Goodson, 1981: 69; also Goodson, 1992: 4). 'By implication, therefore, it matters to teachers themselves, as well as to their pupils, who and what they are. Their self image is more important to them as practitioners than is the case in occupations where the person can easily be separated from the craft' (Nias, 1989a: 202–203). Also Pajak and Blase share this point of view: 'What seems to be most important in the personal lives of teachers, in terms of the effect on the professional life, is a well-developed individual identity and a sense of connectedness to others beyond the self' (Pajak and Blase, 1989: 306). Nias found that teachers, when talking about their job, in fact always talk about themselves. She calls this 'persistent self-referentialism' (Nias, 1989a: 5).

To understand adequately teachers' professional behaviour, one thus needs a thorough analysis of the way teachers see themselves as teachers. We subscribe therefore to the programmatic thesis of Ball and Goodson: 'the ways in which teachers achieve, maintain, and develop their identity, their sense of self, in and through a career, are of vital significance in understanding the actions and commitments of teachers in their work' (Ball and Goodson, 1985: 18).

Symbolic interactionist studies (Blumer, 1969; Nias, 1989a, 1989b) and recent psychological research (Dittmann-Kohli, 1988; Markus and Wurf, 1987; Gergen and Gergen, 1987) give support for a dynamic, interactionist and constructivist notion of self. Self is not seen as static, as a fixed core of personality. We conceive of self as the result of a social construction process, that goes on during the life cycle (see also Hirsch *et al.*, 1990).[4] We define the self as a complex, multidimensional and dynamic system of representations (meanings), which develops over time and is the result of the interactions between the subject and its environment. In this environment the other people, who communicate and interact with the person, who interpret his or her behaviour and react on it, have a central role. The self therefore results from intersubjective processes of interaction and interpretation. Nias, while referring to G.H. Mead, summarises: 'Our "selves" are inescapably social. Deprived of interaction with others we would have no sense of self (. . .)' (Nias, 1989a: 20). The self not only influences the way people perceive concrete working conditions and requirements, but also the way they act.

In our culture a job is a very important element in the definition of a self (see e.g. Hughes, 1958: 43). As we indicated earlier, for teachers the reverse is also true: 'the self is a crucial element in the way teachers themselves construe the nature of their job.' (Nias, 1989a: 13). Therefore self and professional self overlap largely. The notion 'professional self' is the focus of our research. We are interested in the self as far as professional activities are concerned. In our case the distinction is a matter of conceptual emphasis.

A very important part of the professional self is constituted by the knowledge, opinions and values a teacher holds about his or her professional activities (teaching in the broad sense of the word). This 'subjective educational theory'[5] refers to the global interpretative conceptual framework by which teachers make sense of their professional situation. Although some efforts have been made to develop a description of the content of this knowledge system (Elbaz, 1983; Connelly and Clandinin, 1988a), many questions concerning the content of subjective theories, their development and changes remain unanswered. We assume that subjective educational theory is a part of the professional self, and as such a product of the professional biography. We therefore share Elbaz' view that 'story is that which most adequately constitutes and presents teachers' knowledge' (Elbaz, 1991: 3).

From Formal Career to Career Story

The subjective perception of oneself including one's working situation is of central importance in our research. This has implications for the way one conceives of the career. One doesn't therefore conceive of a career as a chronological chain of facts, positions and social roles. We agree with Hughes, who says: 'Subjectively, a career is the moving perspective in which the person sees his life as a whole and interprets the meaning of his various attributes, actions, and the things which happen to him' (Hughes, 1958: 63). From this point of view it is important and necessary to explore the 'professional biography' or 'career story'. A teacher's professional biography results from a narrative retrospective reconstruction of his or her career.

Several researchers link self and biography. Schulze argues that biographical narratives are the most useful sources to understand the self and its development (Schulze, 1983: 314–15; Schulze, 1979: 59–60). Gudmundsdottir studied teachers' pedagogical content knowledge, which she conceives of as 'a narrative way of knowing' (Gudmundsdottir, 1991: 207). She argues that 'Stories are part of our identity and or culture' (Gudmundsdottir, 1991: 207). Recent psychological research also supports this view. Gergen and Gergen, for example, use the notion 'narratives of self'. These narratives reflect events, experiences that are important for the person one is. They are 'continuously unfolding stories in which plot and characters may change as situation and needs dictate' (Gergen and Gergen, 1987: 124). The narrative approach also avoids a cognitivistic bias. The self is not something in the head of people. 'As stories, self-narratives are pre-eminently social. They are essentially communal or participatory events in which the teller is engaging in a public (or implicitly public) act, and in which the target's capacities and predilections must be considered' (Gergen and Gergen, 1987: 125). Markus and Wurf share this view when they argue that people construct a kind of 'current autobiography', which is 'a story that makes the most coherent or harmonious integration of one's various experiences' (Markus and Wurf, 1987: 316). The story is a kind of encompassing structure, to which concrete experiences are connected. As time goes on and experiences change, the autobiographies change as well.

In summary, based on recent educational, psychological, and sociological theory and research, we chose a narrative, biographical approach of professional behaviour and its development. The career is studied from the subjective experience of the respondent. Professional self and subjective theory, as mediating instances between perception and behaviour, are key notions. One important question still remains to be answered: which factors and mechanisms determine the development of the professional biography?

The Development in Professional Biography:
Critical Incidents and Phases

In several biographical studies authors try to identify different (patterns of) phases in the career (see e.g. Hirsch *et al.*, 1990; Huberman, 1989a and 1989b; Sikes, *et al.*, 1985). These descriptions of career development, however, do not answer the question: how does one get from one phase to the next? Which processes or determinants are the motor behind that transition? Sikes *et al.* (1985; also Measor, 1985) try to deal with that question. They see the transition as partly gradual, smooth, and partly discontinuous, disruptive. In this latter transition mode the so called 'critical incidents' are very important. By critical incidents they mean: 'key events in an individual's life, and around which pivotal decisions revolve. They provoke the individual into selecting particular kinds of actions, which lead in particular directions' (Sikes *et al.*, 1985: 57). These critical incidents mostly take place during so-called 'critical phases'. The relation between critical incidents and phases is considered as follows: 'It is during these periods of changing and choosing that critical incidents are most likely to occur. The incident itself probably represents the culmination of a decision-making process, crystallising the individual's thinking, rather than being responsible of itself for that decision' (Sikes *et al.*, 1985: 58; also Measor, 1985: 62). Thus, critical incidents are events that challenge the professional self of the teacher. Assumptions, opinions and ideas about oneself or one's objective educational theory are thoroughly questioned. One has to reconsider the choices, the personal priorities in one's work as a teacher; one has to make decisions that will influence one's further professional biography (development). Retrospectively teachers will mention these moments as important for their professional development.[6] The notions 'critical incident' and 'critical phase' are especially interesting because they can be linked to changes in professional behaviour: as a result of some critical incidents the teacher has to change his usual approach to cope with the new challenges.

The Importance of the Context

It must be stressed here that the biographical approach of professional behaviour also takes into account the structural, cultural and organisational context in which teachers work. Teachers' professional behaviour always takes place within the institutional context of a school. The teacher is a member of a team and is held accountable for his or her job by the principal and external bodies. There are general rules and prescriptions (e.g. curriculum, time tables, etc.) to be respected. But every school is also characterised by its organisational culture. Schein defines this culture as 'the deeper level of basic assumptions and beliefs that are shared by members of an organisation, that operate unconsciously, and that define in a basic "taken-for-granted" fashion an organisation's view of itself and its environment' (Schein, 1985: 6; see also Staessens, 1991a and 1991b). The professional biography is the result of a dialectical relation between the teacher and his (professional) environment. 'As a result of meeting new circumstances, certain interests may be reformulated, certain aspects of the self changed, or crystallised, and, in consequence, new directions envisaged' (Sikes *et al.*, 1985: 2). The personal meaning system (self, subjective educational theory) is constantly interacting with supra-individual meaning systems (e.g. school culture). These supra-individual meanings will be perceived, interpreted and filtered by the respondent and so influence his or her professional behaviour. Or, as Nias puts it clearly: 'No matter how pervasive particular aspects of a shared social or occupational culture may be or how well individuals are socialised into it, the attitudes and actions of each teacher are rooted in their own ways of perceiving the world' (Nias, 1989a: 14).

Research Procedure

Inspired by the grounded theory approach, we consider our conceptual framework as a collection of 'sensitising concepts'. We understand professional development as a lifelong learning process. Professional self and subjective theory mediate between past experiences and the actual professional behaviour. From the research literature we expect the development through the career to be gradual, as well as abrupt. For the latter mode, 'critical incident' and 'critical phase' were promising and useful descriptive notions. This framework provided the base of our research procedure.

Research Procedure: A Cycle of Biographical Interviews

The literature on the 'life history method' (see e.g. Denzin, 1970; Plummer, 1983, etc.) was an important starting point in the development of the research procedure. That procedure is summarised in Figure 13.1. Because we strongly emphasise the subjective perception and the narrative nature of professional biographies, we chose to use biographical interviews. To be able to compare different life histories, the interviews were semi-structured (Denzin, 1970: 235-7). We worked out a guideline for a cycle of three interviews. In the first interview the career of the teacher was explored chronologically. Denzin calls this 'the natural history approach' (Denzin, 1970: 235-7): first one collects objective data in chronological order; these data are then used to explore the career story. The interview was taperecorded, transcribed, coded and analyzed. For the coding we used a code list that had been constructed on the basis of some preliminary interviews (test cases to check the interview guideline); this codelist was refined during the data analysis. The list refers to different aspects which can be expected in the teachers' career stories: the different components of the educational system, formal career, self-perception, professional environment, subjective educational theory, critical incidents and so on.

In the analysis of the first interview we looked for unclear passages, 'white spots' (aspects of the school reality which were not yet mentioned by the respondent) and made tentative interpretations about critical incidents and phases. The second interview consisted of two parts. First, we went back to the chronological story as we reconstructed it during the analysis and asked for more information on unclear points, 'white spots', and checked the tentative interpretations. This is the 'respondent specific part' of the second interview. Then we explored the global career experience by a set of fixed questions (respondent unspecific part). The second interview was also taperecorded, transcribed, coded and analyzed.

Then the data of the respondent were summarised in a synthesis text, constructed along a fixed structure. In doing so, all the relevant data became available

Figure 13.1: *Overview of the research procedure*

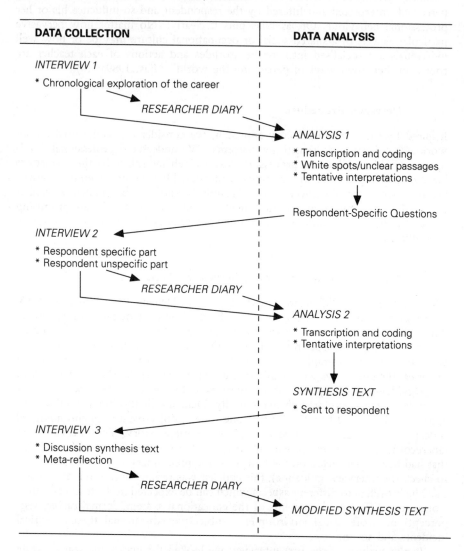

DATA COLLECTION	DATA ANALYSIS
INTERVIEW 1 * Chronological exploration of the career *RESEARCHER DIARY*	*ANALYSIS 1* * Transcription and coding * White spots/unclear passages * Tentative interpretations Respondent-Specific Questions
INTERVIEW 2 * Respondent specific part * Respondent unspecific part *RESEARCHER DIARY*	*ANALYSIS 2* * Transcription and coding * Tentative interpretations *SYNTHESIS TEXT* * Sent to respondent
INTERVIEW 3 * Discussion synthesis text * Meta-reflection *RESEARCHER DIARY*	*MODIFIED SYNTHESIS TEXT*

in a handy format. Further, control by the respondent became possible. The synthesis text was sent to the respondents, who were asked for comments. In the third interview the comments were collected. During this last meeting we also explored how the participation in the research process was experienced by the teacher and we also thematised the autobiographical reflection (meta-reflection) as process. In a final analysis we added to the text amendments, proposed by the respondents and our own final comments to the synthesis text. This led to the 'modified synthesis text'.

The biographic interviews stimulated teachers to think and tell about past experiences and persons who had impact on their career. We call this process 'stimulated autobiographical self-thematisation'. During the interviews we emphasised the importance of the personal character of their story and our non-evaluative stance. We always selected two teachers of the same school. This not only gave us complementary data about the school context, but also constituted an opportunity for triangulation. Data from both respondents could be compared and analyzed for internal consistency.

The interviewers themselves also kept a research diary. After every interview they wrote down observations, tentative interpretations, questions, etc. They also reflected systematically (with the help of a checklist with reflection topics) on the quality of the collected data (interviewer influence, striking behaviours or emotions during the interview, etc.). In meetings of the research team[7] the data, research experiences, analyses and interpretations were discussed intensively.

Interviewees

Interviewees were primary school teachers. Because this was a first study, aimed mainly to check the soundness of the conceptual framework and the usefulness of the research procedure, no heavy demands were made on the selection of the respondents. The teachers' motivation to participate in this kind of research process was the most important criterion. We only selected experienced teachers (at least five years of classroom practice). The interviews took place in 1988–89 with twelve teachers from six primary schools (pupils from 6–12 years) in two districts (three schools in each district). We interviewed eight female and four male teachers. Nine teachers had more than twenty years of school practice, two had eleven to twenty years and one had seven years of practice.

Results: Refining and Consolidating the Conceptual Framework

Through the repeated cycles of data collection, analysis and reflection we refined our initial framework of sensitising concepts. The concepts were made more concrete and meaningful. Also the relations between the notions became clearer. The provisional result of this analysis is presented in Figure 13.2. The two axes in Figure 13.2 emphasise the biographical and interpretative approach. Horizontally time is indicated. The vertical axis refers to different levels of interpretation. The first and lowest level represents the professional behaviour: the daily, observable professional activities. Over the lifetime these 'facts' can be organised in a formal career: a chronologically organised set of the formal positions, tasks, etc. a teacher holds during his or her career. These are facts that can be objectively observed or reconstructed. Because of our emphasis on the career experience (as becomes evident from the narrative reconstruction of the career), we are especially interested in the more interpretative levels. Professional behaviour and formal career constitute the framework that structures the story. Therefore the third level is the professional biography: the teachers' story as we reconstruct it from the autobiographical self-thematisation. One further step in the analysis brings us to the professional self and the subjective educational theory. These are theoretical

Figure 13.2: The conceptual framework

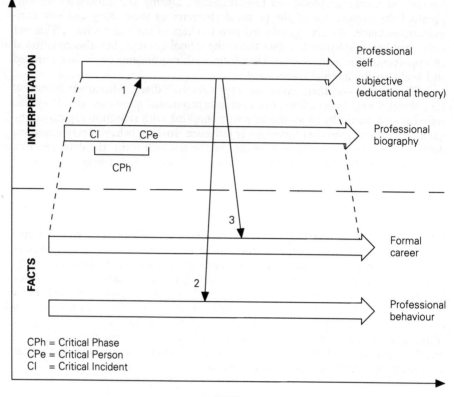

CPh = Critical Phase
CPe = Critical Person
CI = Critical Incident

TIME

constructs. Their content is the result of an interpretative analysis of the career story (professional biography).

Critical Persons, Incidents and Phases: Heuristic Concepts

Initially we expected the analysis of the stories to bring about a list of critical incidents and phases. This didn't happen. When one takes the narrative approach seriously, the critical incidents can only be understood when situated in the career story. The same event or situation can be a critical incident for one teacher, yet not for a colleague, in the sense that it results in a change of professional behaviour. The 'critical' character of an event is defined by the respondent himself and the way he or she copes with the situation. In other words, events can only become 'critical incidents' afterwards, retrospectively. Therefore it is not possible to make a general list of potential critical incidents.

We also learned that the definition of critical incident as an often dramatic key experience (a biographical hinge) in the career was too narrow. Most respondents experienced their career mainly as a gradual evolution, without real ruptures. However, some past experiences or situations were remembered in great detail and described as having a serious influence on their self and their professional behaviour. These situations were clearly distinguished by the teachers from the numerous other events, situations and so on. Critical incidents therefore can also be understood as 'distinctive, having a strong personal meaning'. They are often described as very detailed anecdotes, with an exemplary, illustrative, legitimative or explanatory function. Teachers also used these experiences to structure their career story. One could say that the respondents used their critical incidents as heuristics during the autobiographical self-thematisation. But also for the researcher 'critical incident' proved a useful heuristic concept during the analysis and reconstruction of the career story. When we fed the reconstruction back to the respondents (synthesis text), the interpretation of certain events by the interviewer as critical incident or phase improved the self-understanding by the teacher of the career.

An important completion of the original framework was the identification of the 'critical persons'.[8] We found out that respondents often mention specific individuals who had an important impact on their professional biography. Their presence and their behaviour strongly influenced the professional self and the subjective educational theory of the respondent. Mostly they were teachers at the teacher training college, older colleagues whom they had met during the first years of teaching, principals or inspectors.[9]

Two criteria in the analysis were used for the definition of an event, person or phase as 'critical':

1 the respondent refers to the event as a very meaningful situation (expressions as 'that was very important to me'; 'I never forgot how miserable I felt then . . .'). The fact that the respondent himself retrieves this situation from his memory and presents it as a meaningful event, is already a clear indication of the importance.

   An event is also critical when the researchers' interpretation of an event as critical is confirmed by the respondent. In his analysis and interpretation of critical incidents, the researcher also uses (apart from the content of the narrative) para- or non-verbal behaviours of the respondent during the interview (intonation, emphasis, mimic, gesticulation) or formal aspects of the narrative (overload of details, striking pauses or changes in the story tempo, abrupt endings, etc.);

2 when the meaningfulness of the incident is linked to the professional self, subjective educational theory or professional behaviour. The respondent has to attribute to the event an impact on self, subjective theory or professional behaviour. This will become clear in the concrete description and interpretation of the event.

   The same is true for critical persons and critical phases. In the latter case, we do not refer to specific events, but to a certain period of time, which is depicted by the respondent as very meaningful to his professional thinking and behaving.

Let us now turn to some examples, in order to illustrate the key concetps.[10]

(a) Critical incidents.

Anita is a female teacher of the first grade in a primary school (pupils are 7-years old). When returning to her class, after she had been at home for some time (pregnancy), she discovered that the children had made almost no progress in reading during her absence.

> The principal had taken someone from the nursery classes to substitute me. . . . The kids couldn't read. Absolutely nothing. On the second day of my return the principal came into my classroom and complained about the poor reading results of the children. She blamed me for it. And I — I wasn't completely recovered from pregnancy and birth, because I had had quite a difficult time then . . . and I started to cry. Oh, I felt miserable! If this would happen now, I would frankly say what I think . . . I never forgot this. It was so unfair!! How could I help it . . . I hadn't been at school. . . .

The intonation, the vehemence with which she recalls this more than ten-years-old event, witnesses the deep indignation and humiliation she felt at that time. The rest of the interview data also teach us that Anita highly values recognition of her work by others. This event illustrates this in a reverse way. The message in this narrative could be described in terms of a general principle (formulation): 'you don't have to accept groundless reproaches, but you must stand up for your dignity. Because, unfounded accusations make you doubt your professionality; they make you feel bad and negatively influence your work.'

Anita also refers to a difficult class she had some years ago. It was a large group of pupils and Peter, one of the kids, had behavioural problems. That year Anita started to doubt her own competence and she almost gave up her job. One incident illustrates the conflict and its resolution in a condensed way.

> . . . one day I had to fight with Peter, you know. Really fight. Afterwards I stood there . . . trembling all over. I handed out papers to do a writing exercise. Peter took the sheet, crumpled it up and threw it on the floor. I ordered him to pick it up. He refused, put his head on his arms and didn't move. I again ordered him to pick it up. No move. Then I said: 'Listen, you won't go home until you've picked up the sheet.' And then he started to fight. Took his bookcarrier and started to hit me. I really had to use force to make him sit down again. I said: 'Peter, pick up that sheet'. Finally, he did it . . . and that was the point . . . I broke his resistance. Afterwards I've had only very few problems with the kid. You know, that is exactly what makes it so difficult: stick to your point. It's much easier to give in, but then you'll always have the same troubles again. . . .

This story illustrates also what Sikes *et al.* call 'counter incidents'. These situations look like critical incidents in their constellation, but the way people cope with them is different. A counter incident is succesfully mastered. It usually follows a critical incident. It can mark the end of a critical phase. The counter incident shows that a new situation, task, challenge is succesfully 'countered' (Sikes *et al.*, 1985: 63 ff.). This experience made it clear to Anita that she was still able to handle difficult classes ('I am still competent to do a good job'), although she had been doubting about herself (critical phase).

(b) Critical persons.
Fred recalls a primary school teacher, he met when he was an undergraduate in teacher college. The way this teacher handled the young kids (first grade) seemed silly to him at that time.

> . . . I thought it was ridiculous. I really asked myself: has he gone insane? But now, after I've been teaching the first grade for some time, I notice that I've developed the same style: not becoming childish, but talking so that these young children understand what you mean. And then you get the best results. I had to learn that first. And one can only learn that by spending some time in a first class. An outsider who sees and hears it might think that I'm not normal, but this is the only normal way to behave in this situation. . . .

Only later did Fred appreciate the teacher's competence and realise that he himself behaves in the same way as his mentor teacher did. At the same time, his own experience makes him aware of the danger of the misjudging that threatens outsiders when observing the teaching of young children. It also makes him aware of the way he is perceived by others.

(c) Critical phases.
As Fred started his career, the school was being built up and they had to work in poor material circumstances. But the school team was young and highly motivated to make the best of it:

> . . . my class was in a kitchen, that hadn't been installed as such yet. Later we shared the great hall as room for four classgroups. Everyone had his corner. So these first five years I witnessed many problems. Everything that could eventually happen, every kind of difficulty you can image, I had to cope with: . . . the building, children from different ethnic groups, organisational problems and so on. . . . But we were young, we were all young and that was a blessing. We helped each other . . . we were a magnificent team and we still are. . . .

This period is still influencing the functioning of the school nowadays. Teachers share information and materials, work periodically together, etc. Cooperation among colleagues is highly valued in the school. This became clear again when a new critical phase occurred. Frequent changes in local politics resulted over the last five years in a constant coming and going of principals. There was no continuity in the principal's office, so the teachers had to take care of it themselves. The team actually runs the entire school. The teachers stick together to save the achievements of the past and to face new difficulties (criminality, ethnic conflicts between children of different nationalities, decreasing number of pupils, etc.). Fred, who had plans to change school, decided to stay and stand by the side of his colleagues in these hard times.

The example illustrates how professional biography, self and subjective educational theory are interwoven with the school culture. The school had been built

up by an enthusiastic young team, which strongly put its stamp on the functioning of the school.

Critical Incidents, Persons, Phases and the Professional Self

The arrows in Figure 13.1 indicate that professional biography in general and
critical incidents, phases and persons in particular influence the professional self
and the subjective educational theory. This was already illustrated with the help
of interview fragments. It is important to notice that this link is constructive. It's
not an objectively observable cause-effect-relationship. The causal link is construed by the respondent themself: in the reconstruction of their biography, event
X or person Y receives the status of 'critical incident' or 'critical person'. The
arrows in the figure have to be understood in this sense: they indicate subjective
interpretations of causal relations. We just remember here the adagium of Thomas
(one of the founding fathers of the life history research in sociology): 'If men
define situations as real, they are real in their consequences' (Thomas, 1928: 571,
cited in Denzin, 1970: 220–1).

Agnes: Synopsis of a Career

Finally we present here a summary of one teacher's career story. Agnes (twenty-
eight years of practice) had a rigorous education, at home as well as in the boarding school (secondary school and teacher training college). She was taught docility
and obedience. The boarding school system almost completely seperated her from
the reality outside school. Others always chose and decided for her (*self*). But at
teachers college, two teachers opened up this isolation a bit. One of them had
travelled a lot and told the students about her experiences. Both teachers were
very involved in their job and were sensitive to the questions and interests of the
students. They also behaved according to their ideals. Agnes talks about them as
reference figures (*critical persons*).

The first years of her career were quite hard for Agnes. She felt too young
for the adult life that had been kept hidden to her for such a long time. Further
she didn't feel herself competent to handle the complex class reality in a proper
way. Especially, when pupils had problems she experienced this as a personal
failure and it made her anxious (*critical phase*).

After about ten years, Agnes got married and had to leave school. At that
time married women were not allowed to teach in catholic schools (*formal
career*). Agnes had four children. Apart from the household and caring for the
children, she also participated actively in a local socio-cultural organisation for
women. This work brought her into contact with women from different social
classes. It made her conscious of the differences in background when children
enter school and how these differences influence their educational chances (*subjective
educational theory*). As her children grew older, Agnes slowly became discontented
with her life as housewife (*self*). A meeting of her old classmates constituted a
turning point. Several women of her former class had gone back to teaching (the
restriction for married women had been abolished). Agnes decided to follow their
example (*critical incident*). She found a new job very soon, but experienced a hard

second induction phase (after being home for more then ten years) (*critical phase*). The curriculum had changed, but also the children were different. Agnes experienced them as more emancipated, but also more impudent and with less respect to her as a teacher. But she also noticed that her experience as mother had made her more patient. She could better understand the kids and treat them more empathetically (*self and subjective educational theory*).[11] Further, the combination of the mother and teacher roles demanded a thorough reorganisation in the household. Fortunately Agnes got strong support from a colleague. That colleague helped her hold on (*critical person*).

Some years later, Agnes' youngest son experienced severe learning difficulties at school. The boy was also in weak health. After being in a sanatorium for some time, the boy went to a school for special education. These experiences brought Agnes to change her attitude profoundly towards children who didn't do very well at school. She realised that some kids simply are not able to understand everything and that you have to accept this as a teacher (and don't blame yourself for it) (*self and subjective educational theory*). On the other hand Agnes paid much more attention to these kids than before and tried to develop a proper pedagogical approach for them. She learned a lot on this point from the contacts with the teachers from her son's school (special education) (*professional behaviour; subjective educational theory*).

Becoming a grandmother also meant an important turning point for Agnes (*critical incident*). She wanted more time for herself and her grandchildren. This made her choose a part-time job (*changes in self influence change in formal career; see arrow 2 in Figure 13.2*). Observing the way her children treated their own children helped Agnes to think further about and articulate her own ideas about education, children and teaching . . . (*self, subjective educational theory*).

Although the narrative richness of the career story is lost to a great part in this synthesis, it still illustrates the usefulness of the conceptual framework to capture a career story.

Professional Self and Subjective Educational Theory

From the analysis of the career stories we were able to fill in more concretely the content of the key notions 'self' and 'subjective educational theory'.

Professional self.
Earlier we described the professional self as a complex, multidimensional and dynamic system of representations, that develops over time as a result of the interactions of the person with one's environment. The self influences the way people perceive concrete situations and their daily behaviour. The dynamic and complex nature of the self has been illustrated already. Now we will more concretely describe the multidimensionality. From our analysis of career stories, we distinguished several aspects in the professional self:

- *self image*: is the teachers' answer to the question: who am I as a teacher? It can be inferred from general self descriptions;
- *self esteem*: is strongly interwoven with self image. It is the 'evaluative' self experience. The teacher makes a personal assessment of the quality of his

professional behaviour. One could say that the self-esteem is an indication of the self-image/ideal self-image–ratio. In the example of Agnes we saw how the self-esteem increased as Agnes started to see that other factors (e.g. intelligence) than her own competence were also determining the pupils results;

- *job motivation*: refers to the motives that make people start a teacher's career, stay in the job or leave it. It was striking that the decision to start teacher education for most of the teachers was not a personal choice. For women with lower and lower-middle class backgrounds teaching was one of the few jobs that were considered appropriate for women at that time. Furthermore, teacher education at that time was integrated or closely linked to secondary education. Other teachers chose this career after they failed at the university. Only three of the twelve teachers (the youngest) said their choice to become teachers was deliberate.

- *job satisfaction*: refers to the degree to which teachers are satisfied about their job situation. The most important factor in this satisfaction is the results of the pupils. This gives a feeling of professional competence. The appraisal of the parents is connected with it. Good relations with colleagues, with whom one often works together for many years, are important as well as the principal's supporting attitude. This satisfaction derived from the social contacts is often described in terms of feelings of acceptance within a team, without losing one's autonomy in the classroom. An important theme concerning dissatisfaction — especially for male teachers — is the decreasing social status of the teacher.

- *task perception*: refers to the content of the job as perceived by the teacher. Implicitly this is always normative and connected to self-esteem. The question not only is 'what must a teacher do?', but 'what must a teacher do to be a good teacher?' Of course teachers have to teach the curriculum. But during their careers, teachers also can bring in personal pedagogical accents. Changes in the family situation of their pupils (divorces, both parents working full time, etc.) are perceived by teachers in terms of new educational tasks (even not imposed by school authorities). Fred, for example, understands his own career development as an evolution from the position of a strict teacher (emphasis on cognitive knowledge and discipline) towards the position of a friend and educator, who flexibly adapts himself to the specific group of pupils (emphasis on values, feeling at home, being happy at school as a condition for learning).

- *future perspective*: refers to the expectations teachers have towards the future development of their career and job situation. The changes in self-image, job satisfaction, task perception, etc. that teachers expect to take place, form an essential component of their professional self. The orientation towards the future is implicitly present in the professional self and is therefore part of the background from which teachers behave and make decisions.

Just like the professional self itself, these aspects or components are analytical constructs. We can generally describe them, but their content and meaning (importance) can only be understood with reference to the career story as a whole.

Subjective Educational Theory

Above we described the subjective educational theory as a part of the professional self: a system of representations that are directly connected with teachers' professional activities. The distinction self — professional self is theoretical-conceptual. For, when a teacher thinks about concrete teaching strategies, he always does so in terms of his own behaviour in concrete classroom situations. Here are some interview fragments as illustrations:

Anita describes her opinion about the best way to handle parents:

> . . . I think parents are much better off when they hear the truth about their kid. Of course, you have to be kind and be tactful, but straight anyway. Also the reports . . . that's what takes so much time: if you want to write a critique, it must be true, but the formulation should not hurt. And that's a serious task. I really think parents should be told the truth. I've always done so. . . .

Anita teaches the first grade. She talks about the most successful approach towards these young kids:

> . . . finally I have much better results when being patient and good than if I would snap at them. That leads nowhere. The kids get blocked and things are finished. They need a good atmosphere, feel at ease and they must know that they can ask any question. I put much energy into that. To make them know that they can ask questions if they don't understand something. Then I take them with me and explain it once again. But you should never get angry with them, because then they break up the relationship and things are finished. You can't reach them anymore.

Positive valuing has the best results, because you witness the progress of the children. And it makes you feel good as a teacher.

> That's why I'm so happy to be in the first grade. You see the children make tremendous progress. You see it happen, every day. It makes me feel good and I enjoy it.

This attitude is also valued by the parents. For example, by the parents of a girl with poor results and learning difficulties.

> And they told me . . . 'last year, when she was in your class her results weren't good either, but you had always some good thing to say. Now all we get to hear is negative.' You see? I think, you should tell the truth to the parents, but it's the way you do it. . . . In fact, no matter what a child's results may be, there is always something you can say that's good. They always have positive sides . . . always. . . .

The interview fragments show that opinions or teaching principles never stand on their own. Teachers talk about them by telling concrete stories they experienced themselves, where the complex interaction of the teacher and his environment becomes clear. The teaching principles are embedded in narrative scenes, with various participants playing their roles (parents, colleagues, pupils . . .). One could summarise the second extract as: a child-centred approach, where attention for the wellbeing of the children brings about better learning results for the pupils and more satisfaction for the teacher. But the narrative form not only describes the general principle more concretely, it also augments and legitimates it with concrete practice experiences. The positive results of the children and the appraisal of the parents legitimate (in the eyes of the teacher) the child-centred approach. This validation indeed not only functions in a cognitive way, but has also an emotional side: it reinforces the feeling of effectiveness, competence and so enhances the job satisfaction of the teacher. Narratives that refer to subjective educational theory thus not only have a descriptive component, but always an evaluative, argumentative or explanatory component too. The principle the teacher explicates as the basis for his professional behaviour is immediately confirmed by examples that show the legitimacy, the effectiveness and the appreciation of the principle.

The content of subjective theories (as reconstructed from the career stories) proved quite idiosyncratic (many differences between the teachers), which conforms our basic assumption that subjective theories (as part of the professional self) result from the individual biography (see also Nias, 1989a: 14). Therefore a narrative, autobiographical and contextual approach seems to be the most appropriate way to understand teachers' thinking and practice. One stays closer to the way teachers spontaneously think and talk about their practice: narrative, embedded in concrete contexts, evocative, suggestive, metaphorical and so on (see also Connelly and Clandinin, 1988a: 70). In other words: we respect the teachers' own voice (Elbaz, 1990). By doing so we also avoid too cognitivistic and rationalistic an approach, which would make us lose sight of the emotional, irrational and unconscious elements in teachers' thinking and acting.

Discussion and Further Research

A very positive experience related to this first study was the great motivation and willingness of the teachers to tell their life stories. Probably the form of the study made this easier: the semi-structured nature of the interviews gave the necessary structure, while at the same time leaving space for the teachers' own stories in their own words; the interviewer took an attitude of active and acceptive (not judging) listening; the cycle involved several contacts, etc. But it remains striking how quickly teachers were willing to talk about themselves very openly. Perhaps we should interpret this as a confirmation of Nias' conclusion that the person of the teacher is of crucial importance in his professional life (Nias, 1989a: 202–3). If teachers get the chance to talk about themselves as a teacher to an interested, non-evaluative listener, it seems that they take that chance with pleasure and commitment. This doesn't, however, absolve the researcher from taking into account the motives of the respondent, while analyzing and interpreting autobiographical materials. Allport already warned of this in 1942 (Allport, 1942: 69; see also Hoerning, 1980: 679). Hoeppel emphasises the 'intention to communicate' (*Mitteilungszweck*) (Hoeppel, 1983: 311), that is inherent to every autobiographical text: the storyteller/writer addresses an audience (see also Elbaz, 1991: 6). Autobiographical self-thematisation, therefore, is intrinsically a social, interactive event (see also above: narratives of self). Interaction also means influences on the collected data and the collection process by the researcher. To get valid information from the analysis, the researcher has to keep this in mind. We tried to avoid this bias by systematic reflection by the interviewer after the interview and by gathering contextual information from other sources (colleagues, school-leader, documents, etc.).

Another important aspect of working with autobiographical self-thematisation is the inherent subjectivity of the data. The data are verbal reports about the personal interpretation of lived (objective) situations (Schulze, 1979: 53). Moreover, autobiographical data always suppose a retrospective reconstruction. It is not the facts and experiences as such that are important, but rather the subjective interpretation of those facts by the teacher and the coherence with other experiences. Legewie rightly notes that in the autobiographical reconstruction feelings and unconscious motives also play their part (Legewie, 1987: 177). The functioning of human (autobiographical) memory, personal interpretation by the respondent and the role of unconscious processes, constitute a cluster of important themes and questions that have to be considered thoroughly if the biographical approach is to be methodologically well grounded.

Finally, the relation between reflection (thinking) and action remains very complex. The interplay of professional self and subjective educational theory on the one hand and the concrete professional behaviour on the other, is not to be understood purely (probably not even mainly) in terms of intentionality. Human behaviour cannot be explained completely by understanding its subjective meaning for the person involved. This meaning is not only constituted by the intentions and aims of the actor, but also by unconscious motives and 'latent structures of meaning' (*latente Sinnstrukturen*) (see A.O. Oevermann *et al.*, 1979), that exist independently from the actor's consciousness. Also Legewie warns us that the determinants of human behaviour are only partly transparant to the actor (Legewie, 1988: 18). Much of analysis and theoretical work remains to be done on this point.

We refer here to the distinction Argyris and Schön (Argyris and Schön, 1980 and 1978) make between 'espoused theory' and 'theory-in-use'. Human behaviour (i.e. teachers' professional behaviour) is determined to a great extent by the 'theories of action' (subjective educational theory). Through reflection this theory can be thematised and made more explicit. This results in the 'espoused theory'. But what people say they do (and why) often differs from the 'theory-in-use', the theory of action that can be inferred interpretatively by observing the actual behaviour. The confrontation of espoused theory and theory-in-use offers possibilities for professional growth, according to these authors. Through reflection on the theory-in-use people can learn to act more effectively. They can become more aware of their theory-in-use and direct more succesfully their behaviour (Schön, 1983).[12]

The biographical perspective on professional behaviour could join this approach and offer opportunities for professional development. Autobiographical self-thematisation can make teachers aware of their professional self and subjective educational theory (espoused theory), its origin and development. By confronting this with information about their theory in use (e.g. feedback based on observation), teachers can reach a greater conformity between theory in use and espoused theory, which could result in more effective professional behaviour (Day, 1981). This increase in effectiveness will in turn increase the job satisfaction and the feeling of competence (self-image, self-esteem). The third interviews (meta-reflection) in our first study already gave us indications for this process, but this should be studied further in a form of action research. Teacher pre-service and in-service training can contribute interesting perspectives here (see also Kelchtermans, 1991).

Our own ongoing research aims at a further 'grounding' of the developing theoretical framework. Based on the experiences in our first study, we started a second. The research procedure was refined, systematised and supplemented with classroom observations. We selected a more homogeneous group of respondents, to make comparison easier. We hope to be able to report further on how Flemish primary school teachers experience their career, how their professional self and subjective educational theory (as indicators for professional development) originate and develop through the career. Our experience so far has taught us that the biographical approach and the method of autobiographical self-thematisation lead to challenging, interesting and promising knowledge about teachers' thinking and practice.

Notes

1 I thank Professor Dr Roland Vandenberghe and Professor Dr Danny Wildermeersch (Catholic University Leuven) and Dr Gertrude Hirsch (Eidgenössige Technische Hochschule, Zürich) for their comments on an earlier draft of this article.

2 We prefer the notion 'professional behaviour' to 'teaching'. Since professional activities involve more than just classroom teaching. For example interactions with the school leader, cooperation with colleagues, contact with parents and local administration are also part of the job. The term 'professional' is used in a general, descriptive sense to indicate everything which has to do with the job activities (see also, for example, Huberman, 1989a, 1989b).

3 For a review of the different approaches in the study of teachers in general, and the biographical approach in particular, see Terhart (1990a and 1990b). In order to be complete we also have to mention the German research line of the so called 'pädagogische Biographieforschung' (educational life history research) (Baacke and Schulze, 1979 and 1985; Schulze, 1983; Hoeppel, 1983). This notion refers to a diversity of educational research projects and theoretical frameworks. What these authors have in common is their interest in social change. They all share the view that an encompassing program to change society, necessarily has to involve the subject. To achieve an emancipatory project, one must not only analyse the societal conditions of human life, but as a necessary complement also the biographical experiences need to be taken into account. These authors explore several narrative techniques for data collection and analysis and made efforts to give their research approach a methodological and epistemological legitimation.

4 By not using the notion 'identity' we avoid conceptual discussions, because this term has very different meanings depending on the anthropological and philosophical basic assumptions.

5 This knowledge system is referred to by various notions in the research literature, e.g. 'implicit theory' (Clark and Peterson, 1986); 'practical knowledge' (Elbaz, 1990); 'personal practical knowledge' (Connelly and Clandinin, 1988a).

6 In his work with autobiographical data in Germany (strongly inspired by psycho-analytic theory) Schulze (1979) comes up with a similar notion: 'kritische oder Signifikante Ereignisse'. Critical incidents, in his view, always involve a certain constellation or configuration of well known (familiar) circumstances, that

suddenly or deeply change and therefore have a strong emotional effect on the respondent, and lead to an elementary reaction to master the extraordinary situation (Schulze, 1979: 84–85). Using the psychoanalytical theories on traumas, Schulze tries to depict how these critical incidents function in the development of personal identity. He concludes that critical incidents are always gaps or ruptures in the socialisation process, which are often experienced as traumatic, but at the same time also provide a chance for personal growth.

7   The team consisted of Ann De Jaegher, Myriam Indenkleef, Geert Kelchtermans and Roland Vandenberghe.

8   The idea of 'critical persons' is also implicit in the work of Sikes *et al.* (1985).

9   This finding is supported by Nias' work on reference figures and their influence on teachers' self (Nias, 1985).

10   All the interview extracts are translated from the original tape transcripts. We tried to translate them as accurately as possible. The codes refer to the transcripts. All names are pseudonyms.

11   The impact of parenthood on professional self and subjective theory is a theme that returns with almost every teacher. This has also been observed by other researchers (e.g. Hirsch *et al.*, 1989: 272, 320–1; Huberman, 1989b: 53–4; Pajak and Blase, 1989: 292).

12   Argyris and Schön also developed training programs, based on reflection to increase the effectiveness of the professional behaviour (Argyris and Schön, 1980; Schön, 1983 and 1987).

References

ALLPORT, G.W. (1942) *The Use of Personal Documents in Psychological Science*, New York: Social Science Research Council.

ARGYRIS, C. and SCHÖN, D. (1978) *Organizational Learning. A Theory of Action Perspective*, Reading, Massachusettes: Addison-Wesley Publishing Company.

— (1980) *Theory in Practice. Increasing Professional Effectiveness*, California-London: Jossey Bass.

BAACKE, D. and SCHULZE, T. (Eds) (1979) *Aus Geschichten Lernen. Zur Einübung pädagogischen Verstehens*, München: Juventa.

— (Eds) (1985) *Pädagogische Biographieforschung. Orientierungen, Probleme, Beispiele*, Weinheim: Beltz.

BALL, S.J. and GOODSON, I. (Eds) (1985) *Teachers' Lives and Careers*, London, Philadelphia: Falmer.

BLUMER, H. (1969) *Symbolic interactionism. Perspective and method*, Englewood Cliffs, New Jersey: Prentice Hall.

BUTT, R.L. (1984) 'Arguments for Using Biography in Understanding Teacher Thinking', in HALKES, R. and OLSON, J.K. (Eds) *Teacher thinking*, Lisse: Swets and Zeitlinger, pp. 95–102.

BUTT, R. *et al.* (1986) 'Personal, Practical, and Prescriptive Influences on a Teacher's Thoughts and Actions', in LOWYCK, J. (Ed.) *Proceedings of the Third Conference on Teacher Thinking and Professional Action*, Leuven: University of Leuven, pp. 306–28.

CLARK, C. and PETERSON, P. (1986) 'Teachers' Thought Processes', in WITTROCK, M.C. (Ed.) *Handbook of Research on Teaching. Third Edition*, New York-London: Macmillan, pp. 225–96.

CONNELLY, F.M. and CLANDININ, D.J. (1988) *Teachers as Curriculum Planners. Narratives of Experience*, New York: Columbia University-Teachers College.

Geert Kelchtermans

— (1988) 'Narrative Meaning. Focus on Teacher Education', *Elements*, **19**(2), pp. 15–18.

DAY, C. (1981) *Classroom-Based In-Service Teacher Education: The Development and Evaluation of a Client-Centered Model*, University of Sussex Education Area. Occasional Paper No. 9, University of Sussex.

DE JAEGHER, A. and INDENKLEEF, M. (1990) 'Loopbaan leerkrachten basisonderwijs biografisch benaderd. Empirisch onderzoek en aanzetten tot theorievorming', (The Career of Primary School Teachers from a Biographical Approach), Leuven: Faculteit Psychologie en Pedagogische Wetenschappen (unpublished report).

DENZIN, N.K. (1970) *The Research Act. A Theoretical Introduction to Sociological Methods*, Chicago: Aldine Publishing Company.

DITTMANN-KOHLI, F. (1988) 'Sinndimensionen des Lebens im frühen und späten Erwachsenenalter', in BIERHOFF, H.-W. and NIENHAUS, R. (Eds) *Beiträge zur Psychogerontologie*, Marburg: Philipps-Universität Marburg, pp. 73–115.

ELBAZ, F. (1983) *Teacher Thinking: A Study of Practical Knowledge*, New York: Nichols Publishing.

— (1990) 'Knowledge and Discourse. The Evolution of Research on Teacher Thinking', in DAY, C., POPE, M. and DENICOLO, P. (Eds) *Insight into Teachers' Thinking and Practice*, London: Falmer, pp. 15–42.

— (1991) 'Research on Teacher's Knowledge: The Evolution of a Discourse', *Journal of Curriculum Studies*, **23**(1), pp. 1–19.

GERGEN, K.J. and GERGEN, M.M. (1987) 'The Self in Temporal Perspective', in ABELES, R.P. (Ed.) *Life Span Perspectives and Social Psychology*, Hillsdale: Erlbaum, pp. 121–37.

GOODSON, I. (1981) 'Life History and the Study of Schooling', *Interchange*, **11**(4), pp. 62–76.

— (Ed.) (1992) *Studying Teachers' Lives*, London: Routledge.

GRANT, C. and SLEETER, C. (1985) 'Who Determines Teacher Work: the Teacher, the Organization, or Both?' *Teaching and Teacher Education*, **1**(3), pp. 209–20.

GUDMUNDSDOTTIR, S. (1991) 'Story-maker, Story-teller: Narrative Structures in Curriculum', *Journal of Curriculum Studies*, **23**(3), pp. 207–18.

HIRSCH, G. (1990) *Biographie und Identität des Lehrers. Eine typologische Studie über den Zusammenhang von Berufserfahrungen und beruflichem Selbstverständnis*, Weinheim: Juventa.

HIRSCH, G. et al. (1990) *Wege und Erfahrungen im Lehrerberuf. Eine lebensgeschichtliche Untersuchung über Einstellungen, Engagement und Belastung bei Zürcher Oberstufelehrem*, Bern: Haupt.

HOLLY, M.L. and MCLOUGHLIN, C. (1989) *Perspectives on Teacher Professional Development*, London-New York-Philadelphia: Falmer.

HOEPPEL, R. (1983) 'Perspektiven der erziehungswissenschaftlichen Erschliessung autobiographischer Formen der Selbstreflexion', *Zeitschrift für Pädagogik. 18. Beiheft*, Weinheim-Basel: Beltz, pp. 307–12.

HOERNING, E.M. (1980) 'Biographische Methode in der Sozialforschung', *Das Argument*, **22**(123), pp. 667–87.

HUBERMAN, M. (1989b) 'The Professional Life Cycle of Teachers', *Teachers College Record*, **91**(1), pp. 31–57.

HUBERMAN, M., GROUNAUER, M. and MARTI, J. (1989a) *La vie des enseignants. Evolution et bilan d'une profession*, Neuchâtel-Paris: Delachaux et Niestlé.

HUGHES, E.C. (1958) *Men and Their Work*, New York: Free Press.

KELCHTERMANS, G. (1990a) 'Die berufliche Entwicklung von Grundschullehrern aus einer biographischen Perspektive', *Pädagogische Rundschau*, **44**(3), pp. 321–32.

— (1991) 'Leren van je eigen geschiedenis. Autobiografische reflectie in de lerarenopleiding (Learning from Your Personal History. Autobiographical Selfthematisation in Teacher Education)', *VELON Tijdschrift voor Lerarenopleiders*, **12**(2), pp. 4–10.

KELCHTERMANS, G. and VANDENBERGHE, R. (1990a) 'Het biografisch perspectief in onderzoek van het professioneel handelen van leerkrachten (The Biographical Perspective in the Study of Teachers' Professional Behaviour)', *Pedagogisch Tijdschrift*, **15**(3), pp. 126–39.

LEGEWIE, H. (1987) 'Sinnfindung und Sinnverlust in biographischen Selbstdarstellungen', in BERGOLD, J.B. and FLICK, U. (Eds), *Ein-sichten*, Tübingen: DGVT, pp. 173–81.

LEGEWIE, H., WIEDEMAN, P.M. and VAN DIEPEN, M. (1988) *Arbeitsmaterialien zur Durchführung und Auswertung offener (biographischer) Interviews* (internal document), Berlin: T.U. Berlin, Fachbereich 2 Gesellschafts-und Planungswissenschaften, Institut für Psychologie.

MARKUS, H. and WURF, E. (1987) 'The Dynamic Self-Concept. A Sociological Pychological Perspective', *Annual Review of Psychology*, **38**, pp. 299–337.

MEASOR, L. (1985) 'Critical Incidents in the Classroom. Identities, Choices and Careers', in BALL, S. and GOODSON, I. (Eds), *Teachers' Lives and Careers*, London, Philadelphia: Falmer, pp. 61–77.

NIAS, J. (1985) 'Reference Groups in Primary Teaching. Talking, Listening and Identity', in BALL, S. and GOODSON, I. (Eds), *Teachers' Lives and Careers*, London, Philadelphia: Falmer, pp. 105–19.

— (1989a) *Primary Teachers Talking. A Study of Teaching as Work*, London-New York: Routledge.

— (1989b) 'Teaching and the Self', in HOLLY, M.L. and McLOUGHLIN, C.S. (Eds) *Perspectives On Teacher Professional Development*, London, New York: Falmer, pp. 155–72.

OEVERMANN, U. *et al.* (1979) 'Die Methodologie einer "objektiven Hermeneutik" und ihre allgemeine forschungslogische Bedeutung in den Sozialwissenschaften', in SOEFFNER, H.-G. (Ed.) *Interpretative Verfahren in den Sozial- und Textwissenschaften*, Stuttgart: Metzler, pp. 352–433.

PAJAK, E. and BLASE, J. (1989) 'The Impact of Teachers' Personal Lives on Professional Role Enactment. A Qualitative Analysis', *American Educational Research Journal*, **26**(2), pp. 283–310.

PETERSON, W. (1964) 'Age, Teacher's Role and the Institutional Setting', in BIDDLE, B. and ELENA, W. (Eds) *Contemporary Research on Teacher Effectiveness*, New York: Holt, Rinehart and Winston, pp. 264–315.

PLUMMER, K. (1983) *Documents of Life. An Introduction to the Problems and Literature of an Humanistic Method*, London: Allen Unwin.

SCHEIN, E. (1985) *Organizational Culture and Leadership. A Dynamic View*, San Francisco: Jossey Bass.

SCHÖN, D. (1983) *The Reflective Practitioner. How Professionals Think in Action*, London: Temple Smith.

— (1987) *Educating the Reflective Practitioner. Toward a New Design for Teaching and Learning in the Professions*, San Francisco: Jossey-Bass.

SCHULZE, T. (1979) 'Autobiographie und Lebensgeschichte', in BAACKE, D. and SCHULZE, T. (Eds) *Aus Geschichten lernen*, München: Juventa, pp. 51–98.

— (1983) 'Auf der Suche nach einer neuen Identität', *Zeitschrift für Pädagogik. 18. Beiheft*, Basel: Beltz, pp. 313–20.

— (1985) 'Lebenslauf und Lebensgeschichte. Zwei unterschiedliche Sichtweisen und Gestaltungsprinzipien biographischer Prozesse', in BAACKE, D. and SCHULZE, T. (Eds) *Pädagogische Biographieforschung*, Weinheim: Beltz, pp. 29–63.

SIKES, P., MEASOR, L. and WOODS, P. (1985) *Teacher Careers. Crises and Continuities*, London, Philadelphia: Falmer.

STAESSENS, K. (1991a) *De professionele cultuur van basisscholen* (The Professional Culture in Primary Schools), Leuven: Leuven University Press.

— (1991b) *The Professional Culture of Innovating Primary Schools: Nine Case Studies*, paper presented at the AERA-Meeting, Chicago.

Geert Kelchtermans

TERHART, E. (1990a) 'Lehrer werden — Lehrer bleiben: berufsbiographische Perspektiven', Lecture 'Hochschultage für Lehrerinnen und Lehrer, University Lüneburg. Manuscript.

— (1990b) 'Sozialwissenschaftliche Theorie-und Forschungsansätze zum Beruf des Lehrers: 1970–1990', *Zeitschrift für Sozialisationsforschung und Erziehungssoziologie*, **10**, pp. 235–54.

ZEICHNER, K.M. (1986) 'Lehrersozialisation und Lehrerausbildung. Forschungsgegenstand und Perspektiven', *Bildung und Erziehung*, **39**(3), pp. 263–77.

Chapter 14

The Importance of Learning Biography in Supporting Teacher Development: An Empirical Study

Christopher Day

This chapter reports the findings of research which was undertaken over a two-year period with teachers from eleven primary schools in the Midlands region of England. The purpose of the work was to investigate the effect of macro-level politics and policies, through which the management of in-service budgets was devolved to schools through a government controlled system of Grants for Education, Support and Training (GEST), upon micro-level individual learning behaviours of teachers. The research revealed that leadership support and school culture factors make significant contributions to the quality of professional learning opportunities which are both school initiated and school centred (Day 1991a; 1993). However, the most important influences on the way in which teachers developed were the teachers' personal and professional learning biographies and their stages of career and life cycle development. 'Biography' as used in this chapter refers to those formative experiences which have influenced the ways in which teachers think about their professional development and what kinds of professional development processes they value.

Whilst the contexts for teacher learning reflect to some extent the parameters within which those who manage teacher learning work, the research provided evidence that in the current market-led model of professional development in which personal and professional need may be predominantly defined by external forces and organisational needs the critical dimensions of teacher development — the opportunities to reflect upon the 'why' as well as the 'how' and 'what' — were being lost, that curriculum delivery (an 'efficiency' concept) was replacing curriculum transaction (an 'effectiveness' concept), that teachers' career development needs were being displaced, and that teaching itself was in practice coming to be regarded as purely a technical exercise as opportunities for developing professional judgment reduced thus disempowering teachers (Day, 1993a). It was found that in a managed system of professional development effective interventions reflected a number of principles for professional development.

Individual Learning Cultures

In discussing school improvement in America, Miller and Lieberman (1988) provide a crucial link between school effectiveness in terms of student growth and the growth and development of teachers; and they highlight the need for leaders of effective schools to, 'attend to the specific culture of the school: its history, people, norms, needs, values. . . .' Yet James Calderhead was able to write authoritatively at the beginning of this decade that 'despite several years of fairly widespread research . . . our theoretical appreciation of teachers' professional development is still probably pretty crude' (Calderhead, 1990). Among the many 'serious impediments' to research and development activity in this area which he cited were: the sheer complexity and uniqueness of teachers' professional development; the lack of clarity over the type of theoretical framework we seek to guide professional development; the value-saturated nature of teaching; the multi-dimensionality of ways in which professional development occurs.

Despite these 'serious impediments' there is much accumulated data which, together, represents a considerable body of knowledge concerning professional development, its purposes, processes, outcomes and management. We recognise, and this research confirms that much learning is on-the-job, *in situ*, in response to classroom actions. The first priority of any teacher is to survive, to learn coping strategies which will allow him or her to work towards increasing his or her effectiveness in supporting student learning. If we are to take into account research on adult learning life cycles, teacher careers, and teacher narrative, then it is clear that learning occurs at different rates and that learning needs differ in relation to age, 'cohort' and period influences so that:

> human development beyond adolescence is a far more continuous, fluid, dialectical, sometimes downright random business once one begins to look at individuals (Huberman, 1989).

However, we are now, 'beginning to understand how teachers' careers play out and which are the most influential determinants, within and outside the institution' (Huberman, 1989 *ibid.*). Michael Huberman has identified 'some reasonably strong trends' which recur across studies. His work reveals increasing complexities of development which he categorises within three broad phases:

1　Launching a career: initial commitment (easy or painful beginnings).
2　Stabilisation: final commitment (consolidation, emancipation, integration into peer group).
3　New challenges, new concerns (experimentation, responsibility, consternation).

Within these career phases, however, were three themes which might be described as 'variables.'

- *Metaphorical* ('drowning', 'settling down', 'disenchantment', 'getting my second wind').
- *Administrative* ('during my training', 'getting tenure', 'moving into the upper secondary').

- *Historical* (major structural reforms in the school system, the repercussions of historical events on school life).

Even this relatively complex conceptualisation does not adequately account for the different levels of learning development and the accompanying support needs. The teachers in this study were self-selecting, and so it was reasonable to assume that all were interested in their own professional development. Almost all had co-ordination or curriculum leadership responsibilities and received an 'allowance' in support of this role. Although their teaching experience ranged from two to thirty-plus years, most had between ten and twenty years experience. In national terms, then, they represented the 'norm', and thus the bulk of the teaching population who may benefit from professional development opportunities of one kind or another.

Methodology

Teachers were asked to write brief autobiographies focusing upon events, experiences and people who had significantly affected their attitudes to their own professional learning; and these were elaborated during a series of interviews. It is not the purpose of this chapter to engage in discussion of the value of biographical research as a means of furthering self-understanding and understanding of others. There is now a significant body of documented work which provides ample theoretical and case study data in support of this (e.g., Ball and Goodson, 1985; Goodson, 1992; Woods, 1986). Whilst school culture will facilitate or constrain the provision of opportunities for planned professional learning, it is likely that the effectiveness of the opportunities themselves, whatever their intrinsic quality, their immediate and longer term impact upon thinking and practice, how they are received by teachers — will be affected by individual teacher culture. It was reasoned that there would be a connection between teachers' own values, learning preferences and practices, and past experiences and influences, whether negative or positive.

Past experiences:

Will give us the details of that process whose character we would otherwise only be able to speculate about. . . . It will describe those crucial interactive episodes in which new lines of individual and collective activity are forged, in which new aspects of the self are brought into being. . . (Becker, 1970).

It was further hypothesised that a connection might also be made between their life and career stages and their perceived learning needs. For example, Wood's (1986) research suggested that 'the formulation of self in the early years may relate to later teaching', and points to the need for more consideration of the part played by parents, home background, other teachers, socialisation, and other factors (Woods, 1986).

An analysis of the principle attitudes expressed towards their own learning by teachers provides interesting data for those concerned with content and process of professional learning opportunities. For the purposes of this chapter these have

Christopher Day

been summarised under three headings — pre-initial training, initial training, and in-service.

Pre-initial Training

The most significant influences on these teachers' attitudes to their own learning were:

- parent(s)   (× 10 teachers)
- their own teacher   (× 2 teachers)
- a youth organisation   (× 1 teacher)

So it appeared that parents were principally responsible for embedding attitudes which were carried forward through life. They were: self-sufficiency, hard work, conscientiousness, caring, enthusiasm and interdependence. It is reasonable to infer that these attitudes are transmitted to children in the teacher's own classrooms. Above all, though, the ethic espoused by these teachers was that of *practicality*.

Initial Training

For five of the teachers this phase had provided theory which was not related to practice. The 'trainers' had provided an 'unrealistic' view of reality. The saving grace had been teaching practice itself. In effect, a view of theory and practice as separate and a view of theory as largely irrelevant had been carried through from college into the school and classroom (see also Knowles, 1992). One of the teacher's comments aptly illustrated this unfortunate dichotomy:

> People promote certain things as good practice ... it doesn't take account of the fact that you've such and such in your class who is prone to 'tantrums' and enjoys winding everybody else up. . . . Lots of things are good on paper — you read lots of books and it sounds really good, but when it comes to the situation you're in it doesn't really work. . . .

In-Service

Not surprisingly, perhaps, the most significant influences upon teachers, post-initial training were:

- colleagues generally   (× 7 teachers)
- particular individual colleagues (× 6 teachers)
- children's learning difficulties (× 6 teachers)
- courses   (× 4 teachers)
- other life experiences   (× 3 teachers)
- self   (× 2 teachers)

The findings correspond to and extend Crow's (1987) work with pre-service teachers in which the sources of influence she identified included role models (their own teacher), previous teaching experiences and family role models (Crow, 1987).

At first sight, then, it may appear that the data simply confirm that teachers are caring, conscientious and highly practical people; that many have had negative experiences during initial or pre-service training, and that most are influenced, in the main, during their working lives, by colleagues at work — and that so long as in-service is largely practical and so long as those who organise and present in-service are caring, enthusiastic people, then needs are likely to be met. However, whilst this is useful information, it provides only part of the picture. It was clear from the learning biographies provided by these teachers that each was at a different stage of their life and career development; and interviews revealed further the connection between biography, learning need, stages of life and career development, and support needs.

How do Teachers Learn?

The teachers responses to the question, 'How do you learn?', highlighted the complexities for the researcher and in-service designer (where they are different) who seek to match content and process to learning needs and levels to learning readiness. Teacher J, described development as:

> ... something you're doing all the time ... as you grow older ... I think it's something you perhaps don't notice so much until you sit down and look back, really. And you think, well now I wouldn't have done it like that ten years ago. . . . I think you must (develop) ... if you don't I think you need to get out, because the children are changing, ... the curriculum's changing ... and I think your teaching styles have got to change with it. If you don't develop ... you won't get away with it, you won't be an effective teacher ... and I think there are certain times when you have to push that development. . . . You've got to be looking to change to suit the children because they change ... and I think for staff to develop there has to be the resources needed. . . .

Teacher D had similar views of learning as a continuous, self-correcting, self-timing activity:

> You start off by thinking that you'll do it 'this' way, but by the end of the first year you don't like the way you've done anything, so you change it in the second year. And by the third year you're still not happy with it. And there's quite a lot of those years where you keep altering. And I can honestly say that you keep altering all the way along, because you find something doesn't work, and if it doesn't work you say to yourself, 'Why doesn't it work? What am I doing that's not right? Is it me? Is it the system? Is it the curriculum? And you start to question. And I think that becomes so automatic that you don't know that you're doing it.

Teacher 'C' stated that, 'All the time I'm learning ... All the time you're reaffirming what you know. You're becoming more confident. But, each day you're learning a new way of doing something that's better than the way you did it before . . .'

For these, and the other teachers interviewed, learning is both a natural and a necessary condition for the maintenance of professional effectiveness. It often occurs at an unconscious, intuitive level, and is associated with reflection. Teacher 'L' engaged in reflection in and out of the classroom as part of her continuing professional learning:

'I'   'Do you reflect on what you do and the reasons for it?'
'L'   'Yes, all the time . . . generally in the classroom situations there are ways of teaching different subjects and new themes that come out of things every year and I try to keep pace with those. Also as your situation changes, like moving to a new school, I had to learn new skills and knowledge and attitudes . . ., you're always reflecting how that lesson could have been better on such and such. . . .'

Another teacher found that her learning came, 'from many different strands'.

I think that when you're a teacher and you have a job to do; there are so many different strands that you have to bring together, weave them in like a piece of woven material. . . .

A fourth linked learning with distancing herself from her immediate reality:

You need to be able to step back from what you are doing . . . and teaching doesn't always give you time to do that. . . . You need more time to reflect than a normal teaching time would give you. . . .

This need for time to distance, to reflect in and on the action is well documented in the literature on professional learning (e.g., Schon, 1983). It is a necessary condition for learning; and evidence from schools in this study suggests that the need for extended opportunities for reflection on, in and about teaching, whilst recognised in cultures of collaboration, is not able to be supported with existing resources.

The learning biographies also revealed that a number of teachers perceived themselves to be at a crucial stage of their life and/or career development, and that while some learning is clearly a gradual, cumulative process, there are critical periods in teachers' lives when particularly significant, 'learning moments' occur, what Kompf in this book calls 'landmarks'. For example, Teacher J, who was looking for more responsibility, had 'learned more recently than in the past . . . as a result of working with one particular teacher . . .' Teacher N's vision of mathematics teaching had been totally changed in one afternoon when he listened to an inspirational lecture; and another teacher's, 'whole approach to ownership', had been changed as a result of experiences on a long higher degree course.

Further interviews with all the teachers provided additional corroboration of the importance of these *critical learning stages*. Teacher J, for example, expressed the need for planned professional development at particular *key stages* in her career:

1   On return to teaching after being away for seven years — 'a lot of things had happened in that time'; and

2   On gaining a management post — 'very different from being a teacher in school, and your position is different. . . .'

Teacher S, having taught for about eleven years, stated that when she began teaching she had found the short in-service training of the kind available then at teachers' centres, 'quite useful', but that as she, 'got further into teaching', she found these less and less useful. She was now at a stage when she needed to, '**take stock**', and that:

> . . . if I now went back to college and took time *out* of teaching — and I feel this more often, that I *need* time *out* of teaching in a school . . . a re-think, a re-train. That would be useful if at certain stages you get time out of the pressures of the classroom. That would be *very* useful. Especially now, when I feel in dreadful need of a change . . . to take stock. It's very hard to change while you're doing the job, or to put it all together. . . .

Teacher O confirmed that, 'There's a need for longer courses at certain stages of your career . . .', whilst Teacher R emphasised the need for in-service which focused on a supporting role rather personal learning needs:

> In the early stages it was very much what was in-service going to do for me personally and nobody else . . . and then moving on to helping me develop my first responsibility as a curriculum leader. Now the way I have to look at it is again personal for me as a teacher but also me as a management leader. . . . So it's changed from being self-centred to school centred . . . is it going to be of any benefit to me and will I be able to pass anything on to either the head or other senior curriculum leaders or other members of staff who are coming to me for help and advice. . . .

Others were concerned with the need, at certain stages of their career, to gain a broader perspective, to, 'step back and look at the whole', learning which could not be accommodated in the 'norms' of school life:

> But you do it (learn) at different levels. In my first year of teaching . . . after so many weeks I'd perhaps take all the children's books and have a good look through . . . looking at how the whole thing was running . . . a sort of reflection on what you're doing and a stepping back from week to week. . . . But now, when I came to this job, I found you're no longer in your own little niche . . . suddenly you're thrust into this whole school . . . you've got to have a real overall school view . . . and . . . this sort of reflection time in your own school isn't as effective as going out and talking to other people from other schools and talking about issues that in a busy school week you don't get to talk about. . . .

Teacher S was also very much aware of the need to avoid becoming 'entrenched', to:

> Step back . . . get out . . . talk to other people about their experiences . . . see a wider view. . . . Because you lose perspective . . . become very

> entrenched in your own little box . . . your own ways and ideas . . . this
> school. . . .

Teacher S stated that whereas 'theory' at initial training level had been irrelevant,
as she accumulated practical teaching experience, she did, '. . . need some sort of
theoretical input . . . based on practical experience. . . .'

Teacher B, also, had found herself in a situation when taking up a curriculum
leadership (co-ordinator) post where she, '. . . hadn't got enough theoretical
knowledge to justify or explain what I'm doing. I knew what I was doing, but
I just couldn't explain it. . . . Up until the last four years all my teaching was from
instinct. . . .'

Teacher M pointed out the danger of taking too much on board in the first
five years of teaching:

> . . . because there's enough to cope with practically in a classroom, get-
> ting used to the job and how you're going to work, and I think any
> courses that help you achieve that and establish yourself, that's what you
> need in the first five years. . . .

Now, after teaching for twelve years she wanted to, '. . . go on a course where
you can take your time to study what's coming up and the way things are going
to be expected to run. . . .'

The data revealed the predominance of short professional development opportunities, whilst at the same time pointing to their limitations — they tend to
provide for immediate practical concerns, relating overwhelmingly to curriculum
implementation needs. Though valued, they were not highlighted by teachers as
providing their most significant learning experiences. Indeed, the detailed evidence from the written 'learning biographies' suggests that they cannot match
informal 'on the job' learning nor the more substantial 'courses' of quality which,
by their nature, build upon the need for extended reflection, information collection, reappraisal, evaluation and planning on a greater variety of levels.

Teachers spoke through their learning biographies and interviews of the
planned learning experiences which had been most significant for their development. One teacher wrote of the learning which resulted from attendance at a two
year part-time diploma course:

> It challenged my attitudes and ideas subtly over two years . . . my prac-
> tice used to be very product based . . . but now I can understand the
> child's work more and value it for what it is . . . you get to a stage when
> you need to have your attitudes educated . . . have opportunities to clarify
> your thinking . . . not carry on doing the same old thing every day. . . .

A second teacher attending a part-time university course had been 'transformed
as a teacher', and was, 'more able to support the needs of the children'. Another
spoke of an extended twenty day course which had been:

> . . . the start of my professional development . . . that opened my eyes.
> I learned to look outside the classroom, how things were affecting the
> work inside the classroom . . . management . . . how schools are run . . .
> and how the staff develop as a staff . . . *Timing was quite critical.* . . .

Yet another had found that attendance at an intensive three day residential course had: 'transformed me as a teacher, opened up new ideas, ways forward, working with staff. . . .' Whilst teachers understood and were sympathetic to the need to respond to national initiatives in the short term, many were concerned that their longer term needs were being 'squeezed out'.

Quality Assurance

In writing and talking of the quality of experience in in-service work, experienced teachers identified 'performance indicators' which were common to all kinds of planned learning. Successful activities had, it seemed, provided for:

- *Process needs*   courses presented a balance of activities, involved working with colleagues, sharing experiences, were well structured.
- *Targeting needs*   were focused upon needs specific to the particular age range taught (i.e. were relevant).
- *Content needs*   increased knowledge/awareness, reinforcing and reassuring current thinking but encouraging participants to see issues from different perspectives.
- *Utilisation needs*   provided direct curriculum development benefits and application to classroom practice.
- *Leadership/modelling needs*   were led by tutors who were well prepared, enthusiastic, caring and aware of group dynamics.
- *Time and energy needs*   were timed for when energy levels were high.

However, the longer or more intensive learning had provided significant additional benefits:

- *Critical friendship needs*:   in-depth opportunities for sharing and building knowledge and skills over time in a supportive but challenging environment.
- *'Vision' needs*:   participants had been enabled to relate their experience of practice to theory, to reconsider critically their assumptions, predispositions, and values (the 'why' as well as the 'how' and 'what' of teaching), and the contexts in which they taught.
- *Skill development needs*:   they were able to develop new skills over time.
- *Intellectual needs*:   they were able to engage in systematic reading which, 'otherwise I wouldn't do'.
- *Personal needs*:   to build self-esteem, 'so important in these days when we're continuously being battered from all sides as regards our skills as professionals'.

Concentration of finance and effort on short professional learning opportunities which predominantly focus upon institutionally defined needs may well, in the long term, result in cultural *isolation* and *parochialism* (Alexander, 1991) and in teachers whose sense of vision and whose intellectual needs are not nurtured. This can only be detrimental to professional development. Figure 14.1 provides a number of principles derived from this research. It proposes that those responsible for promoting effective schools must provide intervention support which is appropriate to teachers' own learning contexts.

Conclusions

The research data revealed five main findings:

1 An optimism among some teachers that the predominant models of short burst learning opportunities were beneficial (provided they met quality assurance criteria).
2 A realisation that the benefits to be gained from short burst professional development activities were qualitatively different (and more limited) than those gained from longer term development activities.
3 A pessimism in relation to continuing opportunities for reflection (as being a necessary but not sufficient condition for learning) at all levels.
4 A need for leaders to plan for interventions into professional development which take account of:
   • individual culture (biography);
   • organisational culture;
   • career and life stages of development (critical learning readiness stages);
   • the need to provide a balance of development opportunities for teachers as persons, professionals, classroom practitioners and school functionaries.
5 Evidence of a trend through the kinds of in-service activities offered away from the operational definition of teacher as 'professional' towards that of teacher as technician. This is paralleled in other developments, e.g. initial teacher training (towards an apprenticeship model); and curriculum development (in which first content and more recently pedagogy and assessment is prescribed).

All research into professional development is a contribution towards a larger investment by government, school leaders and teachers in school effectiveness. From the evidence of the teachers in this research planning for development opportunities which involve school support must be profession rather than service centred. Leadership interventions must, therefore, be designed to:

• enhance individual and organisational growth;
• discourage dependency;
• discourage exclusive use of inward looking INSET;
• encourage reflection on thinking and practice at all levels;
• provide learning opportunities which match career and life stage development needs;
• encourage individual professional development planning;
• promote autonomy within collaborative cultures of interdependency;
• distinguish between outcomes and outputs of INSET in evaluations of effectiveness.

Figure 14.1: *Developing professional learning*

Professional Learning Assumptions	Contextual Variables	Leadership Intervention (Challenge and Support)
Teachers and schools are motivated to learn by the identification of a problem or issue which concerns their professional role. This may be externally generated or arise from classroom or career needs.	The organisational culture. Self-awareness of individual. The individual learning culture.	Teachers should be offered the means to reflect as an essential part of inquiry into their thinking and practice and identification of problems and issues.
Effective learning occurs in response to reflection on and confrontation of past and present values and practices.	Provision of enabling relationships and mechanisms.	Teachers should be offered a range of high quality professional development opportunities off and on-site through which they can begin to engage in systematic inquiry on practice which involves making theory (tacit knowledge) explicit.
Teachers have the capacity to be reflective, but not necessarily self-confrontational.	Conditions of service and/or leadership which do not encourage different levels of reflection.	Teachers should be offered affective and appropriate moral and critical support in processes of internalisation rather than identification or compliance. This support should be provided by key colleagues, so allowing teachers themselves to maintain and enhance autonomy.
Teachers' learning is organic and natural. Development (growth) precedes change (planned action).	Efficacy of need identification procedures. Skilfulness of intervention strategies. Leadership.	Teachers should be offered appropriate support in developing strategies for planning, negotiating and implementing work on their own and others' schools.
Transformation in thinking and practice is a necessary part of a teacher's developing learning process.	Individual career, life and organisational growth stages and influences which form critical 'points of departure'.	Teachers should be supported in the testing or validation of their critical theories through the provision of internal and external learning support (consultancy, networks, brokerage).

Christopher Day

In these ways, authorship and ownership of professional development will become a joint enterprise.

References

ALEXANDER, R. (1991) *Primary Education in Leeds: Briefing and Summary*, Leeds: School of Education, University of Leeds.

BALL, S.J. and GOODSON, I.F. (Eds) (1985) *Teachers' Lives and Careers*, London: Falmer.

BECKER, H.S. (1970) 'The career of a Chicago schoolmaster', in BECKER, H.S. (Ed.) *Sociological Work: Method and Substance*, Chicago: Aldine.

CROW, N.A. (1987) 'Socialization within a teacher education program', unpublished doctoral dissertation, The University of Utah, Salt Lake City. Cited in BUTT, R., RAYMOND, D., McCUE, G. and YAMAGISHI, L. (1992) 'Collaborative Autobiography and the Teacher's Voice', in GOODSON, I.F. (1992) *op.cit.*

DAY, C. (1990) LEATGS: *Evaluation of a Pilot Project for the Devolution of INSET Resources to Primary Schools, 1988–9*, Nottingham: School of Education, University of Nottingham.

— (1991) 'A balancing act', *Managing Schools Today*, **Vol.1**, No.4, December 1991.

— (1991a) *The Professional Learning of Teachers in Primary Schools and the Devolution of In-Service Funding*, Nottingham: School of Education, University of Nottingham.

— (1993) 'Management Support for Teachers Learning', *Journal of Teacher Development* **Vol.2**, No.1, pp.5–13.

— (1993a) 'The Development of Teachers' Thinking and Practice: Does Choice in itself Lead to Empowerment?', in ELLIOTT, J. (Ed.) (1993) *Reconstructing Teacher Education*, Lewes: The Falmer Press.

DES (1990) *Developing School Management: The Way Forward*, HMSO.

GOODSON, I.F. (Ed.) (1992) *Studying Teachers' Lives*, London: Routledge.

HARGREAVES, A. and FULLAN, M.G. (1991) *What's Worth Fighting For? Working Together for your School*, Toronto: Ontario Public School Teachers' Federation.

HMI (1989) *The Implementation of the Local Education Authority Training Grants Scheme (LEATGS): Report on the first Year of the Scheme, 1987–88*, Department of Education and Science 136/89.

HUBERMAN, M. (1989) 'The Professional Life Cycle of Teachers', *Teachers' College Record*, **Vol.91**, No.1, Fall 1989.

JOYCE, B. (1989) *Staff Development as Cultural Change*, Keynote Speech, International Conference of the Hong Kong Educational Research Association, Dec 13–16th, 1989.

KNOWLES, J.G. (1992) 'Models for Understanding Pre-Service and Beginning Teachers' Biographies', in GOODSON, I.F. (Ed.) (1992) *Studying Teachers' lives*, London: Routledge and Kegan Paul.

LIEBERMAN, A. (1989) *Staff Development as Culture Building, Curriculum and Teaching: the next fifty years*, New York: Teachers College Press.

LITTLE, J. (1986) 'Seductive Images and Organizational Realities and Professional Development', in LEIBERMAN, A. (Ed.) (1986) *Rethinking School Improvement: Research, Craft and Concept*, New York: Teachers College Press.

MILLER, L. and LIEBERMAN, A. (1988) 'School Improvement in the United States: Nuance and Numbers', *Qualitative Studies in Education*, **Vol.1**, No.1, pp. 3–19.

NIAS, J., SOUTHWORTH, G. and YEOMANS, R. (1989) *Staff Relationships in the Primary School*, London: Cassell.

WOODS, P. (1986) *Inside Schools: Ethnography in Educational Research*, London: Routledge and Kegan Paul.

Notes on Contributors

Margaret Batten is a graduate of the University of Melbourne and Monash University in Australia. She began her career as an English teacher in secondary schools, and has been involved in educational research for the past twenty years. Most of that time has been spent at the Australian Council for Educational Research, where she is now a Senior Research Fellow, and she has spent two periods of study leave in Scotland, working at the University of Stirling and the Scottish Council for Research in Education. Her doctoral dissertation reported on a longitudinal study of students in traditional and alternative Year 12 courses, a reflection of a long-standing research interest in student and teacher perspectives on senior secondary curriculum and assessment. Her other major areas of work in educational research are concerned with the quality of school life, the professional development of teachers, the nature of teachers' work, the consequences of increased student retention to Year 12, and links between school and industry at senior secondary level.

Hannelore Börger studied Developmental Psychology at the University of Groningen. During and after her study, which she completed in 1990, she performed many assistant educational functions. At present she is doing a Ph.D. at the University of Leiden on the transfer of educational skills.

James Calderhead is currently Professor and Director of the School of Education at the University of Bath. After teaching in both primary and secondary schools, he worked for eleven years in the Department of Educational Research at the University of Lancaster. His research interests focus on teachers' professional learning, particularly the processes of development of student teachers and their implications for the design of pre-service education. He has published four books and over thirty papers in the field, including *Exploring Teachers' Thinking*, and *Teachers' Professional Learning*.

Christopher Day is Professor and Head of Research and Development at the School of Eucation, University of Nottingham. After teaching in primary and secondary schools, colleges of education, and working as a local education authority adviser, he spent two years at the University of Calgary, Canada. His research interests centre upon the professional development of teachers, particularly the interface between teacher thinking and action; the interventionist's role in continuing professional development; and school leadership and culture. He has published ten books and a considerable number of papers in these fields. Recent publications include, 'Insights into Teachers' Thinking and Action' (1990) and 'Managing the Professional Development of Teachers' (1991). He is currently Secretary General of ISATT and chair of the editorial board for the ISATT editions of *Teaching and Teacher Education*.

Pam Denicolo is Assistant Head of the Department of Educational Studies, University of Surrey, England. She chairs the Committee of the Institute for Educational Research and Development and, *inter alia*, leads the Staff Development, Quality Assurance and Research Methods programs for the Department. She has been both a chemistry teacher and a lecturer in the psychology of education and holds a psychology practice certificate but currently her teaching is mainly in the form of staff development and research methods workshops in the Department and for HE institutions and professional bodies in the UK and abroad. Her research interests focus on the use of personal construct psychology and action research in the development of teaching practice and student learning. Recent publications include 'Developing Constructive Action: personal construct psychology, action research and professional development' (with Pope) in *Action for Change and Development*, Zuber-Skerrit (Ed.), Gower, 1991 and *What is active Learning* (with Hounsell and Entwistle).

Mary Lynn Hamilton is an Assistant Professor in the Department of Curriculum and Instruction at the University of Kansas, Lawrence, Kansas, USA. Her research interests focus on the effects of culture on students' and teachers' beliefs and how those effects are manifested implicitly and explicitly in the classroom and the school. Currently she is involved in an ethnographic study of an urban setting.

Marguerite Hansen Nelson is a resource room teacher in the Clarkstown School District in New York. In the past, she worked with young educable students and those who were developmentally delayed. She has also been an adjunct at St Thomas Aquinas College in Sparkill, New York and Fordham University in New York City. Her undergraduate degree was earned from Boston College *magna cum laude* and she is currently completing a doctoral program in educational psychology at Fordham. Apart from her book, *Teacher Stories* (Prakken Publications) she has written many articles which have been published in *The Journal of Creative Behavior*, *The Journal of Poetry Therapy*, and *The International Journal of Instructional Media*, as well as special education publications. She has also received an IMPACT II Teacher Recognition Award. Her research interests include the relationship between literacy and identity, the development of self-concept across the life span, and the cognitive function of metaphors.

Martha S. Hendricks-Lee is a Research Associate in the College of Education at the University of Cincinnati. She is currently finishing a doctorate in Educational Foundations. Her dissertation research is focusing on the role of Professional Development Schools in teacher education reform. Her other research interests include knowledge representation and use in classrooms and teaching and learning processes in non-school settings.

Michael Huberman is Senior Lecturer at the Harvard University Graduate School of Education, and Senior Research Associate at the New England Laboratory for School Improvement (Andover, MA., USA). He is presently on leave from the University of Geneva, in Switzerland. His most recent book, *De la Recherche à la Pratique (From Research to Practice with a user's manual)*, with M. Gather Thurler as co-author, was published in 1992. His previous book, *La Vie des Enseignants* is in press in the UK and will appear in 1993 in the USA. Michael Huberman has also done research and written extensively on teachers' cognitions and learning, on qualitative research methodologies, on knowledge utilisation and on issues of professional development in relation to instruction and pupil learning. In his work at the New England Laboratory, M. Huberman spends part of his time in contact with schools with which the Laboratory collaborates directly.

Geert Kelchtermans works as Research Assistant at the Center for Educational Policy and Education and the Section of Didactics, Department of Educational Sciences of the Catholic University Leuven, Belgium. After research on innovations such as Yena-Plan schools and experiential education in nursery and primary schools in Holland, Germany and Belgium, he took his Ph.D. with a dissertation on the professional biographies of primary school teachers.

Michael Kompf has taught developmental psychology, adult education, research design and educational foundations in the Graduate Department, Faculty of Education, Brock University, Ontario, Canada since 1983. His background in psychology, educational foundations and organisational theory has assisted in the supervision and development of an eclectic array of graduate student research projects and theses. An early and long-lasting interest in personal construct psychology was established during an undergraduate assistantship with Jack Adams-Webber, a former student of George Kelly. His current research interests include alternative constructions of mid-and later life development; ethical issues in naturalistic inquiry; probing psychological space-time continua and developing holographic meta-models of constructs and construct systems.

Rosa M. Laffitte is a lecturer and researcher in the field of Educational Management and Teacher and Institutional Development and Evaluation, and since 1987 has been a lecturer at the Departamento de Didáctica y Organización Escolar of Barcelona University, Spain. Previously she was a headteacher in an international primary and secondary school in Barcelona, and at the present moment she is involved in some international collaboration schemes and in research within the field of comparative education.

Hugo Letiche lectures in management learning at the School of Management, Erasmus University, Rotterdam. His applied research has been in the uses of multimedia and distance learning in management training and consultancy. His academic path commenced with phenomenological psychology, developed into action research/self-evaluation and, since the mid-seventies, has focused on post-modernism. He has published on action research most recently, 'Let the Practitioners Choose' and 'Zelf-Evaluatie' and on post-modernism 'Learning and Hatred for Meaning', articles in MEAD, TATE and ISMO. He feels close to movements in 'humanism and management (social science)' which he sees as being championed by SCOS, ISATT and HEC Montreal.

Maureen Pope is Professor of Community Studies and Education at Reading University. She is a psychologist with a specific interest in personal construct psychology and its applications within teacher education and nursing research. She has been involved in research projects on teacher thinking and professional development and is active in the field of staff development. She has published widely in personal construct psychology and a particular research interest is in developing methods which enable teachers to reflect on and develop their roles at any point in their careers and in relation to external pressures on the profession.

Bridget Somekh is a Lecturer in Applied Research in Education at the University of East Anglia. She is coordinator of the Classroom Action Research Network (CARN), a member of the BERA working group on Curriculum and co-Editor of *Educational Action Research: an international journal.* Her interests include curriculum development, teacher professional development and institutional change. Since 1985, the focus of her research has been on the process of change, in particular in relation to the introduction of information technology into education. Originally a secondary English teacher, Bridget has become increasingly interested in communication, discourse and the presentation of self as significant factors in the culture within which educational change takes place. Bridget has considerable experience of carrying out action research, first as a teacher-researcher in her own classroom and school and later as coordinator of two major projects funded by the National Council for Educational Technology: Pupil Autonomy in Learning with Microcomputers (PALM) and Initial Teacher Education and New Technology (INTENT). She is currently evaluator for the Business Education with Technology project (BITE), directed by Bernard Williams, which is developing software for the use of students of accountancy in universities.

Harm Tillema studied Educational Science at the University of Utrecht. He finished his study *cum laude* in 1977. Until 1983 he was scientific researcher at the University of Utrecht, where he wrote his thesis 'Teachers as designers'. After a period of working as a section coordinator at the University of Groningen he was appointed as senior university lecturer at the University of Leiden. His publications are on the field of teacher education and effectiveness of instruction.

Robert J. Yinger is Director of the Cincinnati Initiative for Teacher Education and Associate Professor of Education at the University of Cincinnati. He received his Ph.D. in Educational Psychology from Michigan State University in 1977. His research has focused on studying the relationships between teacher thought and action, beginning with studies of teacher planning and more recently examining teachers' thinking and action during instruction. He is currently interested in describing the improvisational nature of teaching and learning and in examining the ways in which a practitioner's knowledge and action is embedded in conversation, community and place. He has held appointments as Senior Researcher at the Institute for Research on Teaching at Michigan State University and Visiting Professor at Stanford University.

Index